The Restoration of Ami

Sam Hawksmoor

HAMMER & TONG

Hammer & Tong
https://www.samhawksmoor.com

Cover Image:
zulmaury-saavedra-Keh6vLM7w0-unsplash.com
Back cover logo of Studebaker from Wikicommons

The Restoration of Ami/ Hawksmoor, Sam - 1st ed.

ISBN 978-1-7385181-0-4

“Everything in life is located elsewhere,
and you travel there by automobile.” Anon

CONTENTS

Reviews of Sam Hawksmoor's Fiction:

Another Place to Die: The Endtime Chronicles
'A gripping pandemic rollercoaster ride that demands both a sequel and a film.' Amazon

The Repossession of Genie Magee: (3 Book Series)
'mesmerizing, clever, ... smart dark and graceful'
5 Stars. Bookish'
Absolutely thrilling, captivating and oh-so wonderful!'
Cupcake and a latte"
Exciting and gripping... disturbingly realistic. The ending left me hanging. OMG. I need the second book now.'
Ficbookreviews'
*Winner of The Wirral 'Paperback of the Year'

Girl with Cat (Blue):
'An exciting and fast paced story following the lives of two girls who are inexplicably linked across parallel worlds.'

We Feel Your Pain - So you don't have to: (2 Book Series)
A Delaney & Asha Mystery
'Original idea for a novel and a great read.
Highly recommended!'

The Repercussions of Tomas D
'One small lie - Can change History Forever
'Gripping stuff - the perils of living during the Blitz brought vividly to life' - Amazon.

CHAPTER ONE

The Last Straw

Ami tipped the garbage into the bins at the back of the big house and called Stan over to her. He was sheltering from the rain under the old spruce tree. He looked as miserable as she felt. "I swear it's time, Stan. I'm not staying here another day. Are you with me?"

Stan looked up into her face and nudged his wet nose into her thin cotton dress. He'd go anywhere with her. Anywhere.

She rubbed his ears and knelt down to hug him. "He got his fat hands on me again yesterday. I can't stand the smell of him. He's trying to get me alone. You need to keep watching, Stan. You're all I've got to protect me."

Stan pretended to understand everything she said and licked her hands. Ami sighed and stood up. "I mean it, Stan. If I don't get out of here soon, I'm going to wind up dead or pregnant or both. No one else has got the courage to leave, so it's you and me Stan. We can find a safe place, maybe find my mother. She has to be out there somewhere. There just has to be a better life for us than this." She sighed again, closing her eyes a moment. She looked down at the dog's head and kissed his forehead. "I've got to clean his stinking office now. I'll find you something to eat when I'm through, ok? Now go, stay out of trouble."

She broke free and ran towards Father Tresor's office, glad that he wasn't there today. She hated cleaning his office. You could smell him all over the room and he lived like a pig.

Stan watched her go, wondering if he should follow until he saw her disappear into the office. He knew all too well that he didn't go near there unless he wanted a good kicking, and he wasn't going to risk that again. He sauntered away to find someplace dry.

Ami surveyed the office, sighing at the state of it with half-eaten food and rotten banana skins on the floor. She was about to put it all in the bin when she realized the filing cabinet was open, the key still in the look. She nervously checked out the window in case anyone was approaching. All the kids had heard rumors that there were files on all of them. She gave herself five minutes tops to check, slightly scared at what she might find there. Yes! Under H, a slim file, she gingerly pulled it out and opened it. Letters. Someone had sent her letters! Her heart began to beat loudly, she felt panicky. None of them had been opened. None had ever been given to her. None of the other kids' got letters, ever.

Dare she read them? Was this all there was on her? Just letters? Barely able to breathe she opened one, hands shaking, one eye on the door.

My Sweet Angel Ami ...

She almost stopped breathing. A letter from her mother. She was still alive. How ....? She read more, legs shaking with nerves. This changed everything. Everything.

Maisie stared at her uncle with her usual sour face on. The man was relentless, wouldn't accept reality.

"You can't go, Remy. You're too old and it's too risky. It's dangerous, you're dangerous on the road."

"I have to go, Maisie."

She slipped on a headband to pin back her hair. "No, you don't. It's just a car, Remy, just a damn car. You can't go. Why can't they send whatever it is in the mail or Fed-Ex even."

Remy stared at his late wife's cousin and tried to suppress the anger he was feeling, tough call. Maisie was sounding more and more like his late wife. He appreciated she was only looking out for him, but he had to stand his ground on this.

"It's the last one. It's too precious to go in a package. You know how they toss those things around. It has to be handled with care."

"Why can't you just get a replica. Hell, you told me some guy is making replicas of everything now. It's not worth the risk, Remy. Driving all that way in your old truck. Montreal must be over a thousand miles at least. There's so much craziness out there now. People getting shot for no reason at all."

Remy sighed and sipped his coffee wondering why he let it get so cold. It was the same stupid argument all the time. The whole point of restoring a classic car to its original stock state was not to use replicas. Everything had to be genuine. That's the value of the project. Every nut and screw had to be genuine parts. Collectors wouldn't accept anything else. He checked the time and frowned. Where the hell did the time go?

"I'm sticking to the plan Maisie. I need a replacement steering wheel. Got to be white, the genuine article. Can't exactly fit in something any damn wheel when I've taken the trouble to make sure everything else is original and pristine now, can I?"

Maisie shook her head as she slipped on her shoes. Always the same thing. The damn steering wheel. She knew why he wanted to replace it. They never talked about how his father had died but she knew it has something to do with that steering wheel. She turned to grab her jacket. "You've wasted ten years of your life on that vehicle. Ten fucking years. It must have driven Jean mad."

Remy shrugged. His wife Jean had been more than happy that he had something to do when he retired.

"I'm running late. I made soup for you. Leek, carrot, and onion. It's simmering in the crockpot; it'll be ready by seven. Make sure you eat it all."

"I'll set the alarm."

Maisie rolled her eyes. "Sure, you do that, but I'll bet you won't remember why the alarm has gone off."

Remy wrinkled his nose. Maisie was always snippy about his memory. "I'll remember. I can smell it. I'm hungry already."

He didn't much care for her soups, but they helped him piss at night and anything that helped him go had to be respected. His swollen prostate was the bane of his life. Never got much sleep and sometimes the pain was ...

"You're on the night shift a lot these days," he remarked.

Maisie shrugged. "My choice. Once you get all the patients settled it's quiet for most of the night. I know you're going to the garage. You've been hiding in there so long no one remembers you anymore. You know that?"

Remy scratched his beard. Didn't matter to him at all. Once you retire, you're erased from people's memory. Didn't Maisie understand that yet?

"The same will happen to you one day, Maisie. The moment you stop working at the clinic all those people you think care about you will delete you from their phones. You think you matter, that the

Clinic will fall apart without you, but it won't. Look what happened to Dr Yukov."

Maisie paused at the kitchen door. "You know I won't discuss him."

"Yeah, exactly," Remy pointed out. "Of course, you don't. The moment he started showing symptoms they started to edge him out. At least he fixed my shoulder before he got sick. He was the only doctor there that gave a damn about the patients. So, what he was emotional, at least he was human."

Maisie opened the door. She'd long ago expunged the memory of Dr Yukov, her former mentor. He'd been her major crush at the time, not that he'd ever noticed her. The embarrassment of a man having a very public mental breakdown was something she wanted to forget.

"I'm leaving early tomorrow," Remy informed her. "I'll only drive in daylight. Got all my stops planned. I'll be back in a week at the latest."

Maisie briefly stared at him, trying to suppress her annoyance. "You're so goddamn stubborn." She noticed it was wet outside. "Did you check the weather? I hear there's a storm coming."

"Just rain. Florida sunshine will resume the day after. You could come with me." Remy said, knowing that would be the last thing she'd want to do.

Maisie laughed. "And risk my life in that ancient truck of yours. My god, it's almost as old as you are. Is it even legal on the highway?"

Remy chuckled. His '57 Chevy truck had 250,000 miles on the clock and ran better than anything built in this century, never let him down, except for that time he had a tire blowout during a flood in Mt Dora. Not the truck's fault.

"I'll avoid the highways when I can. Not enough stops for my bladder."

Maisie nodded. That was true. Never enough stops for that bladder of his.

"Got to go. Make sure you text me from wherever you get. Ok?"

"Will do. Drive safe."

She stepped out into the rain and ran towards her Toyota. Remy locked the door and took a deep breath. He needed to pack. Make a list of all the things he needed to do and make sure he had his pills. The guy in Montreal wanted cash. Instinctively he'd suspected a scam, but he had a good rating on eBay, not that you could exactly trust anything online. Didn't like carrying cash, but he needed that steering wheel with the all-important Studebaker icon on the horn. His father's head had made quite an impression on the horn. Didn't kill him right away, the shock of the accident took him a few days later when his heart gave way.

Remy hadn't decided on restoring the vehicle immediately. It had been his father's pride and joy. Bought it from a widow who never drove it and he treated it like precious metal. Couldn't understand why it wasn't considered the best coupe ever built – he certainly rated it so. Only drove it a few times a year to classic car events. He loved showing it off. Just short of ten thousand miles of trouble-free driving over thirty-five years before he'd collided with a deer.

Remy had left the vehicle in his garage for years as a retirement project. He knew the Hawk would be a huge distraction if he got stuck into a restoration too early. Retirement came earlier than expected when NASA Shuttle program came to an end. That's why his wife had been annoyed about how much the restoration was costing. If she'd known it had already blown past $25,000, she'd have been really mad. But he'd seen an identical Studebaker Golden Hawk go for $99,000 at auction, so he knew he wasn't wasting his time. Not that he intended to sell it.

You don't own a vehicle like that without wanting to show it off, listen to the purr of the supercharged 289-cu-in V8. It was the '57 model, once voted the best-looking American vehicle, one of only 41 ever made that year with the standard three-speed manual transmission, twin-traction differential, power steering and power brakes. He'd fitted disc brakes in response to his father's accident. Stopping a vehicle was more important than being too obsessive about original condition. He'd been assured it wouldn't affect the value.

The Studebaker story was one of saddest in auto history in his book. He could never work out why the Hawk hadn't sold in thousands. They'd bet the farm on the Avanti in 1960 and it was easily the most advanced design in North America, but still, few bought them. Crazy. It was his duty to preserve this bit of auto history.

His phone buzzed. He read the text from Maisie. "Don't forget your pills!"

He sighed. Maisie was annoying but meant well. Always meant well. He kept hoping she'd meet someone she liked and move out, but she was very picky, not everyone got her sense of humor.

Remy went to pack and made sure his pills went into the overnight bag first, leaving six tablets out to take before breakfast in the morning. He hated being dependent on blood thinners and all the stuff for his blood pressure and kidneys. Dreaded the six-monthly check-ups and how the doctors always seemed to keep adding new drugs without checking if they conflicted with the other drugs he was still taking. Didn't like to be challenged on it either.

He packed spare trousers and underwear – you could never be too careful with his condition.

An hour disappeared. He heard the alarm go off in the kitchen and at first thought it was a fire alarm ... then remembered Maisie's soup. He sighed, glancing at his bed. The overnight bag was packed. He'd gotten lost in a moment of reverie about Jean. That time they'd got stranded when he'd taken her fishing. She'd not wanted to go and after they'd been stuck with a broken engine for fourteen hours, never went out on the ocean again. The coastguard had found them eventually and towed them back. Didn't catch any fish that day either.

The soup wasn't so bad although he ate it without relish. He suddenly remembered he hadn't opened the safe. He went to get the cash the guy had asked for. He could have asked for more. It wasn't as if there were many other spare Hawk steering wheels. He'd looked into *mystudebaker.com* and could have bought a steering wheel without the horn ring for just $250 but it wasn't white. He'd looked into restoring the one in the car, but it was cracked, and the white enamel had peeled. A head travelling at sixty miles an hour can make quite an impact and his Pa had never retrofitted seatbelts. Finding someone with a spare white steering wheel in perfect condition was a rare thing. He prayed it was genuine. Worth driving all the way to Montreal to check at least.

He'd learned pretty early on in the restoration project that he needed expert help. Somethings you can do with sheer hard graft, but he drew the line at upholstery. Fortunately, he'd found Ramone, ex-upholsterer who'd worked twenty-five years on Cadillacs before retiring to Florida. Ramone loved the Studebaker as much as he did and sourced the exact white leather they needed. Ramone confessed to him that putting it all together had been the most satisfying job he'd ever done. He also pulled in all kinds of people who knew about suspension, rewiring and welding. That's where the money had gone.

They all loved working on the Hawk, but they all needed paying for their time and expertise. He'd learned a lot – they had all been generous in teaching him what he needed to know, but his old hands weren't so flexible anymore.

He caught a glimpse of himself in the mirror. Needed to shave and trim his beard. Didn't like seeing himself up close: being reminded he was in his seventies now. Too late for vanity. You just had to accept this was the wreckage of a life lived. No restoration project was ever going to return him to 'like new'.

He put the money into the inner pocket of his jacket. No need for anyone to know it was there.

He checked the route map once more. Just over fifteen hundred miles. The guy in Montreal claimed he had a yard full of Studebaker spares and odds and ends. Been collecting for years, sourcing stuff from a secret Studebaker graveyard he claimed. He owned a Lark, which to Remy's way of thinking was not something you wanted to boast about. They sold thousands more Larks than Hawks, but it was an act of desperation to even build it, let alone sell it. He couldn't imagine why anyone bought one if they could have had a Hawk or an Avanti. Undercapitalized, the company had merged with Packard but that didn't save them and now few people even remembered either of them.

He knew he was being pedantic about the steering wheel and if he didn't damn well hurry up and finish the reno he'd be dead before he ever got to drive it. He had to hope the guy in Montreal was genuine. Fifteen hundred miles of skepticism lay before him.

He remembered to charge his phone. Maisie would be checking up on him. He'd rigged up a hands-free arrangement in the truck on her insistence. 'You have no idea how many people wind up dead using a cell when driving.'

CHAPTER TWO

Emergency Stop

It was raining hard in the morning. Thunder rumbled overhead. He stuck to Route 1 and cursed the heavy rain, the remains of Hurricane Cynthia currently battering the gulf coast of Florida and heading inland. After only ninety minutes on the road, he needed to stop already. At least he'd left the main settlements behind. He pulled over at the entrance to some place called The Farmstead. There was a long drive leading off into the distance, so he knew he'd have time to go and get back in the vehicle before anyone saw anything.

Couldn't avoid the rain. And, of course, it wouldn't come out right away. The more urgent it was, the harder it was to get the flow going. He winced as he waited, rain soaking his cap and jacket. He'd finally finished when a dog came running out of nowhere. Nice looking fella, a Collie mix of some kind, one blue eye, the other gray. Looked drenched. Seemed friendly. Looking at him and the truck expectantly.

"Where the hell did you come from, dog?"

"Wait up!" He heard a young voice shout out. "Waaaait."

Remy climbed back up into his truck to get out of the rain, the dog followed, just scrabbled up after him and sat on the passenger seat, as if he did this all the time. He keenly looked out of the window towards the long drive.

"Well, you're a cheeky so and so," Remy declared, surprised at the dog's boldness. "Whatever you do, don't shake." Remy told the dog, reaching to the back of his seat and pulling out a tattered red towel which he threw over the dog and rubbed him down. "This was Rascal's. You can probably still smell him. Dead three years now."

She was standing outside the truck looking for her dog. Young kid, soaked to the skin, inappropriately dressed for the weather. She stared with surprise to see him already in the truck. "Best get in," Remy shouted through his driver's side window. "Door handle sticks. Need to pull hard."

She moved fast – pausing only to stare at him – making a swift assessment that it was safe to get in with him, figuring the dog already made that choice.

"Come on, you'll have to share the dog's towel."

She climbed in, the dog licked her face as if he'd not seen her for weeks. She hugged him back and Remy started up, checked his mirrors before rejoining the road.

"Where you headed?" He asked. "That's some cheeky dog you got there. Just jumped right on up, like he does it every day."

She didn't reply immediately. She looked exhausted as she tried to regain her breath and rub the rain out of her hair. She'd obviously been running from the moment she'd spotted the truck. Remy judged she was around fifteen. Hard to know these days, but he reckoned he was right. She smelled of roses which he thought was odd, but it was a lot better than what the wet dog smelled of.

"Not the easiest place to catch a ride I imagine," Remy said. "Dog got a name?"

"Does it matter?" The girl asked wearily kicking off her wet shoes.

"I imagine it does to the dog."

"Stan. His name is Stan." She brushed her dark brown hair away from her eyes and looked for something to blow her nose on. Remy pointed out a box of tissues by her feet.

The rain was coming down in sheets now and he needed to concentrate. The wipers were pretty slow and primitive. They hadn't really got windshield tech down to a fine art in '57.

"Can you actually see the road?" The girl asked, staring at him, clearly worried.

"Not so much, but we're only going twenty right now. If this thing hits anything, it will survive."

The girl rolled her eyes, wiped more rain from her face and shook out her hair. The dog leaned into her to get warm.

"Stan seems pretty used to getting into trucks." Remy commented.

The girl hugged her dog. "He likes to ride the tractor on the farm."

"Have you got a name?" Remy asked as they passed a gas station. He saw a sign for Brokenbrook 10 miles. He remembered there was a diner there; or used to be. So many things weren't there anymore. He could use a coffee and wait out the worst of the rain a while.

"I'll stop for coffee at Brokenbrook. You got a destination in mind?"

"H- Haven Ridge." He noticed a hesitation in her reply.

Remy nodded. A good two hundred miles or more.

"Not a happy place since they closed the food processing plant. I seem to recall it was the town's main employer."

The girl shrugged. She had no idea.

"You won't remember it, of course. Plant closed in 2009. Haven Ridge formula milk was sold right across the States. Never did understand why they closed it. Not as if people stopped having babies."

Remy glanced at the dog cleaning himself. "I had a dog just like Stan. He lasted sixteen years. Didn't seem right to replace Rascal, though I wanted to. House never the same without him there."

"What he die of?" The girl asked, then bit her lip realizing this might be a sore point.

"Kidney failure but arthritis mostly. Gets most dogs in the end. People too. Only we like to prolong their agony. I hate to see an animal in pain."

"Stan is two now."

Remy smiled. "Two's a perfect age for a dog. At their best. He loves you. That's good. A person needs a good dog."

The girl wrinkled her nose. "He's not always good. He hates chickens, don't know why. Can't go near 'em."

Remy chuckled. "Must have a grudge. Raised on a farm, he might have got pecked when he was a puppy. Chickens can be aggressive."

The girl frowned. She tried to remember if Stan had any incidents but couldn't think of one.

"Where are you headed?" The girl asked.

"Montreal."

The girl didn't know where Montreal was. Didn't care. She stared out at the driving rain and hoped this old guy could see better than her and she couldn't see anything. She wished she'd had time for breakfast. He'd said he'd stop but she didn't have a dime on her. Not exactly planning this escape too good. She chewed on her bottom lip. That was her worst fault according to Father Tresor. An inability to plan ahead.

He tried to make conversation. "I've been on this road many times; I don't recall noticing any Farmstead sign before."

The girl didn't answer or didn't want to. Remy kept on driving. Well aware the traffic was building up. He really hoped that the diner was still there. Should have remembered the flask. He'd put it out on the table. He wondered what else he'd forgotten. Thank God he'd packed his pills the night before.

"You in trouble of any kind, kid? You seemed pretty keen to get away. No bags. Haven Ridge is a long ways away. I don't want to be in trouble with the law."

The girl still didn't reply. He shrugged and continued staring at the flooding highway. They passed a vehicle abandoned at the side of the road, hazard lights flashing, no sign of any driver though.

"If this storm keeps up there's going to a lot of broken-down vehicles ahead. That diner can't come up soon enough." He wiped the inside of the windshield, annoyed it was steaming up. He opened his window a little but soon regretted it as rain forced itself inside. He noticed she was shivering. "Sorry the heater doesn't kick out much heat. Old truck, heaters were considered a luxury back in '57. If you look behind the seat, you'll find an old sweater of mine. It'll swamp you but might stop you from turning blue."

The girl didn't waste any time in grabbing the old sweater out and pulling it on. Remy smiled as it swallowed her. It was covered in oil stains. He always put it on when fixing the truck.

"Stinks a bit, but it's wool, should keep you warm."

The girl snatched a glance at him. "No one's looking for me. Not yet anyways."

Remy noted the 'not yet'. "But you needed to get away."

The girl nodded and reached for another tissue to blow her nose. She stared out of the windshield again. "Yeah, I needed to get away."

Remy nodded, thinking back sixty years or more. "I ran away once when I was a kid. Managed to get about 100 miles before I realized I had no money, no food. Can't remember why I ran now, but I was angry about something."

The girl buried her face into Stan's wet fur asking, "What happened?"

Remy laughed. "I got home about two days later. My Pa didn't say a word, not a one. My mother said, 'I hope you found what you were looking for'. I guess I learned that I wasn't as important in their lives as I thought I was."

The girl closed her eyes. "No one will miss me. That's for sure."

"Someone will, even if they're glad you're gone."

The girl opened her eyes and nodded. "They'll be happy I've gone."

"And the dog? They'll be worried about the dog."

"He's mine." She asserted. "Always has been. Won't do anything for anyone else."

Remy smiled. Rascal had been like that. Totally devoted to one person. "You dock his tail? Collies usually have a nice fluffy tail."

The girl frowned. "Dock?"

"Cut. Y'know. Some people cut dogs tails. I think it's cruel. A tail is there for a reason."

The girl shook her head. "He was born like this. For a while I thought it would grow but six inches is all there is."

"Must be the breed, whatever it is. Good looking fella either way. You know anyone in Haven Ridge?" Remy asked.

"My mother."

Remy nodded with relief, happy to hear that. "That's good."

The girl stared at him a moment wondering where all these questions were going. When she'd finally found the courage to leave, she hadn't really thought about questions and what she'd say to people. She'd had to leave. The way Father Tresor was always looking at her, stroking her. She didn't want to be the next one and there was always a next one. Stan couldn't protect her all the time.

Remy saw the turnoff for Brokenbrook at last and moments later a brightly lit diner still open after all these years. The faded 'Breakfast Served All-Day' sign was reassuringly still visible.

"You hungry? Breakfast on me. You can't take the dog in, but we can take something out for him."

The girl gazed at her benefactor in wonder. He was being nice to her. Why? People were never nice, let alone be nice to her dog.

"Stan will probably howl. He's not used to being left behind. He goes everywhere with me."

"I'll bring him a bowl of water out. They've usually got treats for dogs on the porch, he like treats?"

The girl nodded. Stan would eat anything. He was always hungry. Always.

Remy parked up as close to the entrance as he could. "Run in, don't get wet. I'll catch up. I have to lock up. Leave your window open a crack so Stan can breathe. Don't want the windows all steamed up."

She did as she was told, gave the dog a hug and let herself out of the truck. The dog couldn't believe she'd left him. Remy smiled at the dog. "You be good, OK? Keep her seat warm. I'll bring you some sausages. Bet you'd like some sausages."

Stan began howling before he'd even got to the diner door. The water bowl and treats jar was right where it was supposed to be, and he quickly headed back to the truck to deliver them. The dog ignored the water but jumped on the treats. Remy backed away and locked up again. He was glad of the extra security a dog gave the truck. There were more than a few unscrupulous folks who'd want to steal a Chevy like his. That's why he never resprayed her. No need for anyone to know she had a reconditioned engine and gearbox that was good for another hundred thousand miles. Even had the seats upholstered and recovered in the original dull brown leather. Bought it for nothing when he was twenty-one from a farmer near St Pete. Fifty-four years on the road together. No point in changing anything now.

She wasn't at a table when he got inside, but soon reappeared from the bathroom looking less bedraggled. Only now did he notice she was a pretty little thing. Nervous as hell, like she'd never been in a diner before.

She slipped into the seat opposite him and wasn't sure what to do.

The waitress loomed over them suddenly with the coffee pot at the ready. "Coffee?"

Remy smiled. "We need it. When will this rain ease up huh?"

The waitress shrugged. "They say it's set for the whole weekend. Breakfast special for two? You both look starved."

Remy glanced at the girl and nodded. "Yeah two. Wheat toast and an extra side order of sausages for the dog."

The waitress glanced out of the window at his truck. "I thought I heard a dog howl. Breaks your heart, right? Hard to get them to stop once they get started."

She glanced at the girl. "You alright girl? You're shivering."

The girl nodded. "Got caught in the rain."

The waitress nodded. "Weather ain't what it used to be and that's a fact." She poured them coffee and tossed a few creamers onto the table, turning her head to holler – "Two specials, both with whole-wheat – extra side of sausages." Then she was gone.

The girl stared at Remy in wonder. She pulled open two creamers. "I only had coffee once. You don't get coffee at the farm."

"Well, it's diner coffee. Not like fancy coffee you get at Starbucks, but it will warm you up. Sip it, it's hot."

Remy opened a couple of creamers and poured them into his coffee. The girl had a red raw scar on her neck. He could see she was anxious about the dog, continually staring out the window towards the truck. He was beginning to form opinions about the girl and her circumstances. "You don't have to tell me much, I guess. There's no law that says you have to, but I think you need to tell me something. Everything is new for you. So, I'm guessing you don't get off the farm that much."

She tried to hide behind the coffee cup, sipping it and wincing because it was so hot or bitter or both.

"It's none of my business," Remy continued, "but here's the thing, if we get pulled over for any reason by the law, I need to know your name and you need to know mine. If someone reports you missing, they'll know about it. So, just to be safe and to protect me and that dog of yours, I suggest you might be my grandniece or something. What's your mother's name?"

The girl closed her eyes. She felt dizzy. Questions. She should have anticipated questions. She guessed he wasn't being mean. He seemed kind. Stan would have warned her if he was trouble.

"I don't know my mother's name. Not her first name. Only that she's called Hannan, like me, I suppose."

Remy digested that as he sipped his coffee, deciding it was too strong and needed more creamer to dilute it.

"That's a start. You have an address for her?"

The girl nodded. He only now noticed she had dark green eyes. "And I'm guessing she doesn't know you're coming, right?"

The girl nodded. "I ..."

Remy put his hands on the table, taking a gentle tone. "Here's the thing. My late wife, bless her soul, ran a charity for separated kids. She was big on getting broken families back together, devoted twenty years to it, or more, so I know something about runaways and broken families. I'm thinking you haven't seen your mother in a very long time. That place you just ran away from is a care institution of some kind. And you've been thinking about finding your mother for years but only just recently found out where she lives. And now you want to know why she gave you up. Correct me if I'm wrong."

The girl stared at him open mouthed, astonished he could know this about her.

Remy sat back in his seat. Her reaction told him he was right. "You wouldn't be the first orphan who ran away to find a parent. You won't be the last. I have no special insights kid. My wife was desperate to mend broken homes and hearts. I've seen hundreds of kids pass through her hands, every one of them banking it all on finding an answer, an explanation, an apology, something that will make sense to them as to why they ended up in care."

He offered her a gentle smile. "I promise I'm not being cruel or cynical, kid. I'm trying to say I understand why you're on the road and why it's important to you. I guess you didn't have time to pack a bag. Stan is the farm dog, right?"

The girl nodded. "But everyone knows he's mine."

Remy nodded. "Yep, that I do agree. But tell me, did you think about what your mother might say to you? What happens if she has a new life, new husband, new kids? You don't know why she gave you up. When did you find out about her?"

The girl wiped a tear away. He was saying he wasn't being cruel, but it sounded cruel. But then again, she was used to that and the name calling, the belittling.

"Yesterday. It was my turn to clean the office."

"Ah, and you found something."

She nodded. "Found my file, didn't even know I had one. There were letters. Not many. Five. Her address was on one of 'em. They stopped when I was ten. They never gave 'em to me. She kept saying how sorry she was that she hadn't been to see me."

"She may have had a reason. Did any other mothers turn up at the farm?"

She had to think about that. "Not that I ever noticed. No."

Remy nodded. "So, the last time she wrote to you was what, four, five years ago? I'm assuming you're about fifteen now."

The girl exhaled. "Sixteen soon, don't exactly know the date."

Remy was surprised by that but didn't query it. "Any schooling?"

She rolled her eyes. "Homeschool at the farm. It's shit. I know nothing except how to read and write and grow potatoes. They tell us that we're all going to work at KFC. I don't even know what KFC is. Father Tresor says, 'the service industry needs people like you'. What does that even mean?

"He's being facetious. If you know what that means."

"Mean. I know words. Most books are banned. Charity sends 'em to us and we're supposed to burn 'em. I grab what I can and stash them in the barn."

"Banned books?"

"Fiction mostly. Science stuff too. There's a list of stuff we can't read but there's only me and Paulo who like reading anyways. Paulo will be mad I left without telling him, but he broke his leg last year and it hasn't healed right. No way he can run."

Remy frowned. "Tell me your name. Mine's Remy."

She hesitated. Her name was all she had left. For some reason she was reluctant to tell him. No idea why. It was the only thing she owned.

"How old are you?" She asked, for no particular reason.

"Seventy-five."

She made a quick mental calculation. "You was born in 1950?" It seemed impossible to her.

Remy laughed as he gulped some coffee. "A lot of people were born in 1950. Might surprise you to know a whole bunch are still alive, despite Covid and heart attacks and everything else that life throws at 'em."

The girl looked away at the kitchen hoping the food would come soon. She hadn't eaten in two days. "I'll never get to twenty, let alone seventy-five."

"Sure, you will. Depends, of course."

"Depends?" She queried, looking out towards the truck again, hoping Stan was ok.

"On the choices you make. You're fifteen. A kid can make a lot of bad choices at fifteen. I've seen it many times. If people are looking for you, you might want to change your appearance some. Dye your hair maybe. Y'know, in case they're handing out photos of you."

The girl shrank into herself. This was not what she wanted to hear. "No photos. It's one of the rules."

Remy noted that particular detail. He wondered why that was.

The waitress was approaching with their breakfasts. He smiled as she laid the loaded plates on the table. "Looks good." Remy remarked.

"New chef. He's trying to impress the customers." She answered. "Top up the coffee?"

Remy was about to nod then remembered. “Can’t dammit. Bladder says no.”

The waitress laughed. “Ain’t that a bitch. My husband’s got the same problem.”

“It won’t kill him, but sure as hell is inconvenient,” Remy confessed.

The waitress smiled at the girl. “Get eating girl. Your grandpa needs to feed you up.”

The girl grabbed some toast – she didn’t need prompting.

“Extra sausages will be out in a moment.” The waitress informed them as she departed.

“Eat slow,” Remy told her. “We’re in no rush to get back out into that rain.”

She looked up at Remy a moment. “My name’s Ami. With an i.”

Remy smiled, slicing a sausage, pinning it down with his fork. “Good to meet you Ami with an i. French name. Classy.”

“You speak French?” Ami asked.

“Wish the hell I did. Be easier to negotiate with the guy in Montreal.”

“Montreal is French? You’re going to France?”

Remy laughed. “It’s in Canada. Quebec.”

She shrugged. “Don’t know nothing about Canada.”

Remy swallowed his sausage. “They’ll be mighty upset to hear that,” he said smiling. “And don’t mind me giving you lectures. Ain’t none of my business, but you seem like a bright kid and I’m all for second chances. What’s life like at the farm? You ever get to leave it? I mean …”

She shook her head. “You can’t leave. That’s another rule. Not even if you get sick.”

She stared at her food. She’d never seen such a big plate of food before, couldn’t believe it was just for one person. She tried some of the hash browns and decided she liked them. She wondered how Stan was coping. Couldn’t hear any howling.

“We’re the Children of the Order,” Ami told him after a moment.

Remy looked up at her and frowned. “Order? Like a monastery?”

Ami shrugged. “I don’t know what that is. The farm is where the brothers and sisters send their kids so they can devote their time to serving the Order. Paulo says it’s to make sure we grow up to be devoted to Lord Ramesh. He’s the leader. Even Father Tresor has never actually met him.”

"But you're not devoted."

Ami pulled a face and scoffed. "None of us are. It's shit. We're just slaves growing food we never get to eat. You're supposed to be sent to Charleston when you reach sixteen to serve Lord Ramesh. I've seen 'em drag kids away in handcuffs so they can't escape. No way I'm ever going to Charleston."

Remy stared at her, saw the fierce determination. "So, what do they teach you at the farm, aside from growing potatoes."

"Obey and Praise Lord Ramesh for his endless bounty and devotion to our wellbeing. We have an hour of devotion every morning to praise all the wonderful things he does for us."

"Such as?" Remy asked.

"The food on the table. The clothes on our backs. The love and care of the Brothers and Sisters who raise us and beat us and lock us in solitary if we don't obey and starve us if we don't smile or work or praise Lord Ramesh loud enough." She grimaced. "We live simple, beautiful lives with nature. Sounds great, don't it?"

Ami ate her food with relish now, allowing herself to enjoy it. Paulo always told her. Eat, it might be your last.

Remy didn't think it sounded great at all. Sounded like a cult and he'd seen enough runaways from cults that could never outrun the damage it had done to their minds or souls. His late wife should be sat at this table. She'd instantly know what to do, who to call.

"And this Father Tresor is in charge of the farm?"

Ami nodded. "You'd probably like him. He's all smiles. No one knows how many lies he tells visitors. You'd never know anything is wrong. We have to swear everything is perfect and how much we love Father Tresor, but he's worst one. The Sisters are evil too. See this scar on my neck?" (She pulled the top of the sweater down to reveal more of the red raw scar). "She twisted the skin off because I fell asleep in class. That's the other thing. You always have to get up at first light to feed the animals and I'm a bad sleeper. Always have been..."

"How many kids live there?" Remy asked.

Ami thought about it a moment. "Twenty-four right now, minus me."

"And you don't think they'll come after you?"

Ami drained her coffee and stared right at Remy. "Father Tresor will do what he always does and call the cops. You think they'll believe me when I tell them this holy man was pawing me and touching me up like he couldn't wait to ... I could feel his prick rubbing up against me. He knows no one would defend me, except Stan. He already threatened to have Stan shot. That's when I knew I had to go. There's always some girl pregnant at the farm. Father Tresor isn't the only one. We're like apples waiting to fall off the tree."

Remy tried not to show any reaction. He could hear the repressed anger; she wasn't making this up. He was a pretty good judge of character. "I know people we could report them to."

Ami smirked. "Go ahead. The cops are just as guilty. Paulo could tell you that. It's not just girls who get it. No one's safe at the farm. No one."

Remy looked out of the window and thought the rain might ease off soon. "Why did you wait so long to run?"

Ami shrugged, she'd asked herself that question a million times, always had the same answer. "Where would I go? How many people would believe me? One kid who ran last year was put into solitary for a month when the cops brought her back and she sure wasn't pregnant before she went in there. They break us down until we obey. It gets worse if you get sent to the Big House in Charleston I hear. A lot worse."

Remy didn't know what to say. Even if half of what she said was true, it was bad. All this going on no more than eighty odd miles from where he lived. His late wife would have stormed the place with the Committee in tow.

"How many years have you been there?" Remy asked, wiping his toast into the egg yolk before eating it.

Ami finished her breakfast. She felt stronger now. She didn't mind the questions so much.

"I was five when she dumped me there. Just had a birthday I think, but I can't recall exactly when."

"And you never saw your mother again?"

Ami shook her head. "Don't feel sorry for me. From what Sister Lopez told me life with my mother would have been crazy. She was a real believer. She was a favorite of Lord Ramesh, a real good recruiter for the Order. She said I looked just like her and I'd attract many new members, like she did. As if I'd do that."

"It's a cult, whatever they might think. I'm kinda surprised you're so normal. I've met kids raised by cults before. They are seriously messed up. It's difficult for them to process the damage. You're not like that."

Ami shook her head, a wry smile on her face. "I'm damaged. Believe me, no one who survives the farm isn't damaged. We all pretend to believe the shit they tell us, but there isn't one kid there who wouldn't run if they got the chance, if they didn't believe they'd get brought back by the cops."

"You left."

"I know where to go. I've got Stan and I've got an address."

Remy shook his head. "So do they. Sorry to disappoint you, Ami. But if you know, they know. They could be waiting for you."

Ami scowled. She hadn't thought about that at all.

Remy finished his breakfast wishing he could drink that second cup of coffee. They sat in silence for a while, the wind and rain battering the window. Ami was pensive, digesting what he'd told her. She had no plan other than finding her mother and it was beginning to dawn on her that things were about to turn to shit again.

The waitress brought the sausages out in a paper bag. "I stuck some broccoli in there. Dog's usually go crazy for it."

Remy smiled at her. "You're a star."

She beamed and winked at him. "I know. Totally underappreciated here."

Ami grabbed the food and stood up. "Thank you." She told the waitress. "I'll go feed him now."

"You're welcome girl."

"You'll need the keys," Remy told her, holding them out for her. "Don't let him choke. He's a hungry dog."

Ami nodded and left quickly clutching the food.

"That's a pretty girl you got there, Grandpa. You think the rain will stop soon."

Remy smiled and dug out his wallet. "Well, it's only Florida rain, it's still 65F out there today. What do I owe you?"

"Twenty-four and seven for the side order including taxes."

Remy winced, he seemed to recall it was about half that last time he came by. He paid her and tipped well.

"Come back again. We like hungry customers here," the waitress said smiling.

"Sure will." Remy got up from the table and made his way to the restroom, wondered how far he'd get after drinking that darn coffee. Two highway patrol cops wandered in shaking the rain off their jackets and found themselves somewhere to sit. They greeted the waitress like an old friend.

Ami was crouched in the footwell with the dog when he got back to the truck. She'd covered herself with the blanket.

"What now?" Remy asked as he climbed in.

"Didn't you see 'em?"

"What? The cops? They probably come here for breakfast every morning. I'm pretty sure no one is looking for you yet. Still less two traffic cops who need their morning coffee."

Ami stayed where she was until she was sure he was back on the road. The dog climbed up on the passenger seat and didn't seem put out any. Ami finally followed suit.

"I hope you let him out for a bit." Remy asked.

She nodded. "He's a good boy. Ate everything so fast – I told him to slow down but he never listens."

"Dogs never know where the next meal is going to come from. My Rascal was the same." He looked across at her a moment before returning his eyes to the road.

"Everything you said back there is true? You swear on it? You know I'm going to ask some questions about that place."

Ami frowned. "I ... I'm not a liar. If you speak to Father Tresor..." She looked away and sighed. "Fuck, what am I saying, he'll tell you I lie all the time and I'm a worthless piece of shit, but I swear I told you the truth."

Remy made no comment. "I don't like to rain on your parade, Ami, but you told me your mother surrendered you to the farm when you were five. She may not be the nicest person on earth."

"She wrote to me." Ami said defensively.

Remy nodded. "That she did. Maybe she felt remorse. Hell, if I gave up on a kid, I'd feel bad about it."

Ami glanced at him. "You got a kid?"

"No. My wife liked to care for kids in trouble, but she never wanted kids of her own. I didn't get much choice in the matter. Maybe I preferred dogs anyway. Had three, one right after the other. It gets harder to lose them each time. Hell, I'm still grieving for Rascal."

Ami hugged Stan. She couldn't imagine her life without Stan now. Had no idea how she'd managed to live before he came along.

"When we get to your mother's place. I'll go first. Just in case anyone is waiting for you." Remy said. "You understand? You'll hang back. I'm looking out for you here, Ami."

Ami nodded. At least he was still taking her there. She'd imagined meeting her mother a hundred times. It never went well somehow. Like she was steeling herself for disappointment.

"Meanwhile let's have us some music. Find something on the radio. Anything but rap. Ok?"

Ami looked at the antique radio and wondered how you made it work.

"It's only AM. I was going to fit something new, but never got around to it. Left hand knob turns it on, right tunes it. You've seen a radio before, right?"

Ami grimaced. "Never turned one on. Devil's instrument says Father Tresor."

"Your Father Tresor was dead wrong. The devil's got the best tunes. Everyone knows that." He chuckled as she experimented with tuning.

'Hotel California' came out of the speaker and Remy smiled. "Stay with that," he told her. "You can't go wrong with the Eagles."

Ami listened – amused to see him look happy. The rain started up again, but it wasn't fierce like before and there was a bright rainbow off to the left which lifted her spirits some. She pointed to it and Remy nodded.

"Best make a wish," he suggested.

Ami was skeptical. God knows how many wishes she'd made in her life so far, but only one had ever come true. She'd been in solitary yet again for some stupid transgression of the rules and made a wish for a true friend; one she could trust. Stan was born a week later. She saved him from being sold and he saved her right back. She'd never forget that. Never.

Remy drove on. He reckoned he could do another hour before he'd need to stop again. It was going to be a long drive. He picked up the speed to fifty-five, about all the Chevy could do these days.

"If the phone rings it'll be Maisie. She's a relative living at my house. She'll be checking up on me. She worries a lot." Remy told her.

Ami smiled. "She's probably right to be worried. Who knows what crazy people you might pick up on the road, right?"

Remy laughed. This girl was whip smart. Spent a long time living on her wits, he reckoned. He hoped he could trust her. Of course, that's what Maisie feared the most, him trusting people at face value. The sort of thing people of his age had always done.

"We won't reach your Ma's place till late. I don't like driving at night these days, so I've got a motel booked nearby. 'Bout twenty miles short of Haven Ridge. You'll have to be my niece, remember? If anyone asks."

Ami frowned. "Who's going to ask?"

Remy shrugged. "Who's to know, but I'm taking a risk with you in my truck. Leaving Florida with a minor is probably a felony. That farm back there will know all kinds of tricks to get you back. If they want you back."

"They won't want me back."

"Sure they will. Even if they hate your guts, they won't want you spilling their secrets to someone outside of their control. My wife had to deal with this stuff all the time. Believe me, you don't get free of them so easy."

Ami digested this. She hadn't thought about any risks. "Then why help me?"

Remy thought about that a while. "I'm an old romantic. You're a damsel in distress."

"Damsel?"

"Means young woman. It's an old expression. As long as you're telling me the truth, Ami. I will help you. Understood?"

Ami nodded. She thought about what she'd said so far. The truth. It was kinda funny. The first thing she'd ever learned at the farm was to never tell the truth. It would always end up in a beating. She had the scars to prove it.

Remy glanced across at her and looked at the dog getting comfortable. "Why Stan?"

"What?" Ami looked at him confused for a moment.

"Why did you call your dog, Stan?"

Ami covered her face with her hands in embarrassment. Remy was puzzled at her reaction. "Someone you liked, maybe? It's an unusual name for a dog."

Ami hugged Stan and sighed. "It was my first book. The one that taught me to read. "Who stole the Ham?"

Remy smiled.

Ami took a deep breath before explaining. "About a little girl investigating mysterious disappearances in her home. You can see her searching with her dog, as first the ham sandwich disappears, then a pillow and a rug, some biscuits. She goes room by room making a list. You don't see much of the dog, just a paw or two and maybe his tail disappearing ahead of her, or half an ear," she smiled remembering. "Then at the end she goes to the bottom of the yard and opens the shed door and there's Stan, caught in the act with all his treasures, given to his girlfriend and all her puppies that look just like Stan." She sighed and closed her eyes. The pages from the book were still quite vivid to her after all these years.

"So, Stan stole the ham," Remy remarked.

"I loved that dog in the book. He was so proud of all his puppies," she wiped her eyes, couldn't believe she'd teared up. "So stupid."

Remy put a hand out to stroke Stan's head and rubbed his soft ears. "I would have loved that dog too."

Ami buried her face into Stan's fur and tried not to remember Father Tresor grabbing the book from her and throwing it onto the bonfire. Who stole the ham? Of course, it was Stan. From that moment onwards she had resolved to hide as many books as she could and one day, she swore she'd have a dog of her own called Stan!

Stan lay his head across her lap and sighed. She stroked him and tickled his soft velvety ears. She closed her eyes again and somehow fell asleep.

Remy drove on cursing the inadequate wipers. They were making better time now. He reflected on what he was doing enabling a runaway. Maybe he was being foolish, but she'd looked so forlorn and well the dog had led the way. His fault entirely that he had such a soft spot for dogs.

CHAPTER THREE

Father Tresor

Father Tresor paled when he saw who climbed out of the white Mercedes sedan. Sister Merciless herself, the black-cloaked senior member of Lord Ramesh's inner circle, notorious for her ruthless enforcement of the Order's rules. He wanted to disappear, but uselessly stood there rooted to the spot, aware she was glaring at him with open hostility.

"Why aren't you out searching for her, Father?" She demanded to know, retrieving her silver-topped cane from the vehicle.

Father Tresor swallowed hard. "I hurried back when I heard you were coming."

Sister Mercy approached him, surveying him with her hooded eyes. She sneered.

"Did you now. Lord Ramesh is not pleased with you Father Tresor. Not-pleased-at- all. This is the third child you have lost in a year. You will need to explain this to him, in person, today. They are expecting you in Charleston."

Father Tresor did his best to retain his composure. He knew better than anyone that a summon to see Lord Ramesh in these circumstances would end in punishment or worse, expulsion.

"I've been searching day and night," he protested in his defense.

The Sister brushed passed him towards his BMW and placed both hands on the hood, turning towards him with disdain. "Not even warm. Perhaps you were out on foot?"

Father Tresor's heart sank. Hard to admit now that he hadn't bothered to look at all. Good riddance to the little bitch. His only regret was that he wouldn't be the first to take her.

Sister Mercy strode towards the gathering hall, phone in hand as she answered a call. "I'm beginning my investigation now. No, I suspect he hasn't been looking for her at all." She glanced back at Father Tresor till rooted to the spot. "When exactly did she go?"

Father Tresor had no idea. "During the night. She was still there at midnight when Sister Ryan did her rounds. She took the dog. She was willful. She knew the rules but the dog ..."

Sister Mercy held up her hand to silence him and returned to her phone conversation. "She's out there with a dog. That will slow her down, people will be reluctant to give her a ride with a dog in tow." She snatched a look at Father Tresor again. "Photos? The girl, not the dog."

Father Tresor frowned. "You know we're not permitted..." he started.

"I know you, Father Tresor. I've heard the rumors. Give me your phone. Now. Put the password in."

Father Tresor hesitated, the very last thing he wanted was for her to see his phone. He fumbled, pretending he couldn't find it, cursing this day and why they had sent Sister Merciless of all people. She continued staring at him with extreme impatience. He finally located it in his back pocket and came forward, entered the password numbers, and handed it over.

Sister Mercy opened up the image file and flicked through dispassionately, her eyes resting on a series of skinny naked girls in the washrooms. She looked up him and shook her head with bitter disappointment. "The showers? Really? Is that what you like Father Tresor? Which one of these pathetic creatures is Ami?"

"She's not in those. I don't have a ..."

Sister Mercy pocketed his phone. "So, we don't know what she looks like."

Father Tresor was annoyed now. He'd only recently bought that phone; she had no right... "She's small, dark hair." He couldn't recall anything else about her.

Sister Mercy narrowed her eyes. "In other words, like a million other children. Perhaps you can recall the dog better. Perhaps it has four legs and a tail?"

Father Tresor didn't appreciate her sarcasm. "It's a mutt. I was going to have to have it shot."

Sister Mercy almost laughed. "Of course, you were. The dog was probably the only thing keeping her safe in this godforsaken place. Make your way to Charleston, Father Tresor and do not falter on the way. Unlike the unfortunate Ami, we do know what you look like, and we can find you wherever you might go."

She turned away from him. “I will speak to the children; they will know where she is likely to run to. They generally do. Go Father Tresor, Lord Ramesh does not take kindly to someone losing one of his daughters.”

“Daughters?” Father Tresor queried.

Sister Mercy threw her hands into the air in irritation. “All the children are his sons and daughters, just like we’re all his brothers and sisters. If you don’t know that, you’ve wasted twenty years of your miserable life in the Order. Lord Ramesh loves all his children.”

Father Tresor walked towards his vehicle, his heart sinking further. Why had no one told him Ami was his daughter? Or had she meant that he simply regarded the orphans as his children, like the pigs and chickens were all his possessions. He waited for Sister Mercy to enter the Gathering Hall. Did he have time to purge his computer? Clear out the safe? If he didn’t clear out either of them, he’d be doomed for sure.

He began to walk towards his office when suddenly Sister Ryan appeared from inside the building and locked the door. She walked swiftly towards the Gathering Hall avoiding his gaze. He didn’t have a key. He’d never ever needed to lock the door. That was it, he was screwed.

A window opened in the Gathering Hall. Sister Mercy appeared and called him out “Why are you still here Father? Lord Ramesh is waiting.”

Father Tresor reluctantly returned to his vehicle and climbed in. He swore. All he knew for sure was that if he saw Ami and that damn dog on the road, he’d run them both over.

Sister Mercy stood in the oak-beamed Gathering Hall and surveyed the nervous, fearful children, clearly believing they were all in trouble now and due harsh punishment. She could smell their fear. They all looked starved. This wasn’t part of the plan. They lived on a farm for goodness’ sake, there should be plenty of food to go around. She nodded towards Sister Ryan who had once been apprenticed to Sister Mercy when she first arrived at the Order.

“Who knows Ami best?”

Sister Ryan pointed towards Paulo. All the other kids stared at him, silent, accusing, scared of what was to come from this scary visitor from the Order. Only bad things could come of Ami running away. They all knew the rules. There would be no mercy.

Sister Mercy took Paulo to an adjoining room. He stood before her, one eye on her cane expecting it to come crashing down on his head at any moment.

Sister Mercy had observed his limp and undernourishment. He had a nervous tic and there were still raw scars on his injured leg. She attempted a smile. "I'm not here to punish you Paulo. Or indeed anyone. I am as anxious to know that Ami is safe as you are. Tell me what you know. You're her closest friend, right?"

Paulo nodded; his eyes still focused on her cane.

"Where is she Paulo?"

Paulo shrugged. "She didn't say nothin'. We was supposed to go together."

Sister Mercy noted this detail. She wondered how many others were desperate to leave. So much for the Order's tender mercies.

"Tell me about your leg?" Sister Mercy asked softly. "And remember you are sworn to tell the truth at all times."

Paulo smirked. He knew that wasn't true. Not if you wanted to live.

"Accident," he replied hesitantly. Couldn't tell her an angry Father Tresor threw him off the hay loft when he'd answered back. He probably wasn't supposed to survive.

Sister Mercy closed her eyes a moment digging deep to find some patience. "Naturally it was an accident. We don't break our legs on purpose, Paulo. Don't fear Father Tresor. He's gone. He won't be back. I can assure you of that."

Paulo's eyes widened. He felt a huge weight lift off him. No Father Tresor with his vice like grip forcing the boys to do want he wanted with them.

"Talk to me Paulo. I want to find Ami before harm comes to her. Anything could happen to a young girl out there. You want me to find her, don't you?"

Paulo didn't confess to her that he had prayed that she'd escape and never ever be caught. "She had to go. He was going to shoot her dog."

"Her dog?" Sister Mercy queried. The rules were clear on attachments. No pets. Lord Ramesh could not abide dogs or cats.

Paulo defended Ami. "It's always been her dog; from the day it was born. That's why he'd not gotten her yet. The dog protected her. He knew what he wanted from Ami."

He cast his eyes down to the ground and knew he'd be beaten now. He'd told the truth. It always meant a beating. If not Father Tresor it would be Sister Ryan. She loved a beating.

"And Ami? Was there a specific event that caused her to go yesterday?" Sister Mercy enquired.

Paulo looked blank. "I didn't speak to her in a week. I was in lockup again."

"Lockup?" Sister Mercy asked, not sure she'd heard right.

Paulo looked surprised. "Solitary. Bread and water." He smiled a moment. "Must have spent half my life in lockup."

Sister Mercy was shocked. There was no lockup or solitary she knew of. Shunning was permitted, but not locking away. What had been happening in this place?

"Sister Ryan has the key. She's always threatening something or someone."

Shocked, Sister Mercy tried to calm herself. "And what terrible thing did you do to find yourself locked away, Paulo?"

"Sister Ryan said I overfed the pigs. They get hungry when they're expectin'. Might be Brother Davos saying I was falling asleep in class. Always somethin'."

"And Ami? Was she ever in solitary?"

Paulo smiled. "Too smart since she got the dog. She knows they'll shoot him if she's not around to protect him."

Sister Mercy nodded. This Ami sounded interesting. "Can you describe her to me?"

Paulo relaxed, maybe she wasn't going to beat him after all. "She's beautiful. Long brown hair, shining green eyes. Her smile makes you feel like .... I dunno."

Sister Mercy nodded realizing the boy was in love with her. "Can you draw her for me? Are there any artists here?"

Paulo shook his head taking comfort from the fact that they didn't know what she looked like. "Ami's the artist. She makes all the batiks they well at the stall in summer."

Sister Mercy was surprised to learn this. She had it on good authority that it was the Sisters at the Farm who made the batiks. There was a wonderful blue and purple one hanging on her office wall back in Charleston. Lord Ramesh was particularly fond of his.

"So, Ami has talent, like her father."

Paulo nodded, surprised at any mention of any father. Ami was always going on about not knowing who her father might be. Not that he knew his own either.

"Help me, Paulo. I need to know where she might go. It's not safe for a pretty girl out there, with or without a dog."

Paulo desperately wanted Ami to be safe. He didn't, couldn't say anything that would help them catch her, even if he knew. No one was more surprised than him that she'd gone without saying a word. If they brought her back it would be six months in solitary, if they ever let her out again before they sent her to Charleston. Then she'd be lost forever.

"I didn't hear anything. She told all her secrets to the dog." Paulo whispered. "That's the truth. She didn't have any friend here except me and I was locked up."

Sister Mercy got the picture. "You can go now. No wait, show me this lockup. I want to see this jail they put you in."

Paulo was surprised she didn't know where it was. Perhaps this was his reward for speaking the truth, they'd put him solitary again. Yes, that was what it would be.

He turned away from her and led the way. He wished he'd eaten supper first. Never a good idea to go into Solitary hungry.

Sister Mercy followed him out of the building to the back of the barn, shooing stray chickens out of the way as they went.

Paulo stood back as Sister Mercy stared at the solid wooden door to the lockup and the large padlock. She was deeply vexed by this. There was no rule that permitted solitary. Shunning was recommended for transgressions but isolation in this miserable cell with no heating was inhumane – against the very spirit of the Order.

"Who has the key?" Sister Mercy asked again.

"Sister Ryan," Paulo replied.

"Fetch her now. Go boy, don't dawdle."

Paulo ran off, wincing as he put pressure on his damaged leg, wondering if Sister Ryan would comply with the request. She was the worst on for sending you to lockup.

Sister Mercy tapped her cane on the thick metal bars, noting the lack of glass in the window. "Is there anyone in there? Hello? Speak up in there. This is Sister Mercy. Show yourself."

Eventually a pale face appeared at the metal bars, an emaciated wraith barely able to stand.

"You will be set free soon," Sister Mercy promised. "And those who put you here will be punished. You can be sure of that."

Sister Mercy took a photo of the door, padlock and metal bars and sent it off to Charleston with a short message. The Farm would be placed under emergency management or better yet closed altogether. The children would be better served in Charleston and receive proper guidance on how to live their lives according to the rules of the Order.

She looked at her phone and saw the time. None of this was helping her find Ami. More worrying was the plain fact of the matter that no one was out there looking for her. It would not do to have a willful child out there potentially bringing attention to the Order. Lord Ramesh was right to be concerned. And as for Sister Ryan, how was it a promising young woman could stray so far from the path of justice? A long period of self-reflection and discipline would be required. Terrible things had happened here, she remonstrated with herself for not coming down earlier. She suddenly remembered the young child in the lockup.

"We will need a cleansing of this place. I can see that. Don't you worry girl. Upon my word, this is the last time you will be punished."

CHAPTER FOUR

Barn Burning

The motel had certainly seen better days. But the room was clean, and it had twin beds. Remy realized he was taking a real risk now. Picking up a hitchhiker was one thing but sharing a room with a minor. What if she turned on him and accused him of stuff. How the hell would be defend himself?

"You'd better shower, Ami."

She frowned staring at the room with skeptical eyes and the slightly sticky brown carpet. "Why? Do I smell?"

"Mostly of wet dog."

Ami rolled her eyes. "I always smell of Stan. I keep him close, in case, y'know."

Remy knew. "I'm just saying, the shower is there. I'll shower in the morning."

Stan chose the bed nearest the door and Ami joined him saying, "We could have kept going to Haven. It's not so far."

Remy nodded. "We could've. But if there's any surprises waiting for you, I'd rather see them in daylight."

Ami digested that a moment. "You don't think she's going to be happy to see me, do you?"

"Maybe she will, maybe she won't. There's a little restaurant across the way. I'm going there. You can join me after you've showered. The outside deck is semi-enclosed so Stan can join us."

"You seem to know the whole route by heart."

"Been driving these roads with a dog by my side for nearly sixty years I reckon. I know all the places that are dog friendly."

"You've stayed here before? It has to be ancient."

"Motel's been here since 1928. Not much changed either. This was the old motor route for snowbirds before they built the highways. It has its charms. There used to be an alligator farm near here and an aquarium. People came from all over to watch the porpoises perform. It's considered cruel now, but they put on a good show I recall."

He inspected the bathroom. It smelled damp but there were clean towels and even complimentary soap.

"Take Stan with you. He'll only want to join me in the shower. I don't want him wet again."

"He probably needs that shower more than you. I don't suppose you have a lead, since you don't have a collar."

Ami looked at him confused. "He's never been on a lead. He'll go with you if I tell him to."

Remy's eyebrows raised. "If he runs off, I'm not to blame, right?"

She pointed at the door. "Go with Remy, Stan. Understand? Go with Remy."

Stan looked forlorn, then stared at Remy as he went towards the door.

"It's ok. He'll feed you. I promise. Go with Remy."

The dog reluctantly followed Remy; ears flat with disappointment.

"I'm taking the key with me, the door locks itself," Remy told her. "We don't want to get locked out."

Remy looked down at the dog and gently rubbed his head. "Come on Stan. Let's see what they've got to eat."

Ami watched them go, she couldn't believe she let that happen, but she desperately needed to poop. She didn't want Remy to see her wounds either, he seemed to be the type of guy who'd want to do something about it, and she was so close to finding her mother. Couldn't believe she'd just meekly followed him into the motel. She and Stan could have walked the rest of the way. She headed to the bathroom and closed the door, glad to be alone. She stared at the door. No doors in the washroom toilets at the farm, not since one of the kids had slashed their wrists. She was keen to take that shower but knew it would sting. It would take weeks before the scars would heal. Father Tresor sure loved that bamboo stick of his. It cut you fine and didn't leave bruises. No one says no to Father Tresor unless they wanted the stick.

Stan stuck to his heels all the way, turning his head to look back at the motel several times, hardly able to believe he'd been handed over to this man.

"You're a good dog," Remy was telling him. "You need a leak, take it now. We're nearly there."

Stan waited until he found a decent tire to cock his legs against. Remy nodded. "Good boy. Let's go in."

Remy entered the deck area glad there weren't any smokers and the dog quickly settled by his feet under the table. He hoped the service dog policy was still in place.

"Stay here. Ok? I'm going inside."

The dog watched him go but didn't stir.

"Coffee?" The guy asked him from behind the counter.

"Got a menu?"

"On the board." The man informed him. "Fresh chicken noodle soup just made."

Remy smiled. "Sounds good. Give me a minute."

"Take your time. We're open till ten."

Remy put his glasses on to read the chalk board.

Ami stared at her wounds with alarm, some were still bleeding. The bathroom was filled with steam, she'd forgotten to put the fan on. The hot shower had hurt, but she felt better for it. She hoped she smelled better. Didn't like Remy thinking she stank. She wiped the mirror and stared at herself; didn't like anything she saw. No mirrors at the farm in case the devil caught a glimpse of you naked. She was thinking the devil sure wouldn't be impressed with this skinny runt of a girl with all her stinging scars. She let the glass steam up again. She resolved never to look in a mirror again.

Maisie called when he got back to the table with a coffee. He realized he'd forgotten to let her know he was ok.

"I've got good news and bad news," Maisie told him.

Remy's heart sank. Now what? "Give me the bad news first." Remy told her. "I'm sitting down already."

"I'm moving out this weekend." He could hear the excitement in her voice. "I'm sorry Remy, it will seem sudden, and it means no one will be looking out for you, but I've got an opportunity I can't turn down."

Remy stared at his phone a moment, doing his best to hide his elation that she was finally going.

"And the good news?" He asked. He couldn't imagine what on earth had happened to her. Change of jobs? She loved working at the clinic. Maybe a promotion. It was well overdue.

"I'm moving in with Dr Campion. I know it seems sudden, but we've been dating for two months now. He wants me to move in with him."

"Has he tried your cooking?" Remy asked. She'd never mentioned she was dating before. Two months already?

Maisie laughed. "He loves my cooking. So do you and you know it."

Remy was in shock. Maisie had finally met a man who liked her. "Well don't poison him straight away, give it a few weeks at least."

"Don't be like that. Be happy for me Remy."

Remy smiled. "I am very happy for you, Maisie. Seriously. You deserve happiness, you really do. Have I met him? Can't believe you kept this secret from me."

"I didn't want to upset you. I know you don't like living alone. Perhaps you could get another dog."

"Dogs don't make soup," Remy replied, but instantly regretted it in case she changed her mind about moving out.

"I'll leave my recipes for you. Where are you anyway? I hope you weren't driving in all that rain."

"Haven Ridge. A motel nearby. I'm ok. Trucks ok. All is fine. I'll miss you, Maisie."

"I know you will. I promise to stop by when I can. Moving out Saturday. He lives near La Gorce Country Club, North Beach."

"He a golfer?"

"He's promised to teach me. You think it's too late to start?"

"Good exercise for your arms but watch your back. I never took to it myself. But congratulations Maisie. I am very pleased for you." He hoped he sounded genuine.

"You never thought I'd catch a doctor, did you."

"I always knew you'd find the right man eventually. If he's worked with you, he already knows what you're like, so hang on to him."

"Are you kidding? He's a doctor. I'm getting a padlock and chains."

Remy chuckled. She probably wasn't joking. "Leave my key with Jim next door. I haven't got another spare."

"Yeah, I will. Please drive safe Remy. Enjoy Montreal."

"If I ever get there. Good luck Maisie and make sure I get to meet this doctor when I get back."

"You will. I promise you'll like him. He's from Cornwall in England."

"I've been there with my wife. She thought it was so quaint. The roads are a nightmare. That much I recall."

"He's promised to take me there next year."

"Buckle up is my advice. Take care Maisie. You sound happy."

"I am happy. Good night. I'll call again soon."

"Do that. Night."

Remy disconnected and wondered how long this happiness of Maisie would last. Couldn't believe she was finally moving out.

Something on the wall mounted TV suddenly caught his attention. He was staring the news with growing alarm. A fire had burned a barn and a dormitory at an orphanage. Police and ambulances were there. One boy confirmed dead in strange circumstances the reporter was saying and there was a girl missing. A blurred image flashed up on the screen. Alice May Geney they called her. Looked a lot like Ami but he couldn't be sure. The fire had started in the morning. The rain had mitigated the damage to the main buildings, but the Sherriff was talking about suspected arson. He felt angry. This was not what he wanted to hear. He was fooling himself that he was a good judge of people. It seemed Ami was a good liar. No wonder she was so nervous about the cops in the diner. Seemed he was harboring a fugitive. He discovered he was more disappointed that he had a right to be.

Remy searched for the story on his phone but couldn't find much more information. There was the same photo of the girl, but it could have been any girl as far as he was concerned. She was described as vulnerable and wary of people, which could mean anything at all. No mention of the dog which he thought was odd. There was a phone number to call but he didn't call. Not until he'd spoke to Ami or Alice or whoever she really was. He wondered if there was a mother in Haven Ridge at all.

Ami finally arrived. She'd towel dried her hair but had no brush or comb and it was a mess. Stan greeted her enthusiastically and she was stood there smiling at him. Hard to accept this girl was 'vulnerable'. He tried to remain calm, detached.

"I officially no longer stink." She said as she sat down across from him. "Can't say the same for your sweater though."

"Sorry about that but it's keeping you warm," Remy replied. "You think Stan will like rice and chicken or rice and prawns?"

"Chicken. He's never had prawns. Me either."

Remy nodded. "We'll order two chicken noodle soups and two rice and chickens. We'll share it with Stan. Go smile at the guy at the counter, order the food and ask for a dog bowl and some water. He won't bite."

Ami obliged, anxious to get it right. Stan keenly watching her every move. Remy wondered how to tackle the orphanage news but decided to wait. He didn't want a scene even if there were no other diners in the place at the moment.

He had no idea how to deal with this and tried to think of how his wife would have dealt with it. She'd never let the kids get away with anything. Plain speaking and never sugar coat the situation. Kids sometimes couldn't tell the difference between lies and the truth. Ami seemed good, but to burn a barn down; cause a boy to die? What kind of girl was she really? How the hell was she so calm?

Ami returned and made a fuss of the dog. She glanced at him and frowned. "What's wrong? You look angry. What did I do wrong?"

Remy stared back at her deciding to tackle this head on. "You tell me, Alice. You tell me."

Ami sat back in her seat puzzled. "Alice? You forget my name so quick?"

He plunged in despite his earlier caution. "Alice May Geney – wanted for questioning in the case of an arson attack on the orphanage this morning. A boy died in the fire. You probably didn't know that. Maybe you didn't know the kid was in there when you set the fire, but they won't take that into account when the law catches up with you. I guess you weren't going to mention this to me before I drop you off at your mother's. If your mother exists at all."

Ami sat and stared at him in shock. "What? What? A fire? My name ain't Alice whoever you said. I never knew anyone called Alice. I know every kid at the farm. And who died in the fire? What fire? It was raining. Who starts a fire in the rain? I'd never do that. Never. Why would I?"

"You tell me? There's a picture of a girl who looks a lot like you on the TV news. Turn around. It's back on screen right now."

Ami spun around and stared up at the TV in astonishment. There were pictures of the burning buildings and kids being shepherded into a bus. She didn't recognize any of them. The showed the picture of Alice May Geney again and flashed up a phone number to call. Could be anyone. It was kinda fuzzy. It just wasn't her.

"It's not me. It's not the farm. Our barn's twice the size of that one." She glanced back at Remy. "Where is this? The farm isn't an orphanage. I mean they don't call it that. Where is this? It's not me, Remy. Not me. I swear it."

The TV showed an aerial shot of the orphanage and cut to an interview with the owner. She was black and was wiping away tears as she struggled to speak.

"It's shocking, truly shocking. We do so much for these children. I truly can't believe this has happened. I hope they find Alice quickly. She is a very disturbed child."

"Should the people of Gainesville be worried?" The reporter was asking.

Ami let out a gasp. "Gainesville! The farm ain't anywhere near Gainesville. I know that because Paulo came from there. He tried to get back there twice. That's why they put him in solitary. It's not me, I'm not Alice. I've never ever been to Gainesville."

Remy studied Ami's face and saw the tears of relief. He had to admit he'd got it wrong. That Farmstead was nowhere near Gainesville. He felt very awkward now.

The soup arrived and they stared at the steaming bowls of noodles in total silence.

"Enjoy," the man told them. "Nice dog. Looks skinny."

Remy nodded to the man with a weak smile. He still couldn't bring himself to say anything. Ami was shaking. He'd truly believed she's burned down an orphanage. It stripped away all her confidence. She had no idea what to say. How could anyone believe she'd do such a thing but then again, she realized that she'd had many fantasies of seeing the barn on fire and Father Tresor burning along with it. She couldn't claim to be pure of heart.

"How did the boy die?" She asked faintly.

Remy picked up his spoon and started to eat. "Trapped in the barn I guess."

Ami nodded. "I guess they've got a lockup there too."

They ate in silence. Ami devastated by the accusation and Remy feeling guilty he'd been so quick to doubt her. He felt very bad about it. He'd hurt her and she been hurt enough.

Remy finished his soup but could hardly remember what it tasted like. Ami looked so crushed; it made him feel very mean. "I'm sorry, Ami. I'm sorry I doubted you." He finally told her. "I was too quick to judge you. Stupid of me."

Ami looked down at her soup bowl as she chased some noodles around. She finally looked up at him and shrugged.

"Father Tresor says I've got a guilty face. I'm always getting blamed for stuff I haven't done. Always. If that girl burned the orphanage, you can bet she had a good reason."

Remy studied Ami and nodded. "Maybe so, but another kid died in that fire. She'll be locked up forever most likely. People won't want to shelter her."

Ami nodded. "No one ever believes what we say. A boy had a cigarette burned into his forehead last year for answering back. He didn't get any help. Left a nasty scar when it healed. You'd get beaten for complaining anyway, so you don't complain."

Remy's phone lit up momentarily with an alert. He didn't glance at it, but Ami did.

"How does it work?"

Remy looked puzzled. "The phone?"

"I never used one. TV, radio, music, all banned at the farm. Lord Ramesh won't allow anything modern. We're all Luddites according to Father Tresor. Whatever that means."

Remy nodded. "Ned Ludd was a weaver in England around 1800 who led a rebellion against the mechanization of the weaving industry, which was destroying thousands of jobs in the countryside. I guess that bit of history isn't taught anymore. What did you do for entertainment?"

"Entertainment?"

"If you can't watch TV or listen to music, what did you do at the farm to amuse yourselves."

She made a face, being amused was not something she was used to. "We worked. I'm great at growing potatoes. We plant them by hand, one foot in front of the other, dig them up too. We also make stuff for the market stall. People like handmade things. Me and Haini, she's from Europe, do batik wall hangings and stuff like that in summer. It takes hours to do the different dyes and patterns. I'm usually covered in wax or dye. Haini's got real talent for design. They sell 'em for a lot of money, not that we ever seen any of it."

Remy was surprised and impressed. "You've got useful skills there, Ami. A good base to build on. I know you probably don't think that, but believe me, one day you'll be glad you learned how to do that."

Ami shrugged and showed him her slightly purple stained hands that looked rough and raw. "Kills your hands. No heating in the barn in case of fire. Which is ..."

"Ironic." Remy told her. "Given the news today."

"Ironic. I know that word. My whole life is ironic."

The rice and chicken arrived finally. It smelled good and Remy discovered he had his appetite back. The owner produced a bowl for the dog.

"Dogs eat outside. They make mess."

Ami looked up at him with a broad smile. "I'll take him out. Thank you. It smells so good."

The owner nodded. "Enjoy." He looked towards the door as four diners came in shaking rain off their hats. "Welcome. Welcome."

Remy quickly emptied some of the food into Stan's bowl and indicated to Ami to take the dog out.

"I'll keep your meal warm."

Ami grabbed the bowl left without a word, Stan excitedly following her out.

Remy was getting ready for bed. The TV news was all about the hunt for the arsonist girl and some rail crash on the West Coast. There was a new photo of the fugitive girl. Close up she looked nothing like Ami.

Ami stared at the screen. "See, that's not me. She's got pierced ears. No way would they let us pierce our ears at the farm. And she's got a pointy chin. No way that's me." Ami protested.

"I concede that there's little resemblance," Remy replied. "But the first photo they showed could have been anyone."

Ami wasn't impressed. "Is this what TV is? News all the time?"

Remy smiled. "No, there's about a thousand game shows and lots of stuff about serial killers and hero cops that don't actually exist in real life. You haven't missed much."

Ami wasn't sure if he was kidding her or not, but she was kind of happy to know that TV wasn't that compelling.

"I'm just waiting on the weather, then I'm going to sleep. Does Stan need to go outside again?"

"I'll let him out." Ami said.

"He won't run off?"

"He knows who feeds him. He won't go far. Come Stan. Pee. You've got to pee."

Stan went to the door and waited for her.

"You've got him well-trained."

Ami made a face. "I think it's the other way around." She opened the door and the dog dashed outside. She stared up at the sky a moment. "Sky's clearing."

"Should be sunny tomorrow," Remy replied. "Hope so. I'm aiming to be at your mother's place by eight. That way if she's going to work, we're likely to catch her and if she's still asleep well, we'll wake her up. OK with you?"

Ami nodded. She was super nervous about this.

"What if someone from the farm is waiting for me?"

"That's why you're in the truck and I'm the one knocking on the door. Don't worry."

Ami turned to look at him. "I am worried. What if she wants to send me back? I mean, she sent me there."

Stan arrived back inside his little tail wagging. He was happy at least.

"That's the risk, Ami. Unfortunately for you the alternative is child services and that's a whole other world of pain until you're eighteen."

Ami narrowed her eyes. "I ain't ever going back to the farm and I'm not going into care. I can take care of myself. I'm not afraid of hard work."

Remy sighed. "I know. I hope it works out for you kid. I really do." He got up to pee, pausing on the way to the bathroom as Ami got back into bed exposing her bare shoulder.

"What the hell is that on your shoulder?"

"What?" She nervously glanced in case it was a spider or something. "What?"

"That thing, your tattoo."

Ami shrugged. "It's a waso."

"Waso? What in god's name is a waso? Spell it."

"W A S O. It's a bird. Cost me two weeks in solitary for it." Ami informed him.

"They should have locked up whoever did it for a month. More jellyfish than bird."

"They beat him so bad he ended up in hospital. He never came back."

Remy frowned. "That's terrible."

"And you're mean," Ami told him. settling down in the bed, covering herself with the blankets.

Remy sighed and nodded. "I'm sorry. I didn't mean to insult you. I promise. For the record, waso is French for bird and its spelled o i s e a u. I don't happen to know the French for jellyfish, however."

He smiled to himself and headed into the bathroom.

Ami buried her head into the pillow. She still thought he was being mean. She hated being laughed at. Hated it.

Remy reappeared moments later, he could see he'd upset her again.

"I'm sorry, Ami. Jeez, don't mind me. I like you; you've got courage and I promise to behave better. I apologize for everything. OK?"

Ami didn't reply immediately. She wasn't used to apologies either. She heard him get into bed and sigh. She flipped the blanket from her head and moved the dog to one side so she could stretch out her legs.

Remy glanced at her and saw she'd been crying. "I'm truly sorry, kid. I've been stupid from the get-go. I've no idea of the hell you've been through in your life and how much courage it took to finally run. I disrespected you earlier. I knew in my heart it couldn't be you who burned that barn. Just ignore any crap I say. I guess I'm not used to being around kids. I married late. My wife was ten years younger but didn't want a family. Too busy."

"Did you love her?"

Remy looked askance at her. "That's a pretty personal question, don't you think?"

Ami shrugged. She had no idea about what was personal and what wasn't. "If you'd had kids, you'd know mocking them isn't nice."

Remy winced. "I did apologize." He figured Ami was pretty sensitive for a girl raised on a farm.

"It's OK." She replied, wearily. "I know the bird is shit. I cried for days in solitary, and it went septic. Hurt like hell. But I guess it's there forever now."

"Yep, it is. For the record, on reflection, I'm not so certain I did love my wife. Never said that before to anyone, but it's true. Maybe in the beginning, but y'know, she had her work, and I had my job and the dog. In the end we were like most married couples living together but apart. Sort of habit."

Ami digested that and stroked Stan who sighed, wishing they'd all go to sleep. Ami remembered something she'd been told at the farm. "Ms. Spottiswood, she's the teacher who comes in twice a week, she said that love lasts precisely three years, three months and four days."

Remy was astonished and shook his head chuckling at the idea. He looked at Ami and smiled. "I hate to say this kid, but your teacher wasn't entirely wrong about that. Maybe that last four days is pushing it. It's sounds very personal for her."

"She did research on it at the University in Miami," Ami told him earnestly.

"I bow to her scholarship," Remy replied. "I hope when you fall in love it lasts a few days longer than that."

Ami scoffed. "I ain't ever going to fall in love. Never going to happen. I got Stan, that's all the love I need."

Remy nodded. "You're not wrong there. Go to sleep Ami. We've got an early start."

Ami settled down again as Remy switched off the light. He was still thinking about her teacher's comment. Three years, three months and four whole days. He decided he wouldn't mention this to Maisie, she'd only start crossing off the dates until their first row. He turned over to his side. He hoped he'd get at least two hours sleep before he had to get up again.

Remy awoke with a start. The dog was whining, the girl was writhing in the bed, yelling 'no, no, I won't, no, don't ... '

He quickly realized she was having a nightmare. He adopted a soothing voice.

"You're safe Ami, you're safe now."

Stan was still whining, worried and scared for his mistress.

"You're ok too, Stan. Calm down now."

Remy put a hand out to stroke him, but he was uncertain about it, climbing closer to Ami.

"That's it, get closer, let her know you're there with her."

Ami abruptly shot up in bed, still asleep but eyes open, struggling to breathe. "Stan? Stan?"

"He's here with you," Remy told her. "You're safe. Go back to sleep now. Stan protecting you. Go to sleep now. You're safe. Sleep, Ami, sleep."

Ami seemed to hesitate, reached out for her dog and he nervously licked her hands. It reassured her and she fell back fast asleep.

Quiet now. Remy got up, picked up the blanket from the floor and pulled it over her legs, as far as he could go with the dog adopting a defensive posture.

"Sleep now, Stan. Keep her safe."

Remy paid a trip to the bathroom. Wide awake now but sympathetic to Ami. She was strong awake, but no one could hide from their nightmares.

Next morning Ami was first in the bathroom. Remy sat up in bed up and smiled at Stan who was all raring to go already. He suddenly realized there was blood on the sheets in Ami's bed. He reached over and pulled the sheets back. Stan thought it was a game and joined in pulling the blanket off the bed. Remy was puzzled by the blood stains grouped around the top of the sheets.

Ami returned and stopped, staring at him, unable to say a word. Remy looked back at her. "Show me. Show me. You're wounded, Ami. It'll need treatment. I promise I'm not being mean. Show me what they did to you."

Ami took a deep breath and reluctantly revealed the bloody scars on her torso.

Remy winced. "Jesus. We're stopping at a pharmacy first chance we get. You need something on that to help with the healing. Why the hell didn't you say something yesterday?"

Ami dropped her sweatshirt and shrugged. "He's done this to me before. Done it to everyone who says no to him."

"Who is this, Father Tresor? It's disgusting he can get away with this."

Amy nodded. "Ain't nothing you can do about it. He's the law on the farm."

Remy could think of many things he could do about it. And once he got back would make calls. That farm needed to be shut down and fast.

"You alright? You were a bit restless last night."

"I was?"

"Well Stan was a bit anxious. I guess he's not used to sharing a room." If Ami had no memory or her nightmare, he wasn't going to bring it up. "I'm taking a shower. Take Stan out for a walk. We'll have breakfast in an hour. Can you wait?"

"Why an hour?" Ami asked puzzled.

Remy pointed to all the pills he was about to take. "Have to wait an hour after I take all this. Ami, we'll get your wounds treated, OK. They need antiseptic and to be bandaged. I'm not delivering you to your mother like this."

Ami sighed. She wasn't used to get this much attention.

Remy smiled. "Don't look so down. If you're in pain, tell people. You're not at the farm now. You have rights. What the hell did he use to do that? I don't see bruising."

"Bamboo. It cuts fine and doesn't heal easy."

Remy made a face and swore. "That man needs to be locked up and soon. Don't disappear. I'll be ready in fifteen minutes tops."

Ami nodded. Stan was at the door ready for his walk. She put on her old worn sneakers still damp from the rain as Remy swallowed his pills.

"Can I buy a toothbrush?" Ami asked quietly. "I like to brush my teeth."

Remy nodded. "Yep, of course. Sorry I hadn't thought about that. Seems I haven't thought about a lot of things. You have to take care of your teeth. I still have most of mine. Get something for the dog to chew on too. Healthy teeth, healthy dog. That's the way to keep a dog safe."

Ami smiled. She looked over at Stan. "Hear that, Stan? You got to brush your teeth."

Stan pricked his ears; happy she was paying him attention.

Ami felt uncomfortable as they left the coffee shop. "Did you have to make the bandages so tight?"

Remy shrugged. "You're hurt a lot worse than I thought. The antiseptic cream will help you heal but you heard the woman in the drug store. Bind it tight and change the bandage tomorrow. You're going to have to get your mother to help with that. Those cuts will leave scars."

Ami pulled a face. "Match the ones on my back. Shit, it stings."

Remy nodded. "Supposed to."

They both stopped walking as Stan decided to take a dump, spinning around until he faced the right direction. Ami pulled out one of the biodegradable bags Remy had bought her. "I'm going to have to get used to picking up shit now."

"You didn't do it before?"

Ami shook her head. "He used to go to the field to do it. Not exactly any fields around here."

"Yep, fields long gone. But I remember when there used to be orange groves here, all torn up for strip malls. Don't know where they thought the orange juice was supposed to come from after that." He checked his watch. "We'll be there in thirty minutes. You ready for it?"

Ami scooped up the poop and looked for a trash can. "No. I ain't ever going to be ready for it. Can you see anywhere to dump this?"

"Next block, I think. Near the truck."

Ami burped. "I shouldn't have eaten the pancakes. I'm all churned up."

Remy smiled. "You'd feel worse if you hadn't eaten. Big day for you, Ami."

She nodded. "I forgot to say thanks for getting me the clothes and shoes. You didn't have to do that."

"I know. Drug store clothes are practical at least and hard wearing. You can go someplace more fashionable with your mother later."

Ami shook her head. "Fashion? Who cares?" She laughed. "These jeans are dry. The sneakers are sooo comfortable. I never had nice sneakers before. And I got a toothbrush. I'm like ..." She looked at Remy. "I only wore hand me down stuff before. They come and dump it on the floor, and we have to fight over it, never mind what they smell like." She grinned, her face shining. "I'm wearing new, Remy. First time ever. New."

Remy pointed to the dog waste trash and Ami ran over to it, Stan at her side.

Remy remembered what he'd been meaning to tell her. "Stan's going to need a collar. He'll need to be licensed and wear a tag. Local officials can be very particular about that kind of thing. He'll need shots too."

Ami rolled her eyes. "Really?"

"Yes, really. You want a dog you've got to be responsible for it. Make sure he eats one of the chews I bought him for his teeth too."

Ami dumped the poop. She'd never even once considered any of this stuff.

"Does a license cost money?"

"Yep. And you'll need to pay it every year as well. Welcome to the adult world, Ami."

Ami didn't look so happy about that as she got back into the truck.

Remy climbed back in and waited for the dog to settle before he started up.

"Remember what I told you. We get there, you hang back. I'll go first. Just in case they're waiting for you."

"What will you say?"

"I'll ask if she's signed up to the neighborhood scheme."

"What?" Ami looked confused.

Remy smiled as he pulled out of the parking slot. "There's always a neighborhood scheme. I get one of those people every month. I join nothing. Only opens you up to scams and annoying emails and garage sale alerts."

Ami laughed at him. "You're a grump."

Remy nodded. "That I am. When we get to Haven, look out for 34th East. We have to turn left there. I looked it up. She lives in the old factory district. Cheaper housing around there I'm guessing, now there's no factories."

Ami said nothing. Didn't matter if it was cheap, she just wanted it to be there. For her mother to be home and be what...? Happy she escaped the farm or annoyed there would be another mouth to feed – shit two mouths. What if she hated dogs? What if she hated she'd actually found her? Her heart was racing. Why oh why had she eaten the pancakes? She felt like she was going to puke.

"If you're feeling anxious there's some mints to suck on in the glovebox."

Ami searched and pulled out a book – she stared at the title confused. 'Places I don't want to go to and the people I don't want to go with.' "What kind of book is this?"

Remy smiled. "Something Masie gave me to read. Forgot it was there. I think it's her little joke about my general attitude to life."

"Hmmm, well I don't get it." She found some mints and popped one into her mouth. "Why would you go to places with people you don't like?”

“You don’t, but families do it every year at Thanksgiving. You don’t know anything about Thanksgiving either, right?”

“We gave thanks to Lord Ramesh every damn day. That’s enough for me.”

Remy registered that and drove on, warming to his unexpected passenger. He was going to miss Stan when he was gone. If any good was going to come out of this he’d decided that he definitely needed another dog. He’d waited too long.

CHAPTER FIVE

A Lost Hope

"What number is it? Ami? You awake?"

Ami opened her eyes, blinked. Couldn't believe she'd fallen asleep. "What?"

"The street number. We're close I think."

"1602." Ami frantically tried to see the numbers on the run-down houses they were passing. Her heart sank. This was not the neighborhood she'd imagined her mother living in.

Remy was looking for the street signs. "We're in the 1400 block now. I want you to look out for any familiar vehicles from the farm, understand?"

"I'm looking." Ami was already scouring the streets for trouble. Would they really be waiting for her? How would they know she'd seen the letters? She'd put them all back exactly where she'd found them.

"Look out for a beat up old blue Volvo station wagon and maybe Father Tresor's silver two-door car. I don't know the make, but it's got a dent on the passenger door."

"Ok, I'm looking." Remy replied. "Might not be parked close to the house, they wouldn't want to spook you."

Ami stared at every vehicle, astonished at how many of them seemed to be parked on bricks, or burned out. Nothing to impress here. Every house seemed to have patched felt roofs or broken sofas out on the stoops, some Mexican flags in the broken windows. Locals stared with envy at Remy's truck as it cruised by.

"This is not a good place to leave a vehicle unattended," Remy remarked. "I'll do a drive by, then turn around. Put my cap on your head to disguise yourself."

Ami quickly grabbed the cap and jammed it on her head. It was too big, but she didn't care. Her nerves were going to explode any minute. They slowly passed the 1602 mailbox and she let escape a gasp. It wasn't there! The house was gone. A burned-out shell, just the old brick chimney still standing.

Remy slowed and turned around using a driveway a few houses down. He was still processing what he'd just seen.

"It's ..." Ami was trying to say. In all the scenarios of meeting her mother she'd never ever come up with the house being entirely gone.

Remy glanced at her and put a hand to her shoulder. "Sorry kid."

"B.B. But..." Ami stuttered. She seemed to have lost the power of speech.

Remy was checking the nearby vehicles. At least the ones still with wheels attached. He didn't think there was any welcoming committee for Ami. He parked one house away from 1602 and stared at the burned-out wreckage across the way. He felt deeply sorry for the kid and a whole lot of emotions washed over him as he realized she was probably never going to see her mother.

Remy glanced at Ami, saw the tears running down her cheeks. "Whatever happened here happened a few years ago, kid. See the weeds in the yard and the tree growing inside the ruins."

Ami hadn't noticed, couldn't say anything. She felt completely drained of all emotions. Everything had depended on her mother being here, opening the front door, letting her in. Everything. Remy was talking, saying something about making enquiries but Ami instinctively knew that this was the end of the road. She would never see her mother – ever. Something bad had happened to her. She was sure of it.

"Ami? Can you hear me?" Remy was asking for the third time. "Stay put. Keep the doors locked. I'll ask some questions."

"Questions?" She whispered, but he'd already gone and locked his door. She clung to Stan who licked her face, well aware somehow that she needed comforting.

She watched Remy go up to a neighbor's house and ring a bell. He didn't stay long there. He walked past the ruins to the house on the other side, which looked in better shape than many other houses on the street. An older woman came out to greet him. She shook her head a lot and waved her arms around but didn't seem to be hostile. Ami wiped her eyes. Tried not to think about what might happen to her and Stan now. There wasn't even a doorway she could curl up in.

Remy returned after a few minutes and Stan greeted him with a wagging tail.

"One neighbor is new, the other says it was an older woman who lived here before the fire. She was called Agata. She used to work at the factory with her. About sixty she said. She didn't survive the fire. Smoke damage most likely. She wasn't called Hannan though, she was Polish. I can keep knocking on doors, but it wasn't your mother, Ami. I'm thinking she used this postal address for some reason, maybe Agata was a friend. It's not the end of the road kid."

Ami didn't know what to say. It sure looked like the end of the road to her. "You said there has to be a record of my birth somewhere, right?"

"I did."

"Does it mean they also list who my parents are."

"It's supposed to. But things have changed these days. Sounds to me like your mother was a free spirit and may not have done that or indeed not known. Don't get your hopes up, Ami."

Ami shook her head. "It doesn't worry me. No, well I mean, I do worry it might turn out to be someone I don't like or .... Shit, I don't know what I mean."

"Some things are best not known." Remy responded.

Remy started the engine. He wanted out of this neighborhood whilst he still had four wheels. He glanced at Ami and smiled. "For now, you're stuck with me. I'm not leaving you here. When will you be sixteen?"

Ami shrugged. "I never really know. Father Tresor decides. Never on the same date though. That's another reason I had to leave. He could tell me I'm sixteen anytime and then I'll be shipped off to Charleston. So, you don't have time to run, y'know? They're sneaky like that."

"We need your precise date of birth so you can go online and trace your birth and your mother at the same time. Once you have her full name, you'll be able to trace where you were born. Floridahealth.gov if I recall."

He could see Ami was thinking that over. Remy thought about it. Maisie would immediately say he'd gone ga-ga. Picking up strays the moment she was gone, but he couldn't abandon this kid. Certainly, he couldn't let her be sent back to live with a damn cult and be abused.

"You can stay with me until you're sixteen. It's not long. Then you can choose what you want to do. That's your right."

"Choose?"

Remy could see she was still confused. “I’m offering you and Stan a place to stay. No paperwork, no crap with the child authorities. When you’re sixteen you can apply for emancipation rights in Florida. You’d need to be able to support yourself. Maybe you can get a job at the DQ or some place. Start building up some savings and you need to finish your schooling. I know someone who could help with getting you enrolled. Whole lot of stuff to discover, but I’m not ditching you, Ami. You’re a good kid who needs a break. If you want to continue searching for your mother, I won’t stop you.”

Ami took a deep breath and buried her head into Stan’s fur. “She’s dead.”

“Who? The old lady is for sure.”

“My mother. She stopped writing five years ago remember. She’s dead, Remy.”

Remy shrugged as he drove on, stopping at the junction to let a truck go by.

“Maybe she is, maybe she isn’t. Either way I’m offering you a home where no one is going to do anything bad to you. Understand?”

Ami looked at him confused. “But you’re going to Canada.”

“For one day! You’ll wait for me this side of the border. Then we’ll head back home. You can search for her then. Deal?”

Ami had no idea how to respond. No one was ever this nice without wanting something in return. No one.

Remy set off again. “Look, Maisie’s moving out. There’s a spare room with its own bathroom. I’ll expect you to keep it tidy and clean. You’ll pick up any shit Stan leaves around, and we’ll figure out how to live together without getting on each other’s nerves.”

Ami looked up at him. “Until I’m sixteen.”

Remy smiled and shrugged. “As long as you like kid, or until you get sick of living with a grumpy old man. It’s a good offer Ami. You’re far from ready to face the world. You need to get school finished and think about what you want to do with your life. Can you cook?”

“I can make soup.”.

“I’ll teach you other stuff. I used to do all the cooking before Maisie stole my kitchen and I swear my meals were better than hers. You’ll not cause me any trouble. You’ll never lie to me, and no boys can be brought home. No drugs or smokes either. I’m tolerant to a point.”

Ami frowned. “Why?”

"Why?"

Ami nodded. "Why would you be nice to me. You don't know me. You ..."

"Everyone deserves a second chance, Ami. This is what I'm offering you. Besides Stan needs a home. Consider that."

Ami thought about it. She was being stupid for even questioning his offer but all those years on the farm made her distrust everything. "Stan's my dog." She said quietly.

Remy chuckled. "He's definitely your dog. But now he's got a home to guard. Do we have a deal?"

Ami discovered the thing that she was most worried about was him wanting her to go to school. They'd find out she knew nothing. The kids would mock her. She hated being mocked or thought stupid. Hated it. She wiped more tears from her eyes. She didn't even know why she was crying. She never ever cried, but it seemed Remy made her cry all the time.

"Think on it," Remy told her. "We need to find the library if one still exists in this town. They'll have local records. You want to do this now?"

Ami looked up at him confused. "But we're going to Canada."

Remy shook his head. "We're here now. We'll find the library and see what we can find. It's important to you."

"Can we find out something about the woman who died back there?" Ami asked.

"Maybe. Used to be every town had a local newspaper. With luck Haven might have records online. When a house burns you can be sure someone kept a record. We have to assume your mother registered your birth someplace. We're going to need to get you a birth certificate, 'cause you're going to need an ID. Unless you already have one."

Ami shook her head. "No. I'm pretty sure no one even knew us kids existed."

"Someone official knows. Believe me."

Ami rubbed her eyes and exhaled. "I'm scared."

Remy glanced at her puzzled. "You're not scared of anything. What are you scared of?"

Ami stared out of the window as they drove towards the center of town. "I'm scared to find her. I'm scared to know who my father was.

I'm scared of everything. I've dreamt about finding her for years and years and now... I can't see a future."

"Yeah. You feel lost, I get that. I'm right here Ami. I'm not going to abandon you. Don't you fret about that. Ah ha, these look like locals." He abruptly pulled over and wound the window down to address an older couple walking with their groceries towards an apartment block. "Good morning. Can either of you tell me where the town library might be? Or the local paper?"

The couple stopped and stared, startled a moment, unused to being asked anything by a stranger and wary of what he'd want. "That a '57 Chevy?" The silver haired man asked.

Remy grinned. "Sure is. Quarter million miles on the clock."

The man smiled, impressed. "Nothing lasts like that anymore. Library closed a year ago. The Haven Monitor is still going. About five blocks east of here. Lincoln and Pillsbury."

Remy saluted him. "Many thanks to you both. You people have a good day now."

Remy set off with a nod to Ami.

"People like this truck don't they, "Ami said, looking back the couple still staring after the truck.

"It's a living piece of history. Like me. Never be afraid to ask a question. Most people are obliging if you give 'em a chance."

Ami smiled. "You think the newspaper will help us?"

"Maybe. But let me do the talking. We don't want them to get curious as why we're looking. They'd love a human heartstring story about a girl seeking her mother, but let's not make it easy for your Lord Ramesh to find you first."

Ami processed that thought as Remy pulled up outside the old redbrick Haven Monitor building.

The Haven Monitor was a ramshackle affair, last surviving business in a row of empty stores. The middle-aged woman behind the desk lost her enthusiasm for them pretty quickly when she realized they weren't going to place an ad and only reluctantly had pulled up details about the house fire to show them.

Remy stared at the screen with Ami peering over his shoulder. She couldn't see this helped any. The woman died from the effects of the fire. They knew that already.

"And no record of my wife's cousin who was supposed to be living there?" Remy asked the woman. "I can only see the name of the Polish woman who lived there."

The woman behind the desk shrugged. "That's all we have. It wasn't a big story. Houses burn down all the time." She gazed briefly at Remy and Ami with practiced indifference. "Why did you leave it so long to try and find her. It's been four years since it burned."

Remy smiled in an attempt to disarm her. "My wife died and left a bequest to her cousin and well I felt obliged to enquire as to why she hadn't replied to my letters."

The woman softened a tad and pretended to be more sympathetic. "Are you sure she's still alive? She would have definitely had to move on."

"I didn't think to check. She's only in her forties. The family wasn't close. Her name was Hannan. I don't rightly recall her first name. Can you check for any Hannan deaths for me?"

The woman was irritated now. "There might be a lot of Hannan's. I don't have time."

"Only female Hannan's in the last five years. I'd really appreciate it. I'm not so good with computers these days."

The woman was irritated now and rolled her eyes at Ami who remembered to offer her an encouraging smile. She turned as she could hear Stan was howling in the truck.

"I'd better check on the dog," Ami said. She realized she suddenly didn't want to know what had happened to her mother and needed to get out of there.

"That your old truck out there?" The woman asked as Ami fled the scene.

Remy smiled. "Sure is. Not sure which one of us will go first. It's a race these days."

The woman attempted a smile. "You look to be in better shape than the truck at least."

"Wish that was true," Remy confessed, watching the woman enter the births and deaths website.

She scrolled through the names, looking up at him briefly. "How old did you say she was?"

"Her forties. She's got a teenage kid."

The woman nodded. "Jacqueline Hannan. 44. Died as a result of a house fire. Survived by one Ami Hannan. Died same week as the Polish woman. You're right, they must have rescued her from the fire, but smoke's a killer. That your cousin?"

"Wife's cousin, yes." Remy tried to look sad. "Jackie was a bit of wild one in her day. So kind of you to find her. Can I get a print out to show my lawyer?"

The woman reluctantly sent the details to the printer. She jerked her head towards his truck. "That her kid?"

Remy smiled. "That particular wild child is my grandchild who predicted this would be a wasted journey. They get bored pretty quick these days."

The woman nodded. "Kids know nothing. But doesn't stop them having opinions. I don't supposed you want to place a memorial ad in the Monitor?"

Remy sighed. He'd walked into that one. "I should, but as I said, we weren't close. Wonder what happened to the kid?"

The woman put up her hands in surrender. "Families disintegrating, I see it all here. When we close, Haven's history sinks with us."

"Well, you do an important job keeping a community together. At least now I know why she didn't reply to my letters."

"That would be logical. Is there anything else I can do for you?" She reached over to the printer and took out two pages and handed them over. Then returned to what she was doing when he came in.

"Thank you." He offered her a dollar for the pages, but she waved it away. Remy headed to the door. "You've been a great help. I'm sorry it's a dead end, but best to finally know."

"Knowing is what the Haven Monitor exists for." She informed him.

Remy briefly paused at the door. "Thank you again. Goodbye."

He stood on the sidewalk a moment to regain his equilibrium, folding the pages into his jacket pocket. Now for the hard part. Ami was definitely on her own now. Maisie would say he'd lost his mind to take her on at his age. He thought about his wife. She wouldn't have hesitated to find a home and counseling for Ami (she was keen on deprogramming). Nevertheless, he didn't want to pass the problem along. So what he was old, give a kid a home, some security for a few years. 'Never let their problems enter your heart,' his wife would say. 'They always let you down. They're too damaged.'

Was Ami damaged? Sure, how couldn't she be. But Stan loved her, and she loved Stan. That was several years of perfect therapy right there.

He checked for traffic and crossed the road. Stan greeted him like an old friend and Ami gave him a hug. Her anxious face staring up at him.

"I know it's bad news. I just know it," Ami said quietly.

Somehow her saying that didn't make it easier. "She didn't stop writing because she didn't care, kid. She stopped writing because she was gone, Ami."

Ami looked up into his eyes trying to understand that comment.

"She must have died of the smoke in her lungs. One hell of a thing to survive a fire then be killed by the smoke."

Ami took a deep breath. Somehow, she didn't feel sad or sick or anything. She felt relieved, how weird was that? Remy was right. She hadn't stopped writing because she didn't care. She *had* cared. She knew she'd done wrong. But now she'd never know her. She'd never know Stan.

"I am truly sorry for your loss. I really am." Remy said softly. Ami said nothing, just wondering why she couldn't feel anything. Surely, she was supposed to feel something. Her mother was dead.

"Get in the truck." Remy told her. "We'll be in Savannah for supper. You'll like it there. I haven't booked a motel for tonight. Wasn't sure how far I'd get. Don't bottle up your emotions, kid. If you want to cry, cry. You don't have prove how tough you are to me."

Ami frowned; she wasn't sure she wanted to cry. Remy had said 'loss'. Yes, that was what she was feeling. Loss. Something had been taken from her, something that could never be returned.

"At least I know for sure now," Ami replied and hugged Stan on her lap.

CHAPTER SIX

The Judgments of Mercy

Sister Mercy convened the emergency meeting of the Senior Brothers and Sisters at the Order. Lord Ramesh had privately conveyed his wisdom on the matter of Father Tresor and the missing girl. It had been decided that the farm should be sold. Farmland prices were high, and the children could be accommodated within the compound with certain safeguards. They had more than enough land to farm on site and it could only strengthen the Order if they had a more visible link to the food they ate. It was a sound decision in her opinion. Now they had to settle the outstanding issues beginning with the punishment of Sister Ryan.

"It's not a good look to discipline our own. "Sister Brownlee declared. "It can spread dissatisfaction."

Sister Mercy frowned. "She has abused the children. Beaten them and jailed them, sometimes several times and put them on starvation diets. How would you deal with this, Sister?"

Sister Brownlee narrowed her mouth and cast her eyes down to the floor. She had nothing further to say on the matter.

"Expel her," Brother Rafe suggested. "As an example."

Sister Mercy nodded wistfully. "She showed such promise in the beginning."

"But away from the all-seeing eyes of Lord Ramesh she revealed her true personality," Brother Rafe remarked. "We too are at fault for allowing Father Tresor too much freedom. We should have gone down to the farm more often."

Sister Mercy made a note on the pad. "That is true Brother Rafe. But even when I visited, the children were persuaded to praise Father Tresor and the care they received. I freely admit I am at fault for not investigating further. I accept that. As Lord Ramesh tells us, 'A dog will still wag a tail to a man that beats it'. I am resolved to pay lengthy visits to other Order outreach communities over the next few months and be more observant."

"And what of Father Tresor?" Brother Rafe asked. "Has he been found?"

"Not yet. We have blocked his bank cards and I'm sure he hadn't time to access the money he misappropriated. Daisy Towe is auditing the farm accounts and will report next week." Sister Mercy informed them. "Brother Grace has been dispatched to find and retrieve Father Tresor. He will persuade him to return and answer for his actions. Brother Grace can be very persuasive."

"Expelling him will not be optimum for the Order. He might seek to spread negative thoughts."

Sister Mercy nodded, clasping her hands together. "We have other means of punishment. Lord Ramesh is quite insistent he should be held to account within the Order and our rules."

Brother Rafe and Sister Brownlee exchanged glances. They knew what that meant and how humiliating it would be for Father Tresor. More is the point; Father Tresor would know that too. Neither one of them envied Brother Grace's task.

"On the matter of Ami, the missing girl. Have there been no reports of any sightings?"

Brother Rafe checked his notes. "None. Clearly, she was able to get a ride away from the farm. It may have been coordinated with one of the farmhands, but we have no proof, and all were present the night she disappeared."

"A girl and a dog could not travel far," Sister Brownlee asserted. "I have personally driven the route and called in on many homes and shops along the way. No one has seen her."

"Where would she have gone, do you think? Her mother?" Sister Mercy asked.

Brother Rafe shook his head. "Her mother passed away almost four years ago. I visited the last known address and there is nothing there except a burned-out shell. No one has seen her or a dog. She couldn't know the address anyway and according to Sister Ryan has never enquired about her whereabouts."

Sister Mercy frowned. "Do we forget her? Or wait until she's found dead. A young girl who knows nothing of the world. She wouldn't be able to feed the dog, let alone herself and could easily fall prey to some man."

Sister Brownlee put up her hand to speak. "Lord Ramesh has spoken to me on this matter. He believes she will return to us. She has no choice. She will suffer greatly but he believes that in her suffering she will return to us chastened and renew her devotions to the Order. She is not the first to run, sadly. You are right Sister Mercy; we are all at fault for allowing things to get out of hand at the farm. We are always too willing to deceive ourselves because it is convenient to do so."

"I hear you, Sister Brownlee. I hope Lord Ramesh is correct in his assessment. A girl that age is so vulnerable to misfortune out there in this evil world. I hope all of the Order will put her in their prayers this evening. I shall."

"So, it is resolved, we will not search for her?" Brother Rafe asked, to be sure.

"It will be God's will. We have neither the resources or the time to find her and Lord Ramesh is insistent that the authorities are not to be involved. A sheep is not lost forever."

Brother Rafe nodded his head sagely. "Then let us conclude this meeting and concentrate on the flock we do have to hand."

"Indeed Brother. Let's safeguard and redouble our efforts to make sure the children are made welcome when they arrive. Let them know the Order embraces them and cares for them. They are our future, after all."

CHAPTER SEVEN

Escape Plan B

He glanced down at the fuel gauge. He'd need to fill up soon. He needed to be careful. He was running out of cash. Couldn't use his cards as they could trace that too easily, but if there was one thing Father Tresor knew with absolute certainty, he was never going to Charleston. Nothing but pain and humiliation awaited him there. He'd laid low long enough now. It was time to take charge of his life.

He knew there was a desperate shortage of teachers in the Christian schools and colleges. Armed with a new resume that spoke of devotion and duty to children in his care this past twenty years, he was sure they wouldn't go deep into checking his credentials. The small Christian campus outside Tampa had readily invited him to an interview when he'd called about openings. Salaries were notoriously low in this sector, but this job came with accommodation. He'd assumed the identity of Dr Lucca, who had graduated a long time ago from Wheaton. He'd joined the Order some years before and gone to Africa on a recruitment mission. Still out there last he heard. As Dr Lucca he'd be a shoo-in for the job. Let Lord Ramesh set his avenging angels loose on him, they never find Father Tresor. He was gone forever.

His interview wasn't for a couple of days, but he wanted to see the place before he went to his motel. He slowed at the gates appreciating the tree-lined drive and classically proportioned buildings ahead. The soft afternoon light made it all look like a scene from a Harry Potter movie. He smiled to himself as he turned the car around.

CHAPTER EIGHT

Savannah

The road sign said Savannah 80 miles. Remy had stuck to Route 17 as there would be more stops, even if it was longer. At least it ended up in the Historic part of Savannah. He'd seen it all before many times, but he wanted his passenger to see it with her own eyes. He rubbed his neck, it was sore. Maybe Maisie had been right he was getting too old for all this. He glanced at Ami who was staring out at the monotonous view.

"Get used to being bored, kid. It's a long drive. We're headed towards Richmond, Virginia after Savannah. And that's only about half way."

Ami had no concept of distances, this being her first ever road trip. She shrugged. "It's all new to me. You, ok? You keep rubbing your neck."

Remy nodded, wincing as he rubbed it again. "They didn't design these seats for comfort back in the fifties. I'll be alright. Remind me to take some painkillers on the next stop."

Ami nodded. "What does it feel like to be so old. I think you're the oldest person I ever met so far."

Remy laughed, wincing at the pain in his neck, which he noticed had spread to his shoulders. "Well for one thing, you get sore necks and stiff joints on long drives. I'm luckier than most people my age. I'm still upright. My heart still works. I reckon I can go on for ten, maybe fifteen years yet."

Ami stared at him, wearing a heavy frown. "But you're always going to be thinking about dying."

Remy glanced at her wondering if she was making a joke, but he could see she was dead serious. "You got a strange idea in your head, kid. Just because you're old doesn't mean you think about being old or death. I feel no different to when I was fifty. Which, I admit, probably still sounds ancient to you. You don't feel age. You might get frustrated that you can't do stuff like you used to, but it's not like a tree can feel it's tree rings, even if it's been standing for a hundred years. Do you feel fifteen?"

Ami thought about that for a moment. "I don't think I feel anything. No, that's not true. I feel a ton of love for Stan. He makes me want to live. I'd be heartbroken if anything happened to him. But I guess you're right. You can't feel fifteen any more than when I was ten."

Remy nodded. "Of course, the mirror tells the truth every morning. I hate looking at my face these days. Keep wondering where the hell I've gone and who the hell this old guy is with a white beard."

"No mirrors at the farm." Ami told him.

"No mirrors?"

"Devil might see you naked."

Remy nodded but didn't laugh. "Yep, you certainly wouldn't want that." He was suddenly thinking about Rascal who for all those years had sat in Ami's seat keeping him company on the road. He'd been one special dog. "You're right about Stan. I'm pretty sure he loves you just as much as you love him." He pointed to the cubby hole. "There's a little plastic album in there. Take a look."

Ami pulled at a small 6x4 plastic covered album and opened it up. She smiled. They were all photos of Rascal. Running, jumping, hauling, carrying sticks way too big for him, smiling, curled up in Remy's lap or stretched out on his bed fast asleep.

"He was beautiful." Ami said quietly impressed.

Remy smiled. "He was. The one thing you could never do was comb him. Couldn't abide it. I once found three combs and two brushes buried in the yard." He laughed at the memory and how upset Rascal had been when he'd dug them up. "Took me a long time to get over him dying. Long time."

Ami put the album away and gave Stan a hug. "I've got no photos of Stan. Cameras are banned at the farm, along with pretty much everything else. I drew him though. Had to leave the sketches behind."

"Well better than the other way around," Remy told her. He rubbed his neck and left shoulder again. "I have to take a break soon. Need to take those painkillers now. Maisie said I should wear a brace when I'm driving, I guess I didn't listen to her."

Ami leaned back against her door and stared at him. He was rubbing his shoulder all the time now. "Maybe it's a bad idea going all the way to Canada."

Remy shot a look at her. "Now don't you start nagging me as well. If it takes a bit longer to get there, we're in no rush. You got some other place to be?"

Ami shook her head; aware she'd annoyed him. She saw a sign that said Gas-Food-Lodging and pointed it out. Remy nodded.

"I see it." His neck was killing him now. Didn't usually play up so early in a road trip.

Ami could see his head kept dropping, like he couldn't keep awake. She began to grow anxious. "Will the painkiller help?"

Remy didn't answer. He was having to use all his concentration now on keeping the truck straight. He was already in the slow lane and prayed the gas station would turn up real soon.

"Remy? Can you hear me? Maybe you shouldn't drive for a while."

Remy dropped the speed, the pain in his arms was more acute now. The turn off finally appeared and he tried to force his eyes open but ...

Ami realized that Remy had actually fallen asleep. She reached over for the wheel and took the turn off. They were approaching the Exxon gas station a little too fast and she had to find the handbrake. The engine stalled at an awkward angle, but Ami remained calm. She pushed Stan out of the way and with a struggle hauled Remy across to her side of the cab. Not easy to move an unconscious person but she had to get his legs out of the way. She took his place and pushed down hard on the clutch to force the gear box into neutral. She then started it up and straightened it out. She didn't want anyone wondering what was going on.

"Don't know about you Stan, but I need to go. Come on."

She reached over to Remy's jacket and pulled out his wallet. She extracted a twenty and put it back. "I'm getting you some coffee and painkillers, Remy. Won't be long now."

Stan waited for her impatiently outside the store unused to being left out of things.

Ami finally reemerged juggling two hot drinks with a packet of painkillers held in her teeth. She nodded towards to Stan, and they headed back to the truck. Somehow, she had to get the old man to swallow the pills and get him right again. She couldn't let him die. Maybe she was supposed to call for help and maybe they'd help him, but no one would be helping her and Stan. She opened the truck door.

"Wake up, Remy. I got you coffee and pills. Got to get you better." She got two pills down him but not much coffee. He fell asleep again almost immediately. She looked around wondering what the hell to do. She looked back at the old man. "Don't die on me, Remy. Please don't die."

Remy woke, rubbing his face feeling confused as to why he was slumped in the passenger seat, a rug over him, Stan curled up on his lap. He felt thirsty. He noticed they were moving. Ami was sitting on his folded coat driving. She turned to glance at him a moment.

"You feeling any better? Did the pills work?"

Remy felt his neck, it was still sore but different, maybe from the awkward position he was sitting in.

"What? Where are we?"

Ami smiled. "Savannah. It's so old but it's beautiful."

"Savannah?" Remy queried. "But ..." he was very confused now. "But you're driving. You're only fifteen."

Ami grinned. "I can drive. Do it all the time at the farm. Trucks don't move themselves. This ain't so hard to drive. Clutch is real heavy though."

"You can drive stick?"

"Been driving the tractor and the old farm truck since I was twelve. I told you, Stan loves being on the tractor. I can operate a digger too. The kids do all the work on the farm."

Remy sat up and felt his neck and arms, he seemed to be ok again. Had no memory of how all this happened. "Did I take the painkillers?"

"It was a struggle. But you swallowed two in the end. Sorry, I got your sweater a bit wet with the coffee."

Remy felt his sweater, but it was only a little damp, coffee stains didn't matter so much on a black sweater.

"And you drove us here?" Remy asked, although felt stupid for asking the obvious.

"You fell asleep at the wheel. Lucky we were going slow, hey."

Remy processed that information. He'd fallen asleep at the wheel. That had happened before. Maisie was right, he was too old for road trips now.

"Take a right at the crossing. There's a pretty little place to eat you'd like I recall. Jeeze Ami, you got us to the historic district."

"Just followed the road and it's signposted. Driving's not so hard. Can I park anywhere?"

"Find an empty meter. You know how to park?"

Ami giggled. "Yeah. You sound worried. How worried do you think me and Stan were when you fell asleep at the wheel?"

Remy winced. "I hope no cops saw you driving."

"I ain't taking any risks. You need a driver."

Remy nodded. "Seems that way but preferably one with a license."

Ami laughed as she pulled up at an empty space and with ease reversed into it like she'd done it all her life. She grinned with triumph.

"Suddenly I'm really hungry. How's your neck? Stu, he's in charge of the pigs at the farm and got all kinds of pains for some reason. He was oldest person I ever met before you. He swears by Tiger Balm. You can always smell him coming, but it's better than stinking of pigs I guess."

"I guess. Yeah, I remember that stuff. Maybe he's right. I'll put it on the list."

"Oh yeah, I had to take twenty bucks from your wallet to get the pills and the coffees. Not much change."

Remy nodded appreciating her honesty. He put a hand out to Ami and squeezed her arm. "You did good, Kid."

She smiled. "I checked your road map. It's almost five hundred miles to Richmond from here. No way you can drive that today."

Remy took a deep breath. "You're right. Let's see how I feel after I've eaten. We can maybe do another two hundred miles."

Ami was skeptical. "If you say so. Come on, Stan needs to pee. We're going over there?" She pointed towards a restaurant with pink awnings and people eating at outside tables.

"Yeah. Give me the keys," Remy told her. "Go. I have to feed the meter."

Ami looked carefully at his tired worn face. "You sure you're ok? Maybe Canada is too far for you. I can get you back home."

Remy smiled. "I don't doubt it, but if I can, I want to continue. We'll decide after we eat. You go ahead, get us a table outside so Stan can join us."

He watched her go. Excited, happy, full of life. He felt so old suddenly. He'd fallen asleep at the wheel. He could have killed them. What does it feel like to be old, she'd asked. Shameful, right at this minute, downright shameful.

They ate cheeseless sourdough pizza as Remy's gut could no longer tolerate cheese in any form. Ami didn't know any different, she was eating pizza for the first time in her life and was impressed.

"I can't believe I never had pizza before. It's like amazing. I don't even know what half the stuff is I'm eating." She grinned as she stuffed more into her mouth and shared the crust with Stan under the table. "You can cook this at home?"

"You've got peppers, eggplant, onion, pepperoni, looks like olives there. You can buy frozen, but it not the same as fresh baked in a wood-fired oven like here. Sourdough pizza like this is the best – nice and chewy. You're going to find a whole lot of foods you've never tried I guess." Remy smiled. "It's like you woke up after being frozen in time."

Ami nodded. "I read a book about that. A man got frozen for a hundred years and woke up and everything had changed. And everyone looked so weird to him. No one was old and everyone used surgery to stay young forever. They ate strange purple food."

"People must have thought he was weird," Remy suggested.

Ami nodded. "They totally rejected him. I often think about that story."

Remy was delighted to see how animated Ami was about this book. "How did it turn out?"

Ami thought about it a moment as she seized another slice of pizza. "Turns out he was a plumber and just about the only one in the city that still knew how to fix things."

"He must have made a fortune."

Ami laughed. "He did. He got really sad in the end though because he knew that everything in the city was crumbling, and people couldn't see that working to fix stuff was important."

"No robots?" Remy asked. "I thought the future was going to be about robots replacing humans everywhere."

"The book said there was a war against the robots and people banned them when they won."

"That's probably wishful thinking – I suspect the robots will win and ban us. One thing is sure, I'd hate to wake up one hundred years in the future. When I was a kid, the future was exciting and full of people traveling in space and exploring other worlds. It's not going to turn out like that at all."

"Lord Ramesh said there'll be a civil war in America, real soon. He's building a fortress in Charleston to survive it. That's why he has us kids farming so he has a good supply of organic food."

Remy frowned as he picked up the last slice of pizza. "Why is the farm so far away from Charleston? I don't get that. Not much use to him if there's a civil war."

"Father Tresor said the farm was a gift to the Order from one of his followers."

Remy nodded. "Hmm, makes sense. And lucky you getting to learn how to grow stuff organically. There's going to be a good living to be made out of growing organic. You might have hated it there, but you got an amazing apprenticeship, Ami. I kinda envy you."

Ami looked at him with surprise. "Really?"

Remy nodded. "Growing good chemical free food is going to be a critical industry in the future. Don't think farming is second best. My Uncle Rick had some orange groves. He used to moan all the time about his problems there with frost or blight or drought or the market price for orange juice, you name it. I asked him why he didn't just quit, and he looked at me as if I was crazy. "Me quit the best job in the world? Why the hell would I quit?"

Ami stared at him a moment appreciating he was talking to her and sharing stuff. She couldn't remember if she'd ever had a proper conversation with an adult ever before, let alone with someone who thought she was going to be worth something.

She was looking around her at all the young people eating and talking, some reading or writing. She'd never imagined the outside world would be like this. She leaned in towards Remy as she dropped her voice. "Is this normal? I mean the people around us. Don't they have jobs?"

Remy looked around him, then smiled. "Probably Art and Design students. The College owns most of this area. People in the real world don't look as good as this most of the time."

"Could I study here?"

Remy rolled his eyes. "If you win the lottery. It's an expensive business going to college. You'd want to study art?"

Ami shrugged. "I want to study everything."

"You could go to agricultural college. There's one in Miami-Dade and another at the University of Florida in Gainesville."

"But it's so pretty here."

Remy nodded. "Generally, you don't choose your college based on how pretty the campus is, but you're right it is pretty. First, we have to get you into the school system. I'm pretty sure there's a way they can test what level you're at."

Ami grimaced. "I know nothing. God, I'll be laughed at forever."

Remy shook his head. "I think you're the smartest kid I've met in a long time; and I've met quite a few." He drank some water and felt his neck. The pain seemed to have gone for now.

"You ok?" Ami asked.

"Yeah, better. Maybe the pizza helped. I don't think it was my heart. I've got five stents in my arteries. They're supposed to help increase the blood supply to my heart. My neck has been troubling me on and off for some time. Maisie, she's a nurse, says it's muscle wastage. You've got sixty years to find out what that's all about."

"Can't wait. I have to go. Hold on to Stan."

"We've got to get him a collar. We'll stop at the pet food place on the way out of town."

"He won't like that."

"It's the law."

Ami wrinkled her nose and left to go to the bathroom. Remy watched her go and he held onto Stan, bribing him with the remains of his pizza. "She'll be back soon. You're a good boy Stan. She's trained you well."

CHAPTER NINE

On The Bus

Paulo sat on his own on the bus, behind him the girls were afraid, sick with apprehension as to what awaited them in Charleston. Leaving the farm for the first time in their lives filled many of them with fear. They had all heard Sister Ryan's terrible stories of how young people were kept as slaves there waiting to be chosen as one of Lord Ramesh's concubines. Paulo had only one thought in his mind, to never arrive. Somehow, or another he would find a way off the bus. Perhaps when they made the inevitable restroom stop.

He knew Sister Ryan would be watching them like a hawk. He had this fantasy in his head that there would be a miracle and he'd spot Ami and Stan walking along the highway. He knew it was stupid. She'd been gone for days now with no reports of her being found, if anyone had actually been looking.

Brother Andrew had admitted that the chances of Ami surviving out there without getting raped or murdered or both were slim. '*She has no idea how wicked it is out there in so called civilization.*'

Paulo didn't know what to think. He was happy she'd escaped. Something bad must have happened to make her run so suddenly. Unlike everyone else he was glad Stan was with her. He'd die for her if she was attacked. No one got near Ami without Stan getting between them and growling if they looked like getting too close.

A small town was visible in the distance. If he did escape would anyone welcome him? Give him work? Or would they reject a boy with a limp? Sister Mercy had told him that they could reset the bone. He was young, his bones would mend quickly. But would she really help him? Probably just a trick to get him on the bus. They had never done anything for him before. Why would he trust them now?

CHAPTER TEN

A Passion for Wheels

They were back on the road again; Stan was hating his new red collar but couldn't work out how to get it off. Ami was keeping a keen eye on Remy as he drove. He stank of Tiger Balm, and she'd wished she'd never mentioned it.

"Why is it so important you have to go to Montreal? Can't you send someone else?" Remy shrugged. "It's the last thing I need to get for the Hawk. Been restoring that car for ten years now, off and on. Always waiting for some little essential part or another."

"But why? Aren't there enough cars on the road?"

Remy frowned. "There're probably enough songs in the world without anyone needing to compose another. Same with art, why on earth do we need more art or artists? But we keep on creating more. The Studebaker Golden Hawk was one of the most beautiful cars ever designed. Some vehicles can disappear without trace, unloved. There's a lot of emotion attached to a '66 Mustang but by '75 they were designed by people who were philistines. It was no better than a Pinto and that was crap on wheels. No one collects that period for good reason. Find yourself a mint condition 1958 Jaguar XK150 Coupe and heads turn. Some cars inspire passion. The last President had a '67 Corvette convertible, they were designed to be driven by people who loved cars – the '66 Sting Ray is worth nearly $70 thousand now. When I get that steering wheel for the Hawk, it's going to be worth a lot of money. Not that I intend to ever sell it. My Dad bought it, loved it, showed it off and I've slowly brought it back to mint condition. So, in answer to your question. Yes, there are enough cars on the road, but I'm talking about automotive history. Drive a Hawk and people are watching art in motion. It was made in a time when we all thought the world was going to get better, although in 1957 I was just a seven-year-old kid convinced the world was going to explode in one giant atomic big bang when Russia attacked. Nothing could shake that out of me. Stuck with me all my life."

Ami stared at the old man. Saw how he came alive when talking about the cars. She had no idea about any of them and couldn't understand it, but she now knew why he'd be wanting to go all the way to Canada. It was important to him.

"Father Tresor preaches about the coming end of the world all the time. The Coming of the Change, Lord Ramesh calls it. We have to listen to all his preaching every evening during contemplations."

"Father Tresor's thoughts or this Lord Ramesh?" Remy asked.

Amy's lips curled with contempt. "Father Tresor never had a thought of his own in his life. This is all Lord Ramesh's word. He sends it out daily. We listen; or pretend to. Mostly I get to daydream." Amy saw a sign for Charleston up ahead and blanched. "We're not going there, are we?"

Remy shook his head. "No. Don't fret. We're sticking to the highway for the now."

Amy discovered she was suddenly shaking. Lord Ramesh couldn't possibly know how close she was, but it was like she hadn't escaped at all and was reaching out to her.

"You think your mother left the cult?" Remy asked suddenly. "What was in her letters. Did you read them?"

Amy closed her eyes picturing the words and her mother's sloping scrawl.

"She said she'd left. Grown too old to hear the same stupid lies."

Remy nodded. "It takes courage to leave a cult after you've been there a long time. You'll wonder how you'll get by or where you'll live or if you'll ever eat again. It's hard to leave what you know. She would have been with them for years."

Amy didn't know about that. She wondered if she would have ever had the courage to leave the farm if she hadn't read the letters. She'd made her mind up to run the moment she'd read them and seen the address. She hadn't thought once about might happen to her if her mother wasn't there. Only now did she realize how foolish that was. Remy picking her up was pure dumb luck. It could have been a crazy person. It could have been no one at all and they would have dragged her back by now and locked her up in solitary. Might even have shot Stan, just like Father Tresor had promised to do. She concentrated on the road ahead and tried to banish her dark thoughts.

"You never talk about God," Ami suddenly remarked.

"God? What brought that up? I'm not a church goer, never really liked all the rules."

Ami stared out of the window a moment. "All religions are false anyway."

"False?" Remy asked. "I'm suspecting this is coming from Lord Ramesh's teaching, right?"

Ami frowned. "He teaches us that there's only one true path, all others lead to a dead end."

Remy nodded. "This is the guy who had you imprisoned on a farm under the whip of a brutal regime that denied you books and freedom of expression and beat you when you didn't obey. That true path."

Ami remained silent and looked away as she hugged Stan.

"A lot of religions are mean to kids, especially to girls, Ami. Your Ramesh wasn't the only one. Somehow, they feel threatened by girls having knowledge and demanding equality with men. Some like to cover them up, pretend they don't exist. Don't get me started on religion. All I can say is, there would be a lot less pain and suffering in the world without it."

"You mean, no path." Ami suggested.

"Just one path. Good governance. There are politicians out there these days who want to abolish all the guide rails. The FBI, the Department of Education, The Tax Office. You name it. They want to live in a harsh world where profit is everything and the only rule of law is the gun. That's not a path, that's terrorism.

"When I go into the pharmacy to buy my drugs, I want to know there are standards and quality control. I believe in the Food & Drug Administration holding companies to strict standards. I want to live in a society where the Department of Education sets standards for all the kids, not leave it up to the cranks and crazies to decide what knowledge is good or bad. I want the FBI to exist to keep us safe from terrorists and corrupt politicians.

"Standards are my religion. I worked for NASA. We needed to know every nut and bolt was made to exact specifications. We needed to trust manufacturers to obey the law. And there were many failures, I know that, but people were held to account for faults and had to fix them. You might not realize this, kid but trusting to God, which a lot of people do instead of checking the label on something, is not a way to run a civilization."

Ami stared at him a moment. "It's funny what makes you so riled up."

"Funny?"

Ami nodded. "You think about this stuff a lot."

Remy nodded, concentrating on a weaving truck ahead and dropped back a ways in case of trouble. He sighed. "I do. Sometimes our trust in things is misplaced. Sometimes things go wrong, but when they do, you can be rest assured it is more to do with human error than God."

Ami smiled. "That's what Lord Ramesh says."

Remy laughed. "Point taken. But I'm being serious here. Nothing excuses what that man has done to you or the other kids. His religion, his disciples, his responsibility. He had a duty of care to make sure you were being treated right."

Ami sighed. She could see that Remy was right, but she wondered if she'd ever be able to get Lord Ramesh out of her head.

Remy gave a wide berth to the truck as he overtook the truck. Maybe the driver was sleepy or talking on his phone. Either way, an accident waiting to happen.

Remy called it quits when they finally reached the outskirts of Fayetteville. He remembered he still had a valid voucher for a motel in Wyndham and took the turn-off. "There's a Macdonald's nearby but to be honest the longer I can keep you out of one of those the better. We can go over to the Cracker Barrel and get something a bit more nutritious."

Ami had heard other kids talk about MacDonalds and had been curious, but Father Tresor had told them all that it was the origin of all that was sinful out there. 'They sucker you in with deep fat fries and never let you go.'

"Cracker Barrel sounds good to me." Ami replied. "What about Stan?"

"We'll feed him before we go, and he can sit in the truck. I seem to recall the Lodge is pet friendly, might be a fee. Rascal and I stayed there once or twice on our road trips. Remind me on the way back to take you to see Bent Mountain Falls if we make good time. The Virginia mountains can be pretty spectacular this time of year. We pass by Roanoke Falls tomorrow but you have to drive up into the mountains to get to see the actual falls."

"I always wanted to see Niagara Falls."

"Sorry. Not this trip, there's a ton of places to stop or cities to see but I wasn't planning on much stopping. Maybe Thomas Edison's National Historical Park. You ever hear about him?"

Ami shook her head.

"Hmm, well we pass Philly, Washington DC, New York. Maybe tomorrow night we'll see where we are but right now, we've still got a thousand miles ahead of us."

Ami sighed. "I didn't know America was so big. God, I'm so dumb."

Remy smiled. "I want you to study the map tonight. I mean we're following the highway all the way now but it's good for you to know where places are, so it sticks in your head. Everyone relies on sat-nav's which tell you were to go, but they didn't realize they aren't learning the route. Reading a map is another skill you can add to your collection."

Ami glanced at him, "I can't tell sometimes if you're mocking me or not."

Remy put out a hand to her shoulder. "I'm teaching you the old ways. Come that civil war you talked about, it just might come in handy after that."

He found a parking spot outside The Lodge and turned off the engine. "Now cross your fingers they've got a room for us. Bring Stan's bowl. He'll be hungry by now."

CHAPTER ELEVEN

The Counting

Brother Grace was sitting in a coffee shop in Tampa staring at his phone. He was biding his time. Father Tresor's vehicle was parked behind the Avalon Motel. It hadn't moved for a while now. He assumed Father Tresor was in the motel. Of course, he wouldn't be so foolish to be travelling under his own name. It wasn't going to be that easy. So, he watched and waited with a full view of the Avalon. He could be patient. This was his role in life to locate stray sheep and guide them back to the faith, or else.

He reasoned that Tresor would want to eat. He needed to be taken discretely. No need to bring any attention to the Order. If he used his vehicle the tracker would alert him. If he walked, he could be followed. Brother Grace didn't know what the man was doing in Tampa, didn't care. He just needed to come face to face with Lord Ramesh and accept his punishment. It wouldn't be pretty. But it would be quick. Enforcing discipline was just as important as all the touchy feely stuff the others in the Order were supposed to deliver. An Order without discipline was no Order at all. *

Sister Ryan counted them back on the bus. Had she missed one? "Is Paulo here?" She called out.

The kids stared back at her in silence. Only one shaking her head no. They all knew Paulo had absconded they moment he had entered the rest room and didn't come out. No one had said a word to Sister Ryan and as there was only one toilet, it had taken an age to go through all 24 of them. Two girls had wanted to follow him out the window but lacked the courage at the last moment. The gas station was in the middle of nowhere. Where the hell would they go? They all felt that Paulo wouldn't get far, not with his leg. They'd given him a thirty-minute start at least.

Sister Ryan swore, turning to the driver. "Don't let anyone off the bus. I'm going to look for him. The cripple can't have got far."

Sad eyes watched as Sister Ryan stormed back into the gas station in the forlorn hope that the boy was still in the damn rest room.

Paulo lay flat under some fertilizer sacks in the back of an old pick-up truck. He could barely breath with the stench of ammonia. Instinctively he knew he'd made a terrible decision. He wanted to vomit. There was no way he could stay under the sacks. The driver didn't seem to be in a hurry to come back, talking with the guy behind the gas station counter.

Sister Ryan came back outside and surveyed the landscape. There was absolutely nowhere for the cripple to go, nowhere. So, he had to be still at the gas station, chosen specifically for its remoteness from civilization.

An old pick-up truck was driving away. She hadn't had a chance to look in the back. Her heart sank. Was Paulo getting away?

There were no other vehicles except a motorcycle, she ran back to the bus. Sister Mercy would add this carelessness to all the other transgressions she was supposed to have done on her long list. Shit, damn Paulo for doing this. She had a mind to disappear herself.

She yelled at the driver as she got back in the bus. "Follow that pick-up truck. He has to be on there. Get going. Don't lose it."

The bus pulled out of the gas station and lumbered after the pick-up.

Paulo heard the bus drive away and hauled himself out of a trash barrel, picking off sticky bits from his faded hoodie. He surveyed the landscape with despair. He had no idea which way to go. It was bleak endless farmland. It was useless, if he got four miles on his leg, he'd be lucky. Had it been like this for Ami? Sister Ryan had a bet going with Brother Andrew that Ami would be found dead inside of a month. Someone would find her body in a ditch someday for sure.

"Need a ride kid?"

Paulo looked around and saw a guy wearing leathers and a pair of goggles like he was out some war comic. He blinked. Ride in what exactly? There was no car or truck.

Paulo tried to say yes but choked, his mouth was dry and all he could hear in his head was all the dreaded warnings from Sister Ryan and Father Tresor about the treachery of strangers.

"I saw the bus. Those kids looked like prisoners. Never seen such terrified kids in all my life. I'm guessing some religious thing you're all heading to."

Paulo nodded. "I ..."

"Didn't want to go. Have to say I'd have gotten off that bus too. That woman looking after you looked pretty damn scary if you ask me."

"Sister Ryan. She is truly scary." Paulo admitted.

The guy smiled and put on his driving gloves. "I'm heading to St Pete. Not much choice for you I reckon. Stay here and hope you catch a better ride or come with me."

Paulo found his voice at last and smiled, nodding his head. The guy seemed ok, weird but ok. He had no idea where St Pete was or who St Pete might be, but it had to be better than here.

"St Pete would be g-g good," he stuttered, trying to look confident.

The guy nodded and began to walk towards his motorcycle as Paulo followed. "Noticed you limp. You been in an accident?"

Paulo nodded. "Fell off a hayloft."

The guy winced. "Ouch. Then you're lucky to be alive. Hop on. It's a long ride from here."

"Who are ...?" Paulo began.

"Call me Jim. No need to be worried. I'm a bounty hunter. The only people who are scared of me are those people with a price on their head. You haven't got a price on your head, have you?"

Paulo looked up at him and shook his head. Had no idea what he was talking about, but it didn't sound good.

The man smiled. "Then you won't be meeting me one dark night when you least expect it. If you've never been on a bike before, lean on my back and make sure you grip the handles at the rear. You see what I'm pointing at? Fail to do that and you'll fall off. You do not want to fall off."

Paulo nodded. He was going to get free. He was going to St Pete. He said a quick prayer that he'd survive this and wouldn't end up dead in a ditch, like Ami.

Hours later in Tampa Brother Grace was still in the coffee shop across from The Avalon. His patience was finally rewarded when Father Tresor emerged from the motel and squeezed into an old Ford Focus just pulled up out front. He noted the license plate and that the man driving was wearing a dog collar. He hurriedly settled up and headed out to his vehicle to follow. He had no idea what was going down but was mighty curious.

He called Sister Mercy in Charleston as he fired up his Jeep and caught up with the Ford, hanging back quite a distance as they headed out of town. He wanted the good sister to do a little digging. What were Father's Tresor's connections to Tampa, if any. Why exactly was he here?

Twenty minutes from the city Brother Grace noted with some surprise that Father Tresor had been driven to the Christian College of St Joseph's. Was this a friend he was catching up with or, and he favored a latter idea, a job interview? Didn't Father Tresor realize that the moment they wrote for references he'd be exposed as a fraud. Naturally he would be there on false pretenses, possibly under an assumed name. That was the most likely scenario. Brother Grace didn't wait, he turned around. Time to talk to the receptionist at the Avalon and search his room. Whatever was going on, it needed to be stopped. Father Tresor could not be allowed access to any young people any longer.

CHAPTER TWELVE

Sharlene

It was the middle of the night when Ami woke startled by a noise.

"Did you hear that?"

She glanced over at Remy; he was sound asleep. She instinctively knew she had to wake him. Stan was already alert, whining, worried.

Remy was befuddled, waking to find Ami violently shaking him.

"Did you hear that?" Ami repeated. "Hush now, Stan. Hush."

"What?" Remy sat up in bed and tried to reorient himself as the dog whimpered nearby. They were in the Lodge bedroom. It was still dark outside. Ami seemed spooked, listening intently for something.

He heard the sharp cracks of gunshot clearly now. His heart missed a beat.

"Shit. Get dressed. Don't put any lights on. Keep the dog quiet."

Stan was anxious, turning in circles looking for somewhere to run to.

Remy urgently had to go the bathroom. He could hear shouting and screaming more clearly now.

"What's going on?" Ami was asking from the bedroom as she hurriedly dressed.

"Let's hope it's not your damn civil war starting," Remy said finishing up, splashing his face, and washing his hands. "Grab all your stuff together. But do not under any circumstances open the door."

Ami had no intention of opening the door. The screaming was getting louder now.

Someone outside fired up a bullhorn. "Sharlene. I know you're in there with him. You come out right now or everyone gets it."

Remy re-entered the room and began dressing. "It's a domestic issue. This could get bad or ... You probably don't know how dangerous the world is now living back on that farm, Ami. You've heard gunshots before?"

Ami nodded, packing away her pajamas into her overnight bag. "Father Tresor shoots vermin and targets. Shot a deer last year and made us all eat it. I didn't want to."

Remy slipped on his shoes and closed the Velcro straps down tight; he didn't want to stumble at a time like this. He was thinking what was best to do. Stay put was one option, but what if the shooter got in and went from room to room killing people until he found Sharlene? He tried to remember how many mass killings there had been this year so far. Two hundred or was it three? Seemed to him there was one or two killings every week now. But out here?

"We're on the second floor. Can you tell if the shooting is happening above us or below?" Remy asked her.

Ami had no idea. She began to walk towards the window. Remy called out sharply.

"Don't go near the window. We don't know where the shooter is. Lie flat, hug Stan. I'll call downstairs."

Remy shone his phone onto the list of numbers on the wall for emergencies. He had to search for his glasses as the print was so small. He picked up the phone and dialed reception. No answer. He rang off after twenty rings.

"Either there's no one there or they're dead."

Ami was surprisingly calm now. "Do we stay?"

A shot rang out and window glass shattered close by. A woman screamed something in Spanish then fell silent.

"We stay for now. Make sure you're not in the line of fire from the door or the window. Get between the beds, Ami. Now!"

Ami crawled into the narrow space; Stan followed. Remy lay on the floor in the bathroom doorway figuring it was the safest place.

"Someone will have called the cops," Remy said quietly to reassure Ami and himself. "They'll be here soon."

Ami wasn't reassured. Cops always meant trouble. "Father Tresor said the outside world was a place of evil and destruction. I never believed him."

"Yeah, well there's 400 million guns between 300 million people. Everyone wants to settle an argument with a bullet these days. Needless to say, it wasn't like this when I was fifteen. The thing we were most afraid of was getting called up – the draft."

"Draft?" Ami didn't understand the term.

"You could get called up to join the armed services the moment you hit eighteen. It was like some kind of evil lottery where you lose if your number comes up. Lasted until 1973. I was one of the last cohort I guess."

"Did you go to war?"

"I got a deferment as I went to college to study engineering. When I graduated, they grabbed me and sent me to Hawaii. Seems they wanted me in logistics. Never fired a shot in anger as they say. Hell, they even wanted me to sign up for more, but I got offered a job at NASA and spent nearly twenty-five years on the Shuttle program. Now no one barely remembers the Shuttles."

Ami was glad he was talking. It kept her from worrying about the shooter.

Rapid gunfire suddenly strafed the hotel shattering windows. A bullet went straight through one of their windows and skimmed the wall just above Remy's bed.

"Jeez," Remy shouted. "He's outside."

They heard the bullhorn click on again in the deadly silence.

"That was a warning shot, Sharlene. Next one is for you. Come on out NOW!"

Ami closed her eyes tight and clasped Stan close to her. She could feel his heart beating so fast; he was panting with fear. "It's ok, it's ok. I've got you. You're safe with me," Ami whispered into his ear, even she didn't believe it.

Remy was wondering where the cops were. Shouldn't take them long to respond. Unless there were other incidents happening out there. That had been the latest trend according to the TV news. Shooters acting in concert in different locations taking out rivals or ex-lovers or more usually politicians they didn't agree with. Especially politicians.

"Why is this happening?" Ami called out.

Remy sighed. "Put a gun in the hand of an angry man it's going to go off one way or another. I hope the hell Sharlene doesn't go out there. He'll shoot her dead for sure."

Ami hugged Stan; she wasn't sure that made her feel better.

More shots were fired but different in sound, a pistol maybe. It seemed to be coming from inside the hotel now, pretty close by, maybe on the same floor as them. The shooter fired back with a devastating response shattering more glass. People were screaming again.

"I'm not sure we're safe here at all," Remy said. "The shooter's using heavy stuff."

Ami didn't know what he meant. She shook with fear. It was all so loud. She could hear Father Tresor laughing at her. "You wanted freedom? This is what it sounds like, Ami. There's no freedom out there. You have no idea what it's like. Dog eat dog every day."

He was always going on about dogs eating dogs. She was pretty sure Stan wouldn't eat another dog. Might fight one or more likely run away. Eat one? Never.

"You want me to look outside the corridor?" She asked Remy.

"You stay put, kid. You're safe there. We're not moving until the calvary gets here and even then, I'm not sure. Stay put." Remy pulled up his legs, he was uncomfortable and cold on the tiled floor. "You holding up in there?" he asked after a few minutes.

Ami felt Stan's paws, they were hot and sweaty. He was alert to every sound and shill shaking.

"If it's any consolation I'm scared too, kid. We should all be scared."

No more shots were fired after that. Remy figured the guy had either died or driven off to avoid the cops. After a while he decided that lying on the bed he'd paid for would be better than the bathroom floor. He urged Ami and Stan off the floor to go back to bed as well but keep their clothes on, in case. Ami was reluctant but allowed herself to be persuaded. Stan had peed on the floor, but Remy didn't blame him. Poor hound was terrified. He mopped it up with a damp towel and tossed it into the bath. No point in having to pay a fine for some stain that was no fault of theirs.

"Don't let me forget to take my pills in the morning," Remy told her.

Ami nodded. "I won't."

Ami and Stan slept but Remy found it hard to relax. It was only three-thirty am - it wouldn't be light until seven at the earliest. He hoped his truck had survived undamaged. Made him realize that this whole trip was a huge risk. The America he loved was definitely disappearing. No doubt about it. There wasn't just one thing you could blame. Maisie would spout off about toxic social media and the legacy of Trump that poisoned democracy forever, but he knew the sickness had been there for a long time before that. He wasn't sure you could pinpoint one specific event unless, like Maisie you laid all the problems of the world at the doorsteps of the NRA and the Republicans. She was probably right, either way Sharlene was right for leaving the crazy guy.

They woke late. Ami dutifully reminded him about his pills and he was grateful for it. Didn't feel like he'd slept at all, but he guessed he must have had three hours at least. He took a hot power shower which revived him a tad.

It was already nine when they finally worked up enough courage to leave the bedroom and venture downstairs. The reception area was a mess. No one seemed to be on duty and cops were everywhere. Remy spoke with some bewildered representative from the hotel and handed her his key card. He'd already settled the night before with his voucher so didn't have anything to pay.

"We'll email you a new voucher," the hotel rep reassured him. "We're so sorry for the inconvenience."

Remy nodded, noting the word 'inconvenience'. The weeping inconvenienced were watching ambulance crews ferrying out injured bodies on stretchers and bewildered cops were making half-hearted attempts at interviewing people that hadn't a clue as to who or what had gone on during the night, never mind why. One female cop was comforting an inconsolable young blonde woman wrapped in a blanket whom he suspected was the infamous Sharlene, very lucky to be still alive. One of the ambulance crew was checking her blood pressure and he could see she has glass cuts on her face and bare legs.

Ami and Stan were waiting for him by the truck. She pointed to a bullet hole that had gone through the side panel. Remy's heart sank. He checked the fuel tank and was reassured when there wasn't a puddle of gas under the vehicle.

"Let's hope that's the full extent of the damage, Ami. We'll get going and stop for breakfast in about an hour. OK with you?"

She smiled and gave him a hug. "Thank you."

"For what?" Remy asked.

"For keeping and me and Stan safe."

Remy ruffled her hair and grinned. "Nonsense, I did no such thing. You kept me safe. That bullet hole in the wall was just inches away from my head. Get in. Let's get out of this madness before some cop decides he wants to talk to us."

Ami was all for that. Stan was first in, totally calm now, ready for anything. Remy reflected on how happy he was that Stan was with them. God, how much he missed Rascal.

Remy and Ami ate at an old railroad diner that promised the best breakfast in America. Remy had often noticed it when passing by but never had the time to stop there before. It had turned into a nice sunny morning, so they ate outside at one of the tables made out of railroad sleepers. Ami was fascinated about how old everything was. The diner kitchen was built inside an old caboose and there was a proper Pullman dining car attached restored to exactly the way it was back in 1885, all brass fittings and velvet drapes.

"The railroad passes by the bottom fields at the farm" Ami told Remy. "I often dreamt about catching it and just disappearing, but it goes by too fast to get me and Stan up there. One of the brothers said people used to ride the railroads right across America for free. Was he telling the truth?"

Remy nodded. "Yep, the freight trucks anyway. They called them hobos. Seasonal workers mainly I guess, stealing a ride on the empty wagons. They were too poor to buy a ticket for the passenger trains. Had a relative who rode the rails all the way to California when he was young, just for the hell of it. Frank died during Covid. One of those people who wouldn't take the vaccine. He was a real conspiracy nut. Fell for every scam that was out there. I remember my mother was so embarrassed about him she pretended he never existed. Every family's got one of those characters I guess." He smiled. "You ok? You were very calm last night. Proud of you. It's easy to want to panic in a situation like that."

Ami blinked. She only remembered shaking with fear. She ate her scrambled eggs and toasted muffin slowly, they didn't taste like the eggs back on the farm, if they tasted of anything at all. Stan was stretched out on the gravel in a sunbeam, he'd eaten his fill in seconds flat.

Remy ate a bowl of assorted fruits with a side of sourdough toast. "You're not so chatty today," he told her.

Ami shrugged. "I'm still trying to make sense of what happened."

Remy nodded. "You know what it is interesting about last night?"

Ami shook her head. Had no clue.

"Almost nothing on the local news about it. One time that would be national news, but I guess after all that only two people actually were badly injured. Not much thought about the trauma we all suffered. The Lodge will be out of action for weeks and the gunman got away. Although obviously Sharlene will know where he lives. They didn't even mention how long it took the cops to get there. Not that they'd be too eager to drive into a gunfight I suppose." He sighed. "Maybe people are getting used to it. It's like unless twenty people die it's not really news."

Ami threw some muffin to Stan. "You got a gun?"

Remy hesitated before replying. "A handgun. Maisie insisted after some guys tried to steal my truck one day. I'm not keen on guns. My reaction time isn't what it used to be. Just as easy to be killed by your own weapon than stop anyone from taking what's yours."

"Does everyone carry a gun?" Ami asked.

Remy nodded. "Pretty much. That's why it's so crazy these days. In the old days people settled arguments with fists or shouting matches. Now you reach for your gun first."

Ami sipped her coffee. "Moses, he's one of the brothers at the farm. He's got gunshot wounds on his legs and arm."

"How did he get that?" Remy asked.

"At the farm shop. They tried to rob him. I got there a few minutes later bringing new stock. I heard the shooting. Had to wrap his wounds in the batik cloths then run back to get help." She smiled. "He still got the batiks on his wall, blood stains and all."

"So, you saved his life."

Ami shrugged. "I thought he was going to die for sure but he's tough. Taught me how to drive the tractor as he couldn't drive it anymore. We all had to learn first-aid after that. Father Tresor keeps telling us (she adopted a deep voice), 'Come the revolution, help isn't coming. You need to learn this."

Remy pondered on this information. "Yeah, it's getting that way. Come on, we have a lot of miles to make up today. Stan, go pee."

CHAPTER THIRTEEN

The Corn Field

They'd done a good two hours of driving when the traffic ahead suddenly began braking. There looked to be quite a long backup two lanes deep. Remy kept to the verge side aware that he needed to pee and left it too long already.

"What is it?" Ami was asking.

Remy wasn't sure. "Probably be road maintenance. We could be here for some time. Let Stan out for a walk when I stop. Keep your eyes peeled. People get antsy in situations like this."

Ami glanced at him. Wasn't sure what antsy meant but figured it wasn't good. She bailed out with the dog the moment he stopped. Remy switched off the engine, opened his door and climbed up on the footplate to see what was going on. Couldn't see anything. No flashing lights or red flags. Maybe it was a shunt or two. Another driver was trying to do the same next to him. There wasn't any traffic on the other side of the highway which was odd.

"Any ideas what's holding us up?" Remy asked.

"Protest maybe." The driver suggested. "Nothing on my sat-nav about highway maintenance. Always someone protesting about something these days. Anti-oil, anti-something, the secessionists, I'm sick of it."

"I hear ya," Remy agreed. "I don't see any cops up there."

"That's the other thing," the driver complained. "You don't see cops doing their job anymore. Know what I mean?"

The driver was called back inside by someone imploring him not to 'get involved'.

Remy looked back to see where Ami was and saw her talking to someone down the line who was exercising their dog too. Further up towards the blockage people were honking their horns. There was a definite tension in the air. He didn't like the situation at all and besides he needed to piss. He ducked back into the cab and discretely dug out a paper coffee cup he kept for emergencies. With Ami out of the cab he could relieve himself without embarrassment.

He'd only just emptied the contents onto the verge when Ami returned shouting something as she climbed back in with Stan.

"Shooters. Shooters," she shouted, her eyes wild with fear.

Remy looked at her puzzled then heard it now. "What the ...?" He decided he wasn't going to hang around. He restarted the engine. Others were doing the same, desperate to get out of the way, uncertain from which direction the gunshots were coming from.

"What are we gonna do?" Ami was asking. She knew they couldn't go forward or back, they were hemmed in. Remy was desperately looking around trying to assess whether they could get onto the verge and the cornfield that stretched for miles alongside the highway. Ami could see what he was thinking.

"The field?"

"They've cropped it. It's just stalks. This is a tough old bird, Ami. Hang on, a little bit of country driving won't hurt us."

Other drivers were making the same decision and trying to break free of the slot they were in. Remy didn't hesitate any longer and turned the wheel, just making the turn without scraping the vehicle in front. "Hang on." He gunned the motor and sent the truck flying down the slope of the verge looking for way over a drainage ditch.

"We'll get stuck," Ami shouted.

"Hang on to Stan, kid." He had the truck up to speed and saw a small crossing over the ditch, swerved right and they entered the cornfield pitching and bucking as they ploughed further into the field. Ami glanced behind them and saw other vehicles trying the same but many pitching down into the ditch and flipping over. They weren't going anywhere.

"Won't the stalks rip the muffler off?" Ami was shouting. Stan whimpered down in the footwell; his eyes wide with terror. She tried to reassure him.

"They might, but we'll keep going either way. You keep hold of that strap Ami."

Remy wrestled the wheel as he turned to drive parallel to the highway now, the stalks loudly strumming underneath.

Ami's window was down. She could hear more shots being fired. It seemed to her that everyone was firing but at what or who? Her head hit the roof and she yelled out in pain. Stan whined with terror.

The truck lurched and bucked but somehow kept going. A Jeep was running behind them now following in Remy's wake. On the highway she witnessed people fleeing their stalled vehicles and running terrified into the field for safety.

"Who's firing at who?" Ami asked bewildered by it all.

Remy had no idea. "Keep your head down, keep Stan down by your feet. We're lucky the field is dry. Any mud would have sunk us already."

Ami watched Remy wrestle the wheel, he seemed to be kinda enjoying the situation.

Sparks flew off the hood suddenly. Ami let escape a scream.

"They're shooting at us!"

"Keep your head down," Remy shouted as he looked across at the roadblock. They were almost level with the head of the traffic jam now and it seemed to him in the brief moment he looked that there was a pitch battle going on there. The Jeep behind them suddenly stopped – he wondered if they'd been hit too. Remy drove a little faster heading back towards the highway now, well ahead of the roadblock.

"Ami sit up. We're looking for a way out of the field. I don't want to end up in a gully."

Ami sat up, gripped the strap scouring the landscape ahead. "We're clear of the shooting, I think. Shit I'm still shaking."

"Hang on, you're doing well. Keep your eyes focused on ahead." He began to slow. "I don't want to wreck the truck at the last moment."

Suddenly Remy's cell rang. He ignored it. It went to voicemail.

Remy was looking for an off ramp, breathing a little harder now. He noticed a couple of trees near the highway and headed towards those. Another vehicle was following him. The adrenaline was still flowing in his veins, but he knew he'd pay for this excitement later. His heart was beating wildly. He could feel a familiar tension building.

"Over there," Ami was pointing. "There's tracks."

"I see 'em." Remy adjusted his direction to beyond the trees and was eventually relieved to turn onto a well-defined dirt track that headed towards the highway.

"We'll get clear and first chance we get we need to stop and see how much damage we've taken." Remy told her. "You did good kid. How are you liking civilization so far."

Ami glanced at him and laughed. "It's not how I imagined it."

"Yeah. I'm pretty sure God says the same thing most days. You know; that person in the sky who's supposed to watch over us."

"Oh her. Lord Ramesh says she probably lost interest in us a long time ago."

Remy nodded. His sentiments entirely. He guided the truck towards the highway checking his rear-view mirror. "Seems we have more company."

Ami looked back and counted seven vehicles in all.

Remy drove the truck back to the empty highway and kept on going, he wanted to be sure they were well clear of any trouble.

One of vehicles that had followed them out of the field passed them by, honking their horn, and showing a thumbs up to them. Remy followed suit and smiled. They could see the Audi's rear window had been shot out but otherwise seemed intact.

"Nice gesture." Remy remarked, appreciating the thumbs up.

Ami checked on Stan who had unbelievably fallen asleep at her feet. "Stan's asleep."

Remy chuckled, relieved they'd made it around the roadblock. He wasn't interested on what had caused it, just wanted to get away from the problem as fast as possible.

"It's getting to be we're living in the wild west," he commented.

"Cops!" Ami shouted, pointing to the other side of the highway. A stream of cop vehicles were heading towards the blockade, struggling to get through a huge line of trucks and cars held up by the shooting.

"Better late than never, I guess. You ok, kid? Stopped shaking yet?"

Ami stared at him. "You're quite the badass."

Remy frowned. "I am? Where did you learn that kind of language? Badass, funny. Just trying to keep us alive."

Remy's cell rang again. This time he answered it, he knew who was calling.

"What's up Masie? I'm a bit busy."

"I know you're busy you crazy old man. I saw your truck on TV just now. Someone's got live drone footage streaming on the news. I knew it was you the moment I saw the truck bumping across that field."

Remy frowned. He didn't like the idea of being identified. "Well, don't tell anyone, ok? I have enough problems getting insurance these days."

"What the hell are you doing Remy? People were shooting at you."

"Not just me. I don't who the hell it was, but I had no intention of dying back there for whatever stupid cause they've got."

"Are you ok? Where are you?"

"I'm back on the highway. Heading towards Richmond. I'm fine, Masie. You don't have to worry about me. I'm getting used to being shot at these days. Welcome to MAGA America. You voted for these people, remember."

"I'm not going to start that argument again."

"Got to go. Don't watch the news Masie. It only gets you worked up. Over and out."

Remy disconnected. He glanced at Ami, and he could see she wanted to ask questions.

"Ok, that was Masie. You need to know that nothing is private anymore. Always someone with a drone up there watching, filming, judging, with an eye to making a fast buck on-line or on the news. Give it a few hours and someone else will do something stupid and they'll get all worked up about that."

"Drone?"

"Very light aerial reconnaissance vehicle powered by four electric rotors. They can fly up there for hours at a time spying on traffic or cities or just someone mowing their lawn. Police, criminals, the Army, everyone uses them now. As I said, there's no hiding from them."

"So, someone knows you were here."

"If they got my license plate, but that isn't as visible as it is supposed to be. Besides we don't matter in this business. The cops will be dealing with the crashes and injured parties. I'm pretty sure they'll be happy some people managed to escape. They'll have enough to do."

Ami shook her head, bewildered at it all.

Remy glanced at her and smiled. "You did real good kid. Some people would have gone to pieces. You kept your head."

Ami shook her head. "I screamed when they started shooting."

"Perfectly normal reaction. I'm sorry you had to go through it, but we survived the hotel last night, we got through this, hell I'm just hoping there's not a third thing. You'll learn in life that often things happen in threes. No idea why but that's just the way it is. Now try to relax a little. Think about what you want to eat tonight or something."

"Food? I can't think about food. We almost died back there."

"Emphasis on almost." Remy grinned, he felt his pulse a moment.

"Pulse calming down now. Pass me one of those barley sugars in the cubby hole, will you? I need to boost my blood sugar. The sticky ones in the packet."

Ami searched through and realized he was talking about sweets. She unwrapped one for him. "But what about your teeth?"

Remy grinned. "The teeth will survive. I need to keep my heart pumping at the moment, ok?" He took the sweet from her and popped it into his mouth. "And no, you can't have one. Way too much sugar for you. Concentrate on being calm. Be more dog."

He pointed to Stan who was still sleeping despite everything. "You best check he's actually alive. I can't believe he slept through all that."

Ami anxiously leaned down to check and Stan licked her hand before going back to sleep again.

Remy followed up on a question he'd asked earlier. "What did you think life would be like outside of the farm? I'm kinda curious."

Ami considered the question. "You ever heard of a book called Little Women?"

Remy nodded. "Louisa May Alcott. Never read the book but I've seen the movie."

"I always wanted to be Jo March. Not Amy. Jo had courage to do want she wanted to do."

Remy was impressed. "And that's what you thought the outside world was like? A book written a hundred and fifty odd years ago?"

Ami shrugged. "I didn't realize it was so old when I was reading it, wasn't much different to my life on the farm, except how polite people were to each other. There was a civil war going on. People picking sides. Lord Ramesh said we'll all be doing that again soon."

Remy sighed. She wasn't wrong. "Yeah, well welcome to the real world, Ami. Maybe we can find a few books for you that explains what it's like now. Sadly, there's a whole lot of politicians who'd like to keep women locked up in the home again, just like in that book."

Ami looked at Remy carefully. "You sure you're ok to drive."

Remy smiled. "I'm fine. Not expecting anyone to shoot at us for the next fifty miles at least."

"Not funny. I was scared back there."

"If it's any consolation, I was too. If you're not scared when people start shooting, you're a fool."

Ami sighed and took her cue from her dog and closed her eyes a moment. She tried to channel her inner calmness, just like they were trained to do at the farm. Focus, think happy thoughts, find a peaceful space ...

When she opened her eyes again, she glimpsed a road sign that said Richmond was thirty miles away. Remy was listening to news radio.

"How do you do that?" Remy asked her as she stretched her arms.

"What?"

"Turn yourself off. You've been gone half an hour at least."

Ami was surprised that it had worked. She felt calm. Just as she was supposed to.

"Once we get to Richmond, I want to look the truck over for damage. You hungry?"

Ami thought about it a moment. "I am now. Are you sure you're OK?"

"If I was going to have a heart attack, it missed its chance, that's all I can say. Glad no one is checking my blood pressure today." He grinned and patted his chest. "Had quite a lot of serious pounding going on in there a while back."

Ami didn't know what to say but was definitely glad he hadn't mentioned that whilst they were being shot at.

Stan was stirring at her feet. "Give that dog a cookie. He was a star. Some dogs would have gotten hysterical back there, but Stan is a rock."

Ami grinned, hugging Stan who yawned and looked a bit bewildered until she showed him a cookie.

"I suspect Stan already regrets leaving the safety of the farm." Remy told her.

Ami shook his head. "He's happy. At least no one is threatening to kick him." Ami fiddled with the radio and found some music. "This ok?"

Remy nodded. "Beats gunfire."

"Any idea what was going on back there?" Ami asked.

"NPR said it was secessionists. They want the South to secede from the North. You might get your damn civil war sooner than you think. A local station claimed it was a Just Stop Oil protest that got out of hand. But I don't think those oil protesters carry guns. That's the thing now, you can't really trust anything you hear or read. Either way it was stupid."

Ami had no opinion either way. Life outside the farm was a whole lot different to what she'd expected. She looked up at the sky and the fluffy clouds. Clouds calmed her. She was always looking for shapes she could make sense of. She wondered if any drones were still watching them. She'd never considered people could be watching from the sky. It unnerved her.

"What's in Richmond?" She asked after a while.

"Tobacco country. City got rich poisoning three-quarters of the world with cancer."

Ami wrinkled her nose. "Lord Ramesh says smoking is one of the ten greatest sins."

"I'm beginning to think I should be joining this cult of yours. He's not wrong."

Ami laughed. "I can tell you the other nine sins."

Remy smiled. "Maybe later, kid. I've probably committed most of them. Never smoked though. My Pa once offered me a hundred bucks not to smoke before I was eighteen. I was ten at the time. A hundred bucks sounded like a lot of money back then. By the time I was eighteen I didn't want to smoke anyway. He never gave me the hundred though."

Ami looked away frowning. "I don't remember any man being in the house when I was little. I don't remember my mother so much either. I've tried, but I can't quite picture her."

"Sorry kid. Didn't mean to bring you down."

"I'm not upset. Most of the kids at the farm have no idea who their fathers are either. Nothing special about that."

Remy said nothing. He kept his eyes on the road ahead and praying his truck wasn't damaged.

"I am definitely hungry though," Ami added.

Remy grinned. "Me too. You ever had curry? I'm thinking of an Indian place I like."

Ami nodded. "Monday's."

"Monday's?" Remy asked.

"That's when we have curry at the farm."

The lube guy at the Tire & Auto place sluiced the underside of the truck with compressed air and finally emerged carrying a long corn stalk. He was grinning.

"Can't say I've ever had to pull one of these out of an engine bay before." He handed it to Remy as he lowered the ramp setting the truck down.

"Any serious damage?" Remy asked him, tossing the corn stalk in the waste barrel.

The lube guy wiped his hands on a rag. "You're a lucky guy mister. These old trucks were built to last. The mufflers ok. A couple of dents but nothing loose. Tire's look nearly new. You must have had work done recently. She's in good shape."

Remy nodded. "Yeah, had a reconditioned engine fitted and new brakes all round." He was inspecting the bullet scratch on the hood. He'd have get some paint on that before it rusted.

"I'd try to stick to the highway from now on though," the lube guy suggested. "I think you got lucky out there. I heard about the shooting on the radio this morning."

Remy nodded. "News said eight people dead and fifteen injured. I'm surprised there wasn't more. Any word on what the hell caused it? Protesters or Secessionists?"

The lube guy shrugged. "All these crazy people who want secession. Seems to me people are infected with hate. Didn't enough people die in the last civil war? We had a shooter in here last year. Complaining about something we did or didn't do. Just drove in and started shooting."

He pointed towards the backwall and the still visible bullet scars in the cement blocks. "Gavin put him down quick, but the boss wanted him fired because it wasn't good customer optics." He shook his head. "Optics. Can you believe that?"

He grabbed a can of WD-40 and sprayed the bullet scratch on the Chevy's hood.

"That will keep it from rusting until you get back home. Don't leave it too long though."

Remy nodded. "Thanks. Got a bullet hole to fill on the side too. Getting so I'm driving a damn sieve." He shook his head in sorrow. "How much do I owe you."

The lube guy shrugged. "Nothing. I didn't do anything except remove the stalk. If it's any consolation, I'd have taken off across the cornfield myself. You got damn lucky I think."

"Thanks. I know that. Luckier still the field was dry."

The lube guy glanced at the truck again and produced a slightly oil-stained business card. "If you're ever thinking of selling the Chevy, give me a call. I'd give you a good price. You're looking for Studebaker parts, right?"

Remy nodded. "Original stuff hard to find now."

"Try Peabody and Stich. Over on Union Street. They've got a Silver Hawk they're restoring. I drive past them on the way home."

Remy felt a quickening in his heart. "Union Street?"

"Stich is an auto nut. They recondition engines. Don't let him get started on EV's, he'll never stop ranting." He laughed. "Hates Tesla's. Gasoline vehicles won't ever go the way of the horse in his estimation, but I can tell you that at least thirty-five percent of the vehicles we get now are all EV's. Lucky for us they still use tires. A lot of tires they're so heavy."

"Like I say, this truck will see me out. Lucky for me gasoline isn't illegal yet."

The lube guy nodded and made a sad face. "Yeah, but one day it will be, and we'll all be forced to ride bikes. We're in the dinosaur business." He had a sudden thought. "You might find it hard to get a motel. It's the Pickleball Nationals this weekend. Hate that game. Causes more arguments than any other. My kids are mad for it."

"Never played it," Remy told him. "Heart couldn't take it. Hadn't even heard of it until three years ago and suddenly the whole world plays it. Crazy." Remy shook his hand and climbed up into his cab to back it off the ramp. He checked his watch wondering where Ami was. He signaled a thanks to the lube guy and turned the truck around. He needed to fill up and headed across the road to the gas station.

A boy came running up to him with Stan in tow. They both jumped into the cab.

"Sorry I'm late. You want me to fill it up?"

Remy stared at the boy and realized it was Ami. She'd had her hair cut short, just like a boy. The transformation was astonishing.

"What, how?"

Ami grinned at him. "Saw a sign in a window. Free haircut. There's a hairdresser school next block over training people to cut hair. What do you think?" She turned her head to show off the cut.

"Seriously? I'm in shock."

Ami laughed. "You said I should change the way I look. If they're looking for a girl, they're out of luck. I should probably change my name too. What do you think?"

"You make a pretty boy, Ami. Might get the wrong kind of attention, but yeah, they did a neat job. You could call yourself Ollie."

"Ollie?" Ami queried screwing up her face. "You think I'm an Ollie?"

"Well, it would be kind of funny to have a Stan and Ollie in my cab, that's all." He was all smiles suddenly. "Long time ago Stan and Ollie were the most famous names in the whole world. I'll show you them on my phone sometime." He chuckled. "It's a vanished world, but one time when I was a little kid, I watched their movies on the TV and laughed myself sick."

Ami still didn't look impressed. "Beats staring at a wall every night I guess."

Remy sighed, didn't quite know how to respond to that. "If you're filling up, make sure it's gasoline you're putting in there. I'll go inside to pay."

Ami nodded and jumped out to fill up.

Remy shook his head, wondered what he'd taken on here. Chopped her pretty hair off. But he guessed she wasn't wrong to do it, she'd be a lot safer from this Cult as Ollie. He suddenly felt so ancient.

CHAPTER FOURTEEN

Hawk Sighted

Ami stared through the window at the Silver Hawk in amazement. It was hard to believe this was a car at all. "It's like a rocket or something out of a comic book. You own something like this?"

Remy grinned. He'd hadn't meant to stop but couldn't resist when he'd seen the Hawk was in the window of Peabody & Stich. Clearly, they were still restoring it, it had been stripped down to the bare metal, but the car had been rebuilt. Even without a paint job it was beautiful to behold.

"Silver Hawk, one of the best-looking vehicles ever made in the USA," a voice stated behind them. Remy and Ami turned and came face to face with Arnie Stich. All smiles and very bald, his blue overalls emphasized his large pot belly.

"I've got a Golden Hawk," Remy told him. "Almost roadworthy."

Stich looked well impressed. "Have you now. What year?"

"'57. Spent ten years restoring it." Remy answered.

Stich cocked his head to one side. "In Richmond?"

"Coconut Grove, Miami."

Stich nodded scratched his head. "That'll be why I don't know you. I know all the Studebakers in various stages of repair in this city. No one has a Golden Hawk though."

"I'm on my way to Montreal to buy a new steering wheel."

Stich laughed. "Pierre Goulay?"

Remy nodded. Had a feeling that was the wrong answer.

"Don't waste your time. Whatever he says he's got, he's lying. You'll be needing the all-white steering wheel with the chrome horn rim inside."

Remy nodded. "He says he's got one or knows someone who will sell."

Stich pulled a very doubtful face. "Yeah well, they are rarer than hen's teeth. I've got a black one but it's gotta be white for the Golden Hawk. I don't suppose you've come across any Hawk door handles by any chance?"

Remy smiled. "I have two spares. Brand new still in the box."

"Hmm, we'll be talking business about that. Come on inside. Take a look at our restoration. A '57 Golden Hawk y'say. The holy grail of Studebakers. I'm Arnie Stitch by the way. Always good to meet another Hawk man."

Ami laughed. These men seemed so happy discussing doorhandles. It felt so weird to her. How strange it was that two grown men could be so passionate about a car.

Remy and Ami followed Stich into the workshop. It was busy and noisy inside. Men and two women working on engines, sparks flying everywhere. Ami was fascinated, Stan a tad fearful of the noises and being underfoot.

"We recondition V8's mostly and some straight eights or sixes," Stich was saying. "Everyone trying to keep the show on the road before they take it all away from us."

Remy nodded, thinking of the lube guy momentarily.

"You know any good upholstery guys?" Stich was asking. "I'm restoring a '28 Caddy and '36 Hupmobile 618 Touring Sedan. Engineering I can cope with, but it's hard to find good upholstery people these days."

Remy nodded. "I have a good guy in Miami. He redid the whole interior of my Hawk with white leather. Stitching's perfect. Ex Caddy leather worker. I can give you his number."

Stich slapped Remy on the shoulders. "I am so happy you dropped by today. You got a name?"

"Remy, and this here is ... Ollie and Stan."

"Stan and Ollie?" He grinned amused, staring at Ami and the dog with raised eyebrows. "I can't even begin to guess which is Ollie or Stan but welcome. Name's Arnie Stich." They shook hands. "Welcome to the deepest money pit in the USA." Stich declared. "We're going to have to find you a steering wheel. What was Goulay asking?"

"Around two grand," Remy replied.

Stich laughed. "What a bastard. Come on, I'll show you our Hawk."

Ami and Stan followed; she was fascinated at the change in Remy. He was like a kid, staring at everything and clearly excited. She bent down to reassure Stan that it was safe. He stuck to her legs like glue. "Come on Stan. You think I'm an Ollie too?"

Stan didn't mind what she was called as long as she paid attention to him.

Arnie was showing off the Silver Hawk when he suddenly remembered something.

"There's a Golden Hawk wreck over at Makkie's place. He's one of the best vintage restorers in the country. He told me it was a total wreck, but the interior wasn't so bad. A lot of blood maybe but ... he said there's was nothing he could do with it. Whole chassis is twisted."

Remy was interested. "Worth me looking do you think?"

"I'll call him. It's over on the west side of the city. Sad story though. Ravi whatever his name was made millions out of something to do with AI development. He was still under thirty. Spent $40 thou on restoring the Hawk with Makkie. Took it out for a spin and ploughed it straight into a wall. Driven it less than an hour. Cops said it was suicide, but I don't know, it was wet and no one, especially a novice in his first ride should put the hammer down on a wet road. They tend to willow and buck. The drum brakes aren't great at stopping at speed even in dry conditions."

"Yeah, I had power disc brakes fitted. My Pa was always going on about how they understeer." Remy chipped in. "Did his have power steering?"

"Not sure about that. The tires were underinflated. Everyone knows you need them at 32 in front and 30 in the rear. Makkie should have made sure of that, but he's a restorer not a driver. There was speculation in the papers that he lost a fortune in crypto investments and that's why he drove into the wall. I'm thinking he just didn't know how to drive a Hawk with all its quirks. You have to ease into them. The lack of lateral support on the seats doesn't help much either. Should have had bucket seats."

Ami stared at the two men, and it was like they were suddenly speaking a different language. She glanced at Stan who sighed and curled up into a ball at her feet.

Remy noticed her rolling her eyes. "Sorry kid, didn't mean to get carried away."

Ami smiled and flopped down on a bean bag to watch. "I'll get used to it, I guess.

Arnie chuckled. "I'll give Makkie a call now. Want any coffee? It's probably stewed though, brewed it hours ago."

Remy shook his head no. "Ok if I look under the hood?"

"Help yourself." He glanced at Ami. "Kid, there's a ton of magazines from the fifties and sixties if you want to acquaint yourself with some automotive history." He pointed towards some shelves.

Ami politely smiled. "I'll take a look."

Remy winked at her as she ambled over to gaze at yellowing pages and photos of cars.

Together they watched Arnie disappear into his office to make a call.

"You'd buy parts off a wreck?" Ami asked him.

"All the time. Sometimes that's the only way to get genuine parts."

"Kind of spooky though. Isn't it kind of cursed?"

Remy glanced at her surprised. "Cursed? Whatever gave you that idea." Remy squeezed Ami's shoulder. "If every car that ever had a crash was cursed, the restoration business would grind to a halt. We're rescuing a little bit of auto history, one part at a time."

Arnie returned moments later all smiles. "You are one lucky bastard, Remy. He's prepared to sell you the steering wheel. All white. You'll have to negotiate your own price but be prepared to haggle. Makkie knows his prices. By the way, there's a hog roast tonight over at the Longhorn Estate. He's a big vintage vehicle collector. Got two Studebakers and some first edition Ferrari's"

"Longhorn the aviation guy?" Remy asked.

"You heard of him?" Arnie asked, a bit surprised.

"His company were one of original rocket developers. I worked on the Shuttle program for nearly twenty-five years. Engineer."

Arnie looked at Remy with renewed respect. "Well, he'd be tickled pink to see you. He's always talking about the Shuttle program and how everyone got shafted when they shut it down."

"You're speaking to one of the shafted. It was pretty brutal, but it wasn't exactly unexpected. Not much call for rocket men when it happened. Different now, but I'm not sure I'd want to work for the new guys. They're pretty demanding."

"I've heard that. I hope you'll come. Follow the 33 out to Laurel, turn right onto Hungary Road and the Longhorn Ranch is signposted."

"Hog roast," Ami queried, looking at Arnie. "A whole hog?"

"You heard it boy. Best crackling' in Virginia. Make sure your grandpa comes tonight. There'll be fireworks and dancing. Longhorn knows how to party."

Remy wondered what Ami would make of an old-fashioned hog roast. He could just picture it. Lots of beer guts bellyaching about the state of the nation.

"We'll try our best," Remy told him. "You got an address for this Makkie character?"

Arnie handed over a scrap of paper. "Easy enough to find. About three, maybe four miles from here on 16th Avenue. Brick warehouse set back from the road. Got an original Pontiac sign on the wall. Used to be their showroom, back in the seventies."

Remy nodded. "Funny you don't see so many Pontiacs getting restored. Except maybe the '59 Bonneville coupe and the '67 GTO."

"I'd love to find a Bonneville – they were classy," Arnie remarked. "389 Cubic inch Tri-power V8. You got 345 hp out of that beauty. But I've got enough on my plate here. You ever want to sell your Hawk; I'll give you top dollar. I know ten people who'd bid over a hundred grand for it, right now, if it's in top condition."

Remy smiled. "I'll keep you in mind, but I'm intending to drive her, and with any luck avoid walls."

Arnie grinned. "You do that. Seven tonight. Hog roast, be there. You too kid."

Remy signaled to Ami that they were going. He gave Arnie his card. "Thank you, Arnie. Good luck with finishing the restoration. Call me if you want the doorhandles."

"I do, I do. These are rusted out. Hundred bucks each?"

Remy thought about it. "If I get the wheel, I'll send 'em for nothing. You've saved me a trip to Canada."

"It's a long way for nothing. Anything you need, just call. Us Studs need to stick together."

"Studs?" Ami repeated as they got back into the truck, then laughed. "Studs?"

"Studs as in Studebakers. He's a good guy. We're on our way to get a steering wheel thanks to him. Beats going to Montreal. We need to find a place to stay the night. Too risky to drive at night now."

"We really going to a hog roast?"

Remy frowned as he turned right onto Sherman Avenue. "Maybe. Maybe not. Let's get the wheel and decide. You want to go?"

"I never been to anything like that. Dancing? Fireworks?"

"Lots of old guys with guns talking about how to make America great again."

Ami snatched a look at him. "I'm sensing something negative here."

Remy smiled. "Been to a lot of things like that – I'm a democrat. That's on par with admitting you sup with Satan up here."

Ami nodded. "Satan been running my world for all my life, so far. But if you think it's a bad idea." Remy could hear the disappointment in her voice.

Remy nodded. "I'll consider it. But first let's get the wheel, a motel for the night and I need a shower."

Jim Makkie turned out to be preoccupied when they got there. Tall man about sixty with a thin whisp of hair combed over his balding head. He was definitely stressed about something in his private life and not interested in hearing any story. He looked Remy and Ami over and pointed to the back of the former showroom. "Maybe leave the dog in the truck. Lots of oil spills on the floor. The wreck's at the back wall. Didn't know what to do with it. Insurers not going to pay out for a suicide, and no one wants to pay for storage. I'm getting rid of it – if you can find anything you want that isn't bent out of shape, there's tools on the bench. Help yourself. We'll talk money when you're done. OK?"

Remy was about to say more when the man's phone rang, and he walked off to talk privately. It didn't sound like a friendly conversation. Ami took Stan back to the truck looking around at all the half-restored vehicles – genuinely puzzled at this obsession with fixing old beat-up cars. At the farm anything old was used as target practice by Father Tresor.

Returning, she joined Remy at the back of the showroom. He'd paused at a bench selecting an adjustable wrench spanner and a screwdriver. He turned towards her with a smile.

"This should do it. Might need your help. Get your first lesson in car maintenance."

Ami nodded, glad to be able to do something useful at last.

They stared at the wreck in wonder. Remy shook his head. "He must have hit the wall flat out. I don't think I've ever seen a wreck as bad as this."

Ami was staring at the bloodstained interior, all the more spectacular on the white leather. She didn't think there would be a single thing they could save.

Remy leaned in and checked the steering wheel covered in dried blood, his heart sinking a little. "There's something strange about this accident. Normally a driver would be thrown forward at high speed. All the blood spatter is backward. You can see it's clear of blood where one hand was on the wheel when it happened."

Ami didn't want to look too closely. "Can you get the steering wheel off?"

Remy nodded. "Might be bent with the impact but I'm pretty sure I can get it off. I have to pop the Studebaker badge off and check the mounting nut holding it in place. We're in luck, I think. Need to make sure the battery is disconnected so the horn doesn't go off."

"Can you get the blood off the wheel?" Ami asked.

Remy nodded. "Some people use a 5% acetate solution – others WD-40, but we'll try detergent soap and water first. I'm hoping it isn't cracked. We can fix that with epoxy resin and do a respray but that's down the road aways." He tried the driver's door but quickly realized it wasn't going to shift. It was the same with the passenger door. "OK, I'll have to climb in. Check the seat for broken glass for me, will you? Your eyes are better than mine."

It didn't take him long to discover the battery was gone – the engine block had already been removed. The front tires were punctured but not flat spotted, as you would expect from heavy braking at speed. He wondered if the driver had used the brakes at all.

Ami was gingerly pulling out several pieces of glass. Remy held out a small bin for her to dump them in.

"We're lucky we got here now; they've already started stripping it." Remy mused. "Remind me to remove the toggle switches on the instrument panel. They're in better shape than mine."

"Toggles," Ami replied, smirking. "It's like I'm learning a new language."

Remy laughed and pulled out a pair of gloves from his jacket pocket. He didn't want to cut himself on any jagged edges or bits of glass. "I'm going to climb in. Get ready to hand me the tools, alright?"

Ami nodded, amazed this old man could squeeze himself through the gap and fold himself into the driver's seat. Even if he did groan a lot with the effort.

"Does this mean we're not going to France? Oops, I mean Canada?"

Ami asked.

Remy took a moment to get his breath back and grabbed the spanner from her. "If it comes off clean, we're going home tomorrow." He looked down and saw a man's leather shoe was wedged under the brake pedal. It certainly looked to him that the driver had meant to end it all.

He removed the Studebaker badge in the center of the wheel and applied the spanner. It took a few attempts but finally the mounting nut came free. He looked up at a concerned Ami. "We're half way there. I have to disconnect the horn rim wires too." He took out a pair of pliers from his pocket.

Ami leaned in looking thoughtful. "I was thinking about my mother."

Remy was surprised. "You were?"

"You said there has to be a record of my birth somewhere, right?"

"I did." He pocketed the mounting nut.

"Does it mean they also list who my parents are? Both of them."

"It's supposed to. But things have changed. As I told you, might be your mother may not have done that or indeed not known. Don't get your hopes up, Ami."

Ami shook her head. "It doesn't worry me. No, well I mean, I do worry it might turn out to be someone I don't like or .... Shit, I don't know what I mean."

"Some things are best not known," Remy responded. He was sure the front seat had shifted during the crash. The wheel didn't want to come off easily, should just ease off.

"Can I help?" Ami asked watching him struggle.

"I'll be ok." Remy answered breathlessly. He reapplied himself to the task again and pulled. The wheel finally came free. He took time to breathe and savor the moment. He finally had a wheel. Maisie had insisted he just painted a black one white, but here, finally, he had an original white one, just as he wanted. He clipped connecting wires to the horn shaking his head. "They didn't change the wiring. They're all frayed. I wonder what else they didn't do."

"You going to mention it?" Ami asked.

Remy sighed. "Too late now. Let's go pay the man. Take the wheel from me. Don't worry the blood is dry."

"Toggles." Ami reminded him.

"Right, thanks. We're in business, Ami. Now let the haggling begin.

You get the wheel to the truck before he changes his mind."

Jim was slumped head down on his desk. He'd forgotten they were there.

"Finished already?"

"Got the wheel. How much?" Remy asked.

He thought about it a moment. "Five hundred alright with you? You did the work."

Remy nodded, trying not to show his surprise. He'd been prepared to pay way more.

"I'll get the cash from the truck. You ok?"

Jim Makkie shrugged. "You ever get divorced? It's amazing how stuff they didn't care about suddenly becomes important. I may have to sell this place; if it's worth anything at all."

Remy looked as sympathetic as he could. "Sorry. Sometimes it's best to walk away and save yourself a lot of pain."

"Or shoot her and her bastard lawyer," Jim added.

"That is certainly one way," Remy told him. "I'll get the cash. Sounds like you'll be needing it."

Remy left to join Ami at the truck as she soothed Stan.

"We done?" Ami asked.

"You wrapped the wheel like I asked?" He handed her the toggles.

Ami nodded. "It's stashed in the box. I'll put these with it."

Remy withdrew some cash and counted out the notes. "He's not a happy man. I'll go back and pay. You're on guard duty. Do not wander far from the truck."

Ami nodded, watching as Remy walked away again.

Inside Jim handed Remy a photo of the accident as he counted the fifty-dollar notes. Remy stared at the photo in horror. Ravi, the driver, had been impaled by a steel rod in his seat. It explained the blood spatter. Even if he'd wanted to survive the crash, he couldn't have foreseen the metal pole. He handed the photograph back to him. Maybe Ami was right, the car was cursed.

"I hope you find resolution," Remy told Jim. He looked up at him and shrugged again.

"Thanks for money. You going to the Longhorn shindig tonight?"

"Might. The kid seems keen."

"Yeah well, better to be there than on the roads. I've heard there's going to be trouble. All those guys wanting 'National Divorce'. By the time they get it they'll be too old to keep it. Civil war is like divorce, with guns. Too much craziness for me."

Remy had to agree. "It's reckless. You really think it will come to that?"

"That's what they want, and they're well financed. Longhorn is all for it. Kill the liberal elite, abolish the FBI, shoot the woke, bring back lynching. That's why they want to ban teaching history, so kids won't know how bad it all was in the fifties."

"Well, I live in Florida, so we know all about that."

Jim looked out towards Ami standing by the truck. He screwed up his face a moment. "I miss my kid. Only see him on weekends. I know he blames me for the divorce, even though she was the one to move out. You take care of that kid, Grandpa. We only get a precious few years before they reject everything you stand for."

Remy nodded. "In my experience kids will come back to you later, once they realized you were right all along."

Jim shook his head. "I wish I believed that. I really do. Drive safe. Enjoy your Hawk when you get it back on the road."

"Thanks, I will."

Jim watched him go, his mind elsewhere again.

CHAPTER FIFTEEN

Hog Roast

Remy pulled over in the Museum district and turned to Ami. "I have to check my phone and find us a place to stay the night. Can we have an awkward conversation, kid?"

Ami looked at him with surprise. "Awkward? Like one of those talks about the evils of sex or drugs? We get one of those every month at the farm. Of course, they never talk about what the staff get up to or the how much they drink in the staff quarters. I know how much because who do you think has to do the recycling? And I seen 'em passed out on the porch because they can't climb the stairs. If it's one of those conversations I already heard it, Remy."

Remy stared at her with amazement. Then took a deep breath. "It's worse than that."

Ami narrowed her eyes. "Now you've got my attention. Maybe I should cover Stan's ears?"

Remy allowed himself a little smile. She was being defensive, clearly worried about what he was going to say.

"Yes, cover his ears," he told her. "Awkward conversation number one coming right up."

Ami rolled her eyes as Remy rubbed his face. He realized he was dog tired.

"I'm wondering if it's a good idea to take you to the hog roast."

Ami frowned. "You mean leave me in some motel as you go boozin'?"

Remy shook his head. "I can't watch you one hundred percent of the time and ... there's some people who might want to take advantage of you ..."

Ami put her hand out to stop him speaking. "I've been raised on the farm, Remy. I've seen boys getting done. I know this stuff. Shit I've been beaten black and blue for simply helping a girl get to the washroom after she was left bloody. I know what evil looks like, hell I know what it smells like. I've seen everything, Remy. I'm no cute innocent kid. I know I look cute. Shit, I've been told it enough times I wanted to cut my face to stop 'em drooling at me."

Remy bit on his lip. "There's another reason. A political reason."

Ami leaned back against the passenger door. "I don't know nothing about politics."

"Longhorn finances insurrection movements. He's famous for wanting a rerun of the civil war. He wants all the former Confederate States to secede from the North including West Virginia and he's prepared to pay people to cause trouble."

Ami stared at him. "Like the shooters on the highway."

Remy nodded. "Exactly. And all I'm saying is that I'm not one of those people. I believe in the Union. I don't like the obsession with gun culture and I, in particular, dislike people who exploit kids for their own ends, whether it's sex or politics. You cut your hair, somehow you made yourself even prettier and I fear for your safety, Ami. I really do. I'm not saying you have to wear a sack over your head, and I know you're no innocent. You wouldn't have survived as long as you did at the farm if you were."

Remy stopped talking, unable to read her reaction.

"Stan's hungry. I know you're looking out for me, Remy. Let's find a place to stay and then decide. We got to eat right? It's a hog roast. I learned not to get too fond of the piglets early on and cried enough tears over that. Pigs are pretty smart if you let them be."

Remy started the engine. She wanted to go. Well so be it. He gave her his phone.

"Time you learned how to use this. See the bottom button looks like a compass. Click on that and search for dog friendly motel in Richmond."

Ami took the phone and examined it. It was that easy to find stuff?

Remy pointed. "You type in the search engine box there what you want to know. If you make a mistake, it will correct it or at least try."

Ami shook her head in wonder as she inputted 'dog friendly motels'. "It's like magic."

Remy sighed. "I really don't want to get you addicted, but I guess you'll be a freak if you don't know this stuff."

"That's what the cops call us kids. 'The Freak Farm'. Like we're so stupid. Everything is so different as to how I imagined the world would be."

The phone gave her options. She stared opened mouthed as it listed at least ten different motels and hotels that were dog friendly. She laughed in wonder. "Has everyone got one of these?"

Remy nodded as he negotiated a crossroads. "Yep. Even tiny kids. It's not all good, Ami. You ask the wrong question, and it will take you to hell in a flash and there are a lot of people from hell on the internet."

"I like the sound of this one. Mimosa Spring motel. We love dogs. $130 bucks a night special. Tex-Mex Café and secure parking, last two rooms available." She showed the link to Remy and he thought it looked a tad pink but what the hell. The price was reasonable. "Address?"

"2055 Geary and Temple."

"There should be a link that says directions..."

Ami realized she could scroll. "Wow, it shows the route and everything. Shit this is magic."

Remy smiled. "I guess you'll be wanting a phone of your own soon."

Ami grinned as she explored some more. "What if I put in Lord Ramesh?"

Remy frowned. "You might be opening a sinkhole if you do but do it at your own risk kid."

Ami stared at all the links and scrolled down to comments. She fell quiet as she read them.

Remy glanced over at her worried at her silence.

"He's so old," Ami said with sorrow. "People say such horrible things. They say he's fathered a thousand children. Can that be true?" She looked up at Remy confused.

"It's a cult. It's usually about sex and control and ..." He could see her expression. "It doesn't mean he's your father. I mean, I guess he could be but ..."

"All the male members of the Order are called Father," Ami pointed out.

"Catholic priests are called father too. Doesn't mean they are. I mean some are, but most are sworn to celibacy. If you know what means."

Ami gave him a look that told him she knew but doubted it.

"Yeah, well. You've escaped Ami. You're free. Now all you have to do is free your mind from them, which might be the hardest part, after all, it's all you've known till now."

Ami went back to the map. "It says you have to turn right at the next crossing."

Remy smiled. "You're a natural, kid. I guess we're heading to the Mimosa."

Remy was taken aback by the sheer pinkness of the motel. He almost chickened out when he saw the "We welcome LGBTQ+ guests – your home from home." Ami seemed keen however and he found parking. "At least the food should be good," he muttered as he headed to reception. He was glad no one back home could see him checking in.

Two hours later they were back on the road. There were several cars ahead of them as they approached the Longhorn Estate. The treelined avenue spoke loudly of money and there was heavy security at the huge open gates.

"Will they let us in?" Ami asked.

"I won't mind if they don't," Remy replied. "There's way too many confederate flags for my taste on their bumpers."

"And the fish sign. What does that mean?"

"Evangelicals. Stick close to me and even closer to Stan."

Ami nodded slowly. Her head was still full of all the things people said about the Order. Some praised it and she was surprised to discover there were at least thirty thousand disciples across America, all charged with spreading the word. That's what she had been destined for. To be a pilgrim going from town to town, recruiting members to send back to Lord Ramesh to receive his wisdom and guide them through the travails of life. This is what she had run from. She sighed, her stomach churning with anxiety.

She glanced at Remy. He'd showered and shaved and done his best to look smart. She'd been taken aback at the guests and their colorful costumes, but they had made her and Stan very welcome. She reckoned Lord Ramesh would probably have a heart attack if he knew this motel even existed. Now she was excited to be going to a hog roast.

The security guys were taking down license plates and noting names.

"Why?" Ami asked as they waited to be told where to park.

"Longhorn is rich. Someone will be checking names against the plates and if we're spies from the other side."

"Other side?"

"Democrats. Woke activists. Jews. They have a thing about Jews. I'll explain later."

"You're a democrat. You said so."

"I'm a secret democrat. Never registered. Just turn up to vote. That way your name doesn't turn up on a list. For the moment the vote is secret. I'm guessing these people will want to change that soon enough."

"Can I vote?"

"Not yet. They don't teach you about the electoral system at the farm?"

Ami laughed. "Never."

Remy nodded and finally they got the signal to go through. Someone waved them to the side of the house and where to park. There had to be at least fifty or sixty vehicles there already.

"Ok, we're in. If I say we have to leave, no sulks, ok? We go in, we eat, we smile and make nice and leave."

Ami frowned. She realized that he'd only done this for her. "Sorry I made you come."

"You need to see the enemy up close anyhow." Remy told her. "Please don't wander off without me knowing where. Ok?"

"I'm good. Stan will be with me."

"Yes, he will. Now fix on a smile."

Ami rolled her eyes. This was going to be interesting.

Ami walked towards the crowd, Stan sticking close to her side, a little bit anxious about noise of the band and people everywhere. Remy followed behind her, a tad relieved that there was a carnival atmosphere.

Ami surveyed the scene with a critical eye. There had to be well over a hundred people at the hog roast talking loudly at each other but not really listening. She couldn't believe the size of their bellies and the woman looked like old painted dolls, their faces either bloated or so taut they could barely smile as they sucked on their vapes.

Remy was watching her reaction with amusement. "This is what the real world looks like, Ami. Best get used to it."

Ami had spotted some kids sitting on hay bales huddled over their phones oblivious to what was going on around them.

"What are they looking at?" Ami asked Remy.

Remy glanced at where she was gazing and shrugged. "Other people having fun. That's what Maisie tells me anyway. Come on, let's go get something to drink. What would you like, kid. Coke, juice... whiskey?"

Ami wasn't sure. "Orange juice, maybe? I like to squeeze them when they're in season. We had twenty orange trees on the farm. We were supposed to send the oranges to Charleston, but I couldn't resist. Another thing I got beaten for."

"I'm pretty sure they've got everything here." Remy threaded his way through the crowd and got them both there safely. The barman found him a glass of red wine.

"Wine?" Ami asked him, noticing everyone else was drinking beer.

"Can't drink beer. It's a killer for the bladder." He pointed to a cloud of smoke on the distance. "There's your hog roast. Anytime you and Stan feel hungry just head on over there and they'll feed you."

Ami strained to see it over the heads of others but could smell it. Stan could too, sticking his nose in the air to sniff.

"Don't give him any fat," Remy warned her. "He'll just fart all night and we're sharing a room remember."

A bearded man in a wheelchair was making his way towards them. He seemed intent on talking to Remy. Remy smiled at him trying to recollect if he knew him.

"Remy? You're a dark horse. Didn't know you were into this kind of thing."

Remy searched his memory for a name, and it suddenly clicked. "That you Walter hiding behind that beard?"

Walter gripped Remy's hand and shook hard, snatching a curious glimpse at Ami.

"You're nephew?"

"I think technically great nephew. Meet Ollie. What the hell happened to you, Walter? Last time I saw you, you were still doing those marathons."

Walter made a sad face. "MS they tell me. It's progressive. So first the legs go then eventually my arms. Shit it's been a long time since Kennedy. You still got that shack by the beach?"

"Lost it in the hurricane in '99. Moved further south to my dad's old place. It's a little more solid. Good to see you, man." Remy turned to

Ollie. "Walter and I worked on the Shuttle launch team for years."

Ami pretended to be interested, she didn't know what the Shuttle was. "Stan and me are going to check out the hog roast. I don't think I can hold out any longer."

Remy nodded. "Ok. I'll join you there in a moment." He watched her go, then returned his gaze to Walter. "You live in Richmond now?"

"Got a place near the hospital. My niece works there. It helps. God, it must be like twenty-five years..."

"I guess. I thought you'd moved to Houston."

"I did. Then California. Planned a long happy retirement. Ending up in a wheelchair was not part of the plan."

"That's so tough for you. Yeah, I had a heart scare in 2010 myself. They shoved in stents to keep me going. Feel like the Duracell bunny sometimes."

"You were going to restore your Pa's Studebaker. I remember that. Your Pa was so damn proud of that car. I guess he's long dead by now."

"He hit a deer."

Walter looked pained. "Ouch. In the Hawk?"

"Restoration proved a little harder after that. I think I've been working on it for ten years now."

Walter laughed, then coughed, taking a while to recover. Remy noticed his shaking hands.

"You met Longhorn yet?" Remy asked.

Walter nodded. "Quite a guy. Planning big things for America. Big things. So pleased you're here Remy. Wasn't I always telling you that you have to pick a side."

Remy nodded. "You were."

Walter looked around him. "Not much a guy in a wheelchair can do for the movement but believe me, we're taking back control. That's the main thing."

"The Feds might have a say in that," Remy suggested.

Walter dismissed them. "Don't worry about them. We've got the National Guard with us, at least half the army. When it kicks off it, will all be over in a week. The fucking Democrats won't see it coming."

Remy frowned. "You don't think they'll fight it?"

"Not when the cops turn their guns on them. Defund the cops will come back to bite them in the ass."

"You hear about the shooting on the highway?" Remy asked.

Walter seemed to dismiss it. "Oil protesters. I would have shot them too. They have no right to glue themselves to any highway."

"You sure it was oil protesters? I heard it was secessionists."

"Fucking rumors, fake news. Antifa stuff. I know it was oil protesters. Longhorn has a plan for them too. You'll see."

Remy lifted his glass to him. "May you live to see your revolution, Walter."

Walter grinned. "Oh, I will, I will. Come the New Year we take over everything. Jan 6th will be made a public holiday for the martyrs. Going to be total revolution Remy. All the vermin will be rounded up and shipped out. You'll see. Glad you're on our side at last." He drew out a card from his top pocket and pressed it into Remy's hand. "Call me. Lots to catch up on. It's so good to see you man. So many of the old team are gone already."

"Shit yeah, I went to three funerals last year." Remy squeezed the man's shoulder. "I have to catch up with Ollie. It's been good to see you man. Fight that MS. Walter."

"I am fighting. Check out Longhorn's auto collection, Remy. He's got a Cord. Not to mention two Silver Hawks. Must be millions parked over there."

Remy looked impressed. "That I will. Not jealous much at all. Good luck with the hospital. I hope they can find something to help."

Walter nodded. "That's where the real war is, Remy. Big pharma sucking the life out us all. There's a plan for them too. But first, kill all the lawyers, right?"

Remy chuckled. "Yeah … the lawyers. Maybe be some Judges too, huh?"

He moved away from him, pocketing the card, squeezing through a crowd to get to Ami. He didn't want her out of his sight too long. Walter had changed a lot. Another guy lost down the MAGA rabbit hole. He tried to remember if he was always like that but wasn't sure. Maybe getting MS had warped his mind. Or revealed his true nature.

The gleaming hog on the spit was huge. A guy in a chef's uniform was scraping fat off the skin as flames leapt up towards the carcass. Remy could feel the heat. It smelled pretty good, pity he wasn't going to eat any.

Stan was carefully guarding a slice of pork with his paws as he chewed on another. He was in pig heaven. Remy looked around for Ami and couldn't see her.

"You want a hot pork sandwich with apple sauce?"

Remy spun around and Ami was holding a paper plate piled high with food. "Tastes good."

He shook his head. "Heart attack in a sandwich kid. I'll pass and check out the fixings."

"There's hot cornbread, collard greens, roast potatoes. I had four already."

Remy grinned and headed to a table loaded with food and sauces.

"Bet you didn't think you'd meet someone you know." Ami remarked walking over with him.

"No. Took me by surprise." He looked back at Stan, still choking meat down. "Don't let him have any more. He's not used to it and a dog never knows when to stop."

Ami nodded. "I already told him no more. He's like so excited."

"And you?" Remy asked. "This what you expected? That's one big hog, don't you think?" He helped himself to cornbread and greens. Just like he remembered from being a kid. He allowed himself to two roast potatoes.

Ami looked back at the fire. "It sure is big."

"Walter back there used to be one of the fittest men I ever knew. Ran, swam, anytime he wasn't at work, he'd be working out. Hard to see him like that."

Ami shrugged. "Lord Ramesh says that illness is caused by an unpure heart."

"You believe that?"

Ami wrinkled her nose. "I'm already cursed, Remy. My heart is a long way from being pure. Sister Rice told me that a strong-willed person like me would have been burned as a witch back in the day. That filled me with a lot of hope." She laughed. "That true?"

"Believe it or not that was definitely true back in Salem. Women were blamed for bad weather, disease, you name it. History is not a happy place in this country. We're always inventing new ways to make people miserable." He ate his collard greens and surveyed the crowd. "Notice anything about this crowd?"

Ami looked about her. "Everyone is like swollen. How did they get so fat?"

"You'll find that using that word can you get you arrested in some places further north."

"Swollen?"

"The other word."

Ami laughed; she didn't believe him. She looked for a place to put her paper plate. "Do not let me eat anything more. I'm going to explode."

Remy ate as Stan returned to Ami's side still licking his lips.

"Someone else is going to explode first I think," Remy said. "His tummy is distended already. Want to see Longhorn's automobile collection? I know you don't know one car from another, but he's got some impressive vehicles on display."

Ami examined Remy's face. "More impressive than your Studebaker?"

Remy laughed. "Yeah. I'll admit that, yeah. Wait till you see the Cord."

"Cord?"

"The King of the Road. First front-wheel drive luxury car in America. I read he's got an 810 from 1936. If you're not impressed, you'll have to hitch a ride back to the motel."

Ami laughed but wasn't one hundred percent sure he was joking.

Remy finished his food, and they found their way over to the automobile collection on the other side of the main house.

"I don't suppose you found any napkins?" Remy asked with greasy fingers.

"Napkins?"

"Paper to wipe sticky fingers with, not to mention sticky paws."

"Oh, yeah, I saw those but ... sorry."

Remy took out a clean tissue from his pocket and wiped his fingers, handing it over to Ami. "Do not under any circumstances get any greasy fingerprints onto any vehicle. Understood?"

Ami looked at him in wonder. "Wow, you really like cars, don't you."

Remy grinned. "I do. You like the music?"

Ami looked over to where the band was playing. "I don't know much about music. Is it good?"

"It's country. Lots of sad songs about loneliness and heartache. But good dancing tunes too. You have so much to discover, Ami. I'm quite jealous in a way."

"I know. Believe me I know. It's like every day I have to climb a mountain of stuff I had no idea existed. It's …." She searched for the right word. "Exhausting."

Remy smiled. Yeah, it had to be.

Ami was impressed by the two Silver Hawks and a 1934 Mercedes Benz 500 K Roadster. She could see Remy was slightly envious of the collection. Finally, they found themselves standing in front of an all-white Cord 810, admiring the sweeping aerodynamic lines as Remy explained what all the features were and why it didn't seem to have headlights.

"Was it fast?" Ami asked.

"It wasn't the fastest, even though it had the Lycoming V8 engine and a four-speed pre-select gearbox. But think on this, most roads outside of the cities were still dirt. Imagine a beast like this having to suddenly brake on a dirt road. Driving was a big risk in those days. Took a great deal of energy just to stop 'em."

"You must be the shuttle guy," a gruff voice stated from behind them.

Remy and Ami turned to see an imposing man of about sixty wearing a cowboy hat and sporting an impressive Mustang silver belt buckle prominently under his large belly.

Remy introduced himself. "Remy Mitchell and my great nephew Ollie. You must be Mr. Longhorn. Mr Stich pointed me in this direction tonight."

"Yeah, Stich is here somewhere. Another Stud man. He said you might be here. All the Shuttle guys are welcome at my place."

They shook hands. Remy noticed the man had a missing finger.

"Welcome to the Longhorn Ranch. You're the guy with a Golden Hawk I'm told."

"That's me. Almost done with the restoration."

"I heard about you looking for a steering wheel. Nothing escapes me when it comes to Studebakers, getting harder to find original parts these days. You seen my two Studs?" He smiled revealing a gleaming set of perfect white teeth. "If Washington gets its way, they have all of these vehicles off the road by 2030. I hope you're resisting."

Remy nodded. "I sure am. I worry they'll turn off the gasoline tap or tax it out of existence. Be hard to keep them running without it. I hear they're thinking of some kind of subsidy to covert everyone to electric. A kind of job-creation scheme."

Longhorn swore. "That will never happen. You think millions of vehicle owners will just roll over because of a little change in the weather? They won't dare to take away our automobiles. They're killing freedom and we ain't going to take it up the ass anymore. We're taking back control. Those damn oil protesters deserved what they got on the highway today."

Remy nodded and felt obliged to agree. "One has to make stand." He hoped he sounded convincing.

Longhorn looked Ami over and smiled. "We will make a stand and soon. What kind of future will this kid have if we don't? You a patriot boy?"

Ami blinked; this was just like being back on the farm. She knew exactly what to say. "America First, sir. We have to defend our rights. Freedom is nothing without it."

"Too damn right, kid." He glanced at Remy. "You're teaching him right, Remy. Good job. America has lost its way. Our enemies are gathering strength as we dither and prevaricate. If we don't make a stand, it will all be lost. All of it."

Remy rested his hands on Ami's slim shoulders. "It's Ollie's world now. We need to preserve the past, so they know what they hell they're fighting for."

Longhorn punched the air. "Damn right we do. Damn right. You're ok Remy. You Shuttle guys are ok. Walter's here somewhere if you haven't seen him yet. Poor guys a cripple now. You'd never guess he was a marathon winner. You guys got royally shafted when they closed the Shuttle program down. Now it's all about colonizing fucking Mars. Well good luck to that. We're staying put. We have to protect what we've got right here. Musk can have Mars; I just hope he takes all the screwballs with him."

Remy smiled. "Mars is definitely not on my vacation plans."

Longhorn laughed and slapped Remy on the back. "Have fun, enjoy yourselves. Come the New Year we take back control."

Ami watched Longhorn go, backslapping others as he made his way through the partygoers. "New Year?" She asked.

Remy lightly punched her arm. "That's the date for the glorious revolution. Well done with your answer. I was convinced. America First, hey."

"Lord Ramesh keeps telling us on the day of reckoning we shall be saved, and the Order will have to defend America from enemies from all over the world."

"I guess he didn't mention the enemy within, huh. Come on, let's go see the band. Stan will be wanting to poop in about five minutes if I know anything about dogs. You remember that little plastic bag I gave you in case?"

Ami pulled it out of her jeans.

"Keep it handy. Dogs always choose the most embarrassing place to do their business."

"That is so true." Ami was ready and kept her eye on Stan as they wandered towards the music and dancing. Ami simultaneously nervous and excited to see so many people having a good time.

Remy and Stan stood back from the crowd pressing the dance floor. They were watching Ami learning to line dance, a big grin on her face as she strove to keep up and turn with the others.

"You see that, Stan? That's a girl learning how to be happy. Got quite a few years of catching up on that I reckon."

Remy was thinking about Ami's future and feared he wouldn't live long enough to help her find her feet in the world. He'd only known her for a few days and yet it felt like months. 'Never get too attached,' his wife would always say about every kid she felt responsible for, but this felt different. If he didn't step up who the hell would?

Stan interrupted his thoughts as he suddenly began choking and after some desperate moments vomited all that pork he'd wolfed down. Remy was glad the band drowned out the choking sounds as Stan puked his heart out. The dog stared at the mound of undigested meat at his feet as Remy swiftly scooped it up, in case he was tempted to eat it all over again. He looked down at the dog who now seemed quite bewildered.

"I bet you're proud of yourself now, huh? You feel better?"

Stan looked up at him and then puked some more. Remy patiently scooped that up too. "That's enough now, Stan. Enough."

Stan lay down panting, not sure he felt better at all.

Remy turned towards the dancing and was relieved to see Ami laughing and linking arms with a sequin attired attractive woman in cowboy boots. Her face seemed familiar to him but didn't know why. He thought back to the last time he'd been dancing. When the hell was that? Had to be twenty years or more. His wife hadn't like dancing, but she'd had a friend called Dorothy who lived to dance and made sure to get him on a dance floor any chance she got. He couldn't remember if he liked dancing, but he'd liked Dorothy with her infectious laugh and twinkling mischievous eyes.

Ami was suddenly at his side and Stan was jumping up to greet her.

Remy smiled. She looked red faced, breathless and pleased with herself.

"It was hard at first. All my life I never danced before."

"One of the sins, I suppose," Remy suggested.

Ami shook her head. "No music, remember. God, I'm soooo hot now."

"Stan had a moment. Puked up everything he ate."

"Oh, you poor baby." Ami hugged her dog. "I told you to stop eating."

"He'll be hungry all over again soon, but I don't suggest anymore hog roast. Some biscuits in the truck."

Ami nodded, glancing back at the packed dance floor. "That was fun." She looked back at Remy. "You look tired though."

Remy smiled. "If you want to go back on the dance floor I can wait. You were having good time."

Ami gave him a little hug. "Nah, I'm happy. I learned to dance. That woman, the one who was teaching me. She's famous according to other dancers. You know who she is?"

Remy shook his head. "Could be a country star. Good looking woman that's for sure."

Ami took Remy's hand. "Come on, let's go. I'm glad we came. You met a friend too."

Remy nodded. "I was just thinking about that. Walter was so different back then. Always so active. Brilliant mind. God, I used to have friends back then, well work friends anyway. Cook outs at my place at the beach on weekends when we weren't on duty or back in Houston. Seems like ancient history now. Once I met my wife it all seemed to stop. I don't blame her. It was probably time to grow up. I'd postponed it long enough."

Ami linked arms and steered Remy and Stan back to the truck. "Thanks for bringing me here tonight."

Remy put an arm around her. "You're welcome, Ami. I was enjoying watching you with that big grin on your face."

Ami grinned some more and looked for Stan stopping to sniff something. "Come on Stan, keep up."

Remy was thoughtful as he drove them back to the city.

"Now you've discovered dancing, maybe you'll have to think about sports."

"Sports?" Ami asked, puzzled.

"First off you have to learn what they all are, just to fit in. People are pretty obsessed with their sports, so you need to know what's on offer out there. Baseball, basketball, pickleball, football, soccer, which is European football, tennis, marathons, skiing, beach volleyball, squash, golf, surfing, wind surfing, sailing, swimming, and a whole host more. You have to decide which sport you like and pick a team."

Ami looked doubtful. "Pick a team?"

"One you'd support. You don't have to play the sport but believe me, people will ask which is your sport. Doesn't matter which one you pick, but once you do, you get an entry ticket to a tribe. That sort of makes people comfortable knowing what tribe you belong to and decide what kind of person you are."

"Really?" Ami was skeptical.

Remy nodded. "Listen up, this is Civilization Orientation 101. Then you'll need to know some of the player's names. You don't have to be an expert, but you just drop a name in, and it puts people at ease. 'You say... Oh yeah, Brady was the best or he's not the person he used to be.' It sounds kind of cynical, but that's how society works."

Ami shook her head. "What if you meet someone who knows you're full of bullshit."

"That the beauty of it. They will be so keen on expressing their opinions all you have to say is 'Wow, you really know your stuff.' They feel good about themselves and your opinions too."

"So, in other words fake it. Shit I've been faking it all my life so far."

Remy chuckled. "Everyone does it. On-line everyone has an opinion about everything, even if they know nothing at all. I'm old fashioned, I think conversations should be face to face, in a bar or some meeting place over a glass of something. But that makes me a dinosaur."

Ami laughed. "You are a dinosaur."

"I'm guessing you don't know what online is or even half of what

I'm saying."

Ami closed her eyes a moment, suddenly tired. "I know online. Lord Ramesh is online. We have to listen to him give a sermon all the time. Then we watch the brothers and sisters praying and healing. I tuned it out. Needed matchsticks to keep my eyes open. Sister Ryan would crack the whip at us if we closed our eyes."

"Well, being online doesn't have to be so painful. Although I'm going to have to teach you what's good and what to avoid when you do get online."

"Why do I have to belong to a tribe?"

"You just left a tribe, so I'm guessing you're not so keen to join another and learn all their tiresome rules. For instance, another way of belonging is to join a religion. Protestant, Catholic, Methodist, Evangelical or Buddhism, the choice is endless. They welcome you in and bang, you got a social life to go with it and of course you have to obey their rules or be kicked out."

"Hmmm, sports sounds better somehow. Is this all according to the Law of Remy?"

"Yep. Or you can be a loner. However, people don't like loners, people get suspicious of them, as they tend to drift towards conspiracies or illegal drug use and blame society for all their problems."

"So, this is it? Sports or religion?"

Remy shrugged. "No, you've got music, pop rock, metal, country, punk, a whole lot of tribes. Swifties for example. Then there are people who devote their whole lives to worshipping celebrities. There are also gamers; and that's a whole different set of loners who never meet anyone in real life at all. The whole of society is broken down into tiny pieces and all you have to do is find one of the pieces and get to know it. It just makes people happier to know you're either just like them or you are another piece of the puzzle, and they can fit you in there."

Ami reflected on that. "That's what Lord Ramesh says. One day everyone will belong to the Order and conflict will cease to exist and there will be no more strife or pain."

"Hmmm, sounds a little optimistic to me. Did I mention that once you pick a team, you're supposed to hate all the other teams and sometimes it gets a little heated."

Ami laughed. "I know you're messing with me Remy."

"Uh-huh. I promise you this is real. The motel we're staying at tonight for example. You saw some of the other guests in the lobby. You think they'd want to stay someplace else where people will stare or be hostile? No. They chose there because it's safe and they'd be accepted. The moment they decided which gender they wanted to be they joined a tribe and tribes' function best in large numbers.

"You escaped one tribe because it wasn't your choice and they mistreated you. You'll be on a journey now to find a new identity and a new tribe, one that will embrace you."

"You must think about this stuff a lot." Ami said. She stroked Stan's ears. It kind of made sense to her. "But you're alone."

"I'm a widower. There's a heck of a lot of widowers out there. They tried to make me go to a support group, but I avoided all that. Besides I'm a Stud, remember. The moment I drive that Studebaker to a vintage meet, I'll be Mr Golden Hawk, for one day at least."

Ami laughed. "Yeah, you'll be a stud. Funny. But I get it. Does everyone believe this stuff?"

Remy nodded. "Pretty much. Take Stan. On his own, he's a dog, slightly indeterminate breed but he has these amazing eyes. The moment you go walking with him I guarantee you'll make friends with other dog owners; they'll love him. Might not be lifelong friends, but friends, who will trust you simply because of Stan and then judge you on how you treat your dog. There's a whole million sub-division of tribes out there."

Ami cuddled Stan who was feeling better now. "You and me Stan are going to join a tribe."

Remy grinned. "Got it on one. Here endeth the lesson, we're almost there."

Remy glanced at her a moment. "I'm pretty sure people will like you just the way you are. All I'm saying is, don't rush to judgment. The guy who delivers my groceries used to be a soldier who got PTSD, that's post-traumatic stress disorder. He's a good guy who needs the job to survive. Most people will just see him as the delivery guy and won't look beyond that. We don't often see both sides of the story."

Ami stared at him. Remy briefly returned her gaze.

"Take you, Ami. Outsiders will assume you're a pretty kid without a care in the world. You're polite and got a dog that loves you. They'll think she's got it easy. Nice warm home to live in, loving parents or grumpy grandparent at least. No one will look at you and think escapee from a religious cult. It just wouldn't cross their minds."

Ami nodded. "I get it. No judgments, give people a chance, learn to belong."

"Exactly. And the great thing about life is this, you can always start again, reinvent yourself. Never let anyone tell you that you can't do something unless it's, y'know, against the law of course. All it takes is will power and a lot of reading."

Ami smiled. "You should start a cult, Remy. Bet people would join you."

Remy chuckled. "Definitely not on my to do list. We're here." He frowned as he glanced at her again. "You're itching. That dressing needs changing when we get inside. Take a shower and I'll change the bandages."

Ami nodded, she hadn't realized that he'd been watching her, and it was true, she was feeling itchy.

"It's a good sign when it itches. Means its healing. And you probably got a bit sweaty dancing. All good, Ami. I was watching you out there on the dancefloor and I could see how happy you were. Grab all the happiness you can find kid. You deserve it."

Remy drove the truck towards their side of the motel pleased to see his parking spot was empty. He turned around and backed it into the space. He could see Ami was puzzled at his actions.

"In case anyone wants to help themselves to my lockbox. We can hear the alarm better from inside."

Ami nodded. "Stan will hear it for sure. He has super hearing."

"Yeah, my error, I hadn't thought about that. My apologies Stan. You're on duty now dog. That's one precious steering wheel in the back of my truck."

Stan wagged his tail still aiming to redeem himself in Remy's eyes.

CHAPTER SIXTEEN

Tresor Trail

It was almost midnight before Lord Ramesh belatedly gave Brother Grace permission to intercede with full force. He was tired now. Spent more than 30 hours observing Father Tresor. The man had returned to the motel three hours ago. Lord Ramesh had called a committee to decide Father Tresor's fate and it swallowed time. Midnight was a good hour to confront the man, but Brother Grace would have preferred to have done it earlier.

He climbed the stairs to the fifth floor and headed to room 519, The corridor was dark, just one light flickered at the far end. The Avalon had clearly seen better days and he'd observed over the hours he'd waited many single men entering the motel and leaving no more than fifteen or thirty minutes later. He thought he could hear something that sounded remarkably like someone being whipped behind one of the doors. He ignored it and focused on Room 519.

Curiously the door to 519 was ajar, a light on inside. Cautiously he pushed open the door, his heart immediately sinking, the room was empty. Father Tresor was gone.

He raced downstairs and headed around the back of the building to the car park. The BMW was gone, the tracker on his phone patiently showed it was still there in the car park.

Brother Grace swore under his breath. Perhaps the receptionist had informed him that someone else from the Christian College had made enquiries and it had spooked him. Perhaps the interview had gone sour? Either way Father Tresor had bolted and now he would have find yet another identity. A small inconvenience for him but a genuine inconvenience for Brother Grace. If only Lord Ramesh had acted earlier.

He briefly thought about giving chase, but he'd not slept for almost two days. A bed beckoned in an empty room. He went back upstairs and entered Room 519. Perhaps Father Tresor had left a clue as to his next location, but he doubted it. Next time he wouldn't be wasting time about getting permission. He'd end it as soon as possible, hogtie the man if necessary. He wouldn't get away so easily next time.

On the highway out of Tampa Father Tresor cursed his luck. He'd seen Brother Grace on the motel CCTV, the receptionist had given him access. They weren't going to catch him so easily. He was annoyed he wouldn't be able to take up the post at the College. He'd have to change his ID again. His money was running low now. He needed work, damnit.

There would always be someone desperately looking for teaching staff. No one wanted to teach anymore, not for poverty wages. No one wanted to discipline kids, they were all running scared of them. Well, he wasn't scared or woke. He was free of the Order. He'd change the Beemer for something innocuous in the morning. He was heading to Miami. A man could easily hide in a big city like that. He'd have a job in a week, he was sure of it. Brother Grace didn't have a chance in hell of finding him again.

CHAPTER SEVENTEEN

Parting Shots

Remy awoke to the sound of screaming. He glanced over at Ami, but she was sleeping through it somehow. Stan was whining, worried about the noise. There was thumping against the wall. Remy realized it was a couple having sex next door. Loud, exuberant sex. He sighed and went to the bathroom. Stan followed him, still whining.

"It's ok Stan. I'm guessing it's pretty normal around here."

The dog went to his dog bowl and drank some water.

Remy checked his phone for the time. 3am. There was a message from Maisie on there. She'd be on the night shift as usual. He sent a simple reply that he was ok and, on his way home tomorrow. He worried how he was going to explain about taking in Ami to her. Of course, didn't really have to justify himself. Somehow Maisie always made him feel guilty about something or other.

He wondered if he'd be able to get back to sleep with all that noise next door. It sure went on a long time. How Ami could sleep through it, he didn't know. Maybe she was used to noise, after all she'd only slept in a dormitory before this.

He thought about Walter. He should have made more effort. He had his phone number now. He could call him when he got home but now he thought about it he remembered they'd parted on bad terms. In fact, there was the matter of an outstanding loan that never got paid. Five thousand was lot of money back then. Walter's deposit on a '68 Corvette he'd desperately wanted. Bit late to claim that back now. It would appear mean given his MS and all. But it rankled him a little. There had been times since he'd retired when that five thousand would have come in handy. Couldn't believe he'd forgotten all about it. 1997 was a long time ago. Walter had moved on to other research fields. Remy had stayed with the program till 2011 when they laid off nearly 10,000 people. By then, it was a lost cause anyway. He watched Atlantis touch down at Kennedy Space Center that July and that was it. All over. Everyone had lost interest in the Shuttle, and it was way too expensive to maintain. He'd given over twenty-five years to NASA, and it was pretty quickly forgotten as it faded in people's memories. Ami didn't even know it had existed.

He turned over and willed himself to sleep. Stan jumped back on Ami's bed and turned circles until he was comfortable again.

Ami woke at five. Remy was sleeping. Stan was whining he wanted to go out.

She groaned. "It's still dark, Stan. Can't you wait?"

Stan went to the door and scratched it. Waiting clearly was not an option. Ami reflected back at the farm he slept by the door. He wasn't allowed anywhere near the dorm beds of course. Morning prayers were always at 5.30 am. He was still on the 'farm clock'.

Ami quickly got dressed and put her shoes on. Grabbed the key so she wouldn't get locked out. Stan shot out of the door when she opened it. "Don't go far."

Ami loitered by the truck as Stan hunted for the right place to pee. She heard two people loudly arguing outside one of the rooms further along. It sounded ugly. She couldn't see well in the dark but there was definitely some pushing and shoving going on. Someone in a nearby room was yelling for them to shut the hell up. There was sudden sharp crack. Ami glimpsed a flash from a gun and Stan ran off, completely spooked. He bolted away from the parking area towards the highway and Ami momentarily stood transfixed in surprise. She finally set off in pursuit, heart in mouth as her precious dog blindly ran across the road. "STAN!" she yelled after him, but he kept on going. A truck blasted it's airhorn at him as it barreled on by, it didn't even attempt to slow down. Stan managed to reach the far side of the highway unscathed as Ami paused to check for traffic. She launched herself across the highway, thanking the universe for saving her dog as she ran across two lanes to the middle section, desperately trying to see where Stan had gone. "Stan. Stan." She yelled but he wasn't paying her any heed.

It was still dark, too early for much traffic. Stan wouldn't have stood a chance any later than this. She dashed over the last two lanes and ran into what appeared to be a Funeral Parlor parking lot. Her heart was still racing. She was suddenly aware of how cold it was. A digital display on the Parlor wall told her it was 05.16 and 35.6F – We Have a Great Funeral Plan for You and Your loved ones.

"Stan? Where are you? Stan?"

She saw movement in the far corner where some trees and bushes were tastefully arranged around a small fountain. She ran towards it and there was Stan, standing stock still, panting, bug eyed, still in a state of shock. Ami fell on her knees and held him close feeling him shivering and shaking. In all the time they had been together she'd never seen him like this, never.

"It's all right, you're safe now. You're with me. Calm down. Calm down," she said in a soothing voice, holding him tight. "Can you hear me? You're safe now."

Slowly Stan came back to her, he began licking her face with his hot tongue. Ami began to breath more normally, still shaken to the core. Of all the things that happened to her since they left the farm this was the worst. She had no idea how she'd make it through life without Stan. She looked at him shaking her head. "You're supposed to be the sensible one, Stan. You're supposed to look after me. Y'hear me? You can't do this. We're a team. Traffic will kill you."

Stan burrowed his head into her lap and let her fondle his ears, as she held him tight. She whispered to him. "We're going back now. I don't know what happened, but it's not about you, right? No one is shooting at you."

She looked back towards the brightly lit motel. Lights were coming on in many of the rooms and even from this distance she could hear shouting and screaming. Two further shots rang out and she tried to cover Stan's ears, held him tighter. He didn't react. He felt safe. Ami knew they had to get back over there and wake Remy. Police would be coming for sure; she didn't want to be there when they started asking questions.

She looked back at the motel again as she saw movement. A man in a flowing dress was running out of the parking lot towards the highway but collapsed in a heap at the curb. Was he the shooter or the person who got shot? Either way it was bad news, very bad.

"Ok, we're heading back. Stay close. I can't carry you. You understand me? Stay close. Whatever happened is over. We can do this, Stan. Come."

Stan looked up at her as she stood up, still nervous and ready to bolt at the slightest provocation. He was still panting but he was paying attention now.

"Let's go." She grabbed his collar and began to walk towards the highway. The traffic was still light. "We're going to run for it after this next truck. Understand?"

The truck rumbled past and with one last check left and right Ami launched herself across the four lanes at speed. Stan was right with her, practically standing on her shoes. They made it across. The man in the red dress was dead. Blood was pooling under him; a discarded blonde woman's wig lay a few feet away. Ami didn't stop. She kept on going aware that someone was loudly weeping and wailing beside a pickup truck near the motel entrance. Ami kept to the darkness, not wanting to be seen or remembered.

Remy was already up and getting dressed. He looked very relieved she'd returned.

"I heard yelling. I was just going to search for you," he said. He could see she was shaking.

"Did you hear the shots? Stan was spooked and bolted. Nearly got himself squished on the highway."

Remy winced. "He's not used to traffic. You got lucky, Ami. Did anyone see you out there?"

"I don't think so. There's a dead man lying on the curb. He's been shot."

Remy nodded. "No shit. Cops will be coming. Grab your stuff. We're leaving. Things will get ugly. We need to go. If you need to pee, do it now."

Remy packed his pills and sat down to fasten on his shoes as Ami rushed to the bathroom. Maybe he was panicking over nothing, but he wasn't prepared to take the risk again. With a dead body out there, the cops would be asking a lot of awkward questions of everyone.

"Toothbrush?" Remy reminded Ami. "Dog food."

"Got everything. Pills?"

"Packed. Make I sure I take them later. Let's go."

"Don't we have to pay?" Ami asked as she returned and picked up her knapsack.

"I guess there's a reason you have to pay upfront here. Ok, let's go."

Outside they discovered many others had the same idea. Half-dressed, wigs off, bundling everything into their vehicles in a rush to get away.

"Seems like no one wants to answer any questions," Remy commented as he started up the motor.

He swiftly drove them out of there. He didn't pause to look at the dead man, none of their business. He joined the highway just as three police vehicles with sirens blaring approached the motel from the opposite direction. No one attempted to stop them leaving.

Ami looked back at the motel as other vehicles tried to leave but were blocked by the cops arriving. It was like a bad dream. She clutched Stan and tried to unsee everything that had just happened. Her hands were still shaking.

"Did you see anything back there?" Remy asked, his heart racing.

"Heard three shots. Someone was arguing. Saw the guy collapse on the pavement. He was wearing a red dress and had on a blonde wig."

Remy didn't comment on that. He checked his mirror. No one was following.

"Let's get out of this city. I'll stop to take my pills in a moment and then we'll have breakfast a bit later. When it's safe."

"We didn't do anything wrong, did we?" Ami asked.

"No, we didn't. But the cops will want to see ID's and you don't have one. Then they'll ask awkward questions as to why you're there. The sooner we get an ID for you, the better."

Ami stared out into the darkness and the mostly empty streets. She was beginning to understand how hard it would have been for her and Stan if Remy hadn't picked her up.

"You ok, Remy? You didn't get much sleep."

Remy nodded. "I never get much sleep. I was reading how people who don't sleep are at a greater risk of heart attack. I guess it's true. I'm living proof. I'll have a nap later." He chuckled. "When you're young you think napping is a waste of time, but you'd be wrong. Snatching thirty minutes here and there, you'd be surprised how it recharges your batteries."

"Warn me if you think you're going to nap this time," Ami told him sternly.

Remy nodded. "Yeah, sorry about that earlier event." He pulled over at an empty store parking lot. "Pass me the water bottle. I'll take my pills. How come you were awake back there, last I checked on you, you were sleeping like a rock. Are you ok? I know you were spooked by Stan running off but ..."

Ami smiled. "I'm ok now. You said there would be a third thing."

Remy sighed. "I did. I sincerely hope that is the end of it. Jeez kid, you must thinking the whole world is mad. I'm sorry you've been through so much shit. I was looking at you sleeping earlier and how quickly you take things in your stride."

"I'm not really ok but I feel safe with you, I guess. When I finally get to sleep, I can't hear anything. Stan woke me. Stomped on my legs then whined. He knows all the tricks to get me to wake up."

Remy smiled as he dug out his pills and began lining them up.

"Dogs can guilt us into feeding them, walking them, and rubbing their bellies. We fall for it every time."

Ami hugged Stan. "But he loves me back."

Remy nodded. "10,000 years of bonding and they understand us completely."

"Never want to see him bolt like that again though. He wouldn't listen. Just fled when he heard the first shot. I swear my heart stopped."

Remy glanced at her. "You're going to have to train him about traffic. But when a dog panics, they're not thinking. It's instinct. Self-preservation. You can't blame him. But yeah, you must have been shocked. If you'd told me a month ago that I'd be involved in three shootings in a week I would have thought you were crazy. You must be my lucky charm."

Ami smiled. Paulo kept a lucky charm in his pocket all the time. Said it was to keep him alive. It was just a pretty green stone he'd found but he believed it.

Remy swallowed the pills, one by one. He sighed. "There was a time I used to like my trips away from home, whether it was work or just looking for spare parts. Now..." He swallowed another three pills and swallowed hard. "Now it's too risky to leave your home to even go the supermarket. People with their obsessions for guns have turned America into shit."

Ami glanced at him. He wasn't usually this angry. "You ok?"

Remy shook his head. "No. Sorry, I'm cranky and upset. I wanted to have a leisurely morning before we set off and ..." He swallowed his last pill. "I was going to take you to The Museum of Fine Arts. They've got a pretty damn fine collection there. One of the best in the country."

Ami shrugged. "I've never been to a museum."

"We'll have to remedy that in Miami." The thought of that calmed him a little. "We'll plan a day of it. Learning how to appreciate art is important. After all you're an artist, right, with all your batiks you made. I'll take you to Wynwood to see the street art. You'll like that."

Ami laughed. "I wish. I should have kept one."

"What made you even start that? All the wax and dyeing, must take a while."

Ami thought about it. "Haini and me working in the barn away from everyone. We wanted peace I guess and because it was for the farm shop, we could take all the time we wanted. The hard part was getting hold of the cotton and the dyes. I love clouds. See patterns and colors and I guess I wanted to copy that. Stupid really because you can't really copy a cloud but that's why I started."

Remy smiled. It was a good answer. He set off again. Traffic was building on the other side, as the morning rush into the city began.

"I love clouds too," he confessed. "At least I do now. When I was working for NASA, we were in a constant battle with the weather and reading clouds. We used to get some spectacular weather at my beach place. I liked to lie on the dunes and watch the sky."

"I never seen a beach either, or the ocean." Ami said quietly.

"And you've lived in Florida all your life. That's cruel. We will make a list of everything you have never seen or done and tick them off one by one. I'll take you to my old hangout on the way back. You'll see Pelicans fly alongside us. Birds with long beaks to go fishing with. And dolphins. Sometimes they swim close to the shore following the fish. With luck we'll see the next Artemis launch. Rockets to the Moon, Ami."

Ami smiled. She couldn't even begin to imagine that. She couldn't wait.

"You don't have to do anything special for me," she protested.

Remy shook his head. "Kid, nothing will give me greater pleasure than to make you happy and experience all the things you deserve to see. It's a treat for me too. Maisie was right, I've been shut away in that garage for far too long. We'll drive the Hawk to Key West or Cocoa Beach, and I can't wait to show you what you've been missing."

Ami hugged Stan. She could hear in Remy's voice he meant all this. Whether she deserved it or not. "Yeah, I really want to see the ocean," she confessed. "I really do."

CHAPTER EIGHTEEN

The Tractor Museum

Remy searched for a printed copy of the *Richmond Times-Dispatch* to read at the breakfast table but couldn't find one. That was other thing that got him riled up now. Used to be you could buy the *Miami Herald* or *The Washington Post* and linger with it over a cup of coffee for hours. Trying to squint at your phone to read a newspaper just wasn't the same. No one seemed to even notice a whole way of life had disappeared along with all those jobs producing them.

He stared at Ami a moment. "I'm guessing you have questions about this morning."

Ami drank some of her orange juice and sighed. "I never saw a man die before."

Remy nodded. "And nor should you. I'm sorry Ami. Seems every place we go to we run into trouble. It shouldn't be like this."

Ami buttered her toast. "I used to talk to Paulo about what it would be like living away the farm. We had these great plans to get jobs and find ourselves a place of our own to stay. Paulo said people would be happy to help us get started. We'd work hard and be reliable and polite. He'd read that someplace. To fit it we had to be polite, even if we didn't feel like it. He was going to do all the cooking and I'd be this amazing artist and we'd somehow get by. Paulo thought he could get a job as a trainee chef. He worked in the kitchen on the farm and planned all these exotic meals, even though we ate the same shit every day. I never want to see oatmeal ever again, even if it is good for you."

Remy smiled. "One day you'll have a place of your own, make your own rules."

Ami glanced out of the window and wondered about that. "I had a color scheme all picked out. Kids dreams, huh."

Remy sipped his coffee. "I guess they didn't tell you how much it costs to rent a place these days."

Ami let escape a hollow laugh. "Funny, I never once thought about rent, or if anyone would even rent to a couple of penniless kids. I know nothing about real life, Remy. Nothing at all."

Remy ate some of his eggs. "Well, you've got your own room to paint at mine. Hasn't been touched in years. Time to get some practice in."

Ami frowned. "Any color I like? I like white mostly."

"It's your room. It's a nice room, sunny in winter, cool in summer. In fact, you can paint the whole house inside. Don't worry, I'll pay. Been meaning to get started on that since my wife passed away. One of those projects that never seemed to get going."

Ami was doubtful. "You serious?"

"Any color except black. I don't like a dark house. And anyway, how are you going to learn if you don't get started? Who knows you might even make a living out of it."

Ami made a face. "Oh sure. I don't even know how to paint a wall. I don't know anything about paint."

Remy grinned. "It's all on YouTube. Everything you need to know. We'll set you up with brushes and rollers. It'll be a lot of hard work. Not just painting but preparing the surfaces, clearing furniture, covering stuff so you don't splash everywhere. But do it right, I can think of at least four people who'd want to hire a decorator. When you're done, we'll invite them around for Sunday drinks after church, just like my wife used to do."

Ami shook her head doubtful this would happen. "That's a thing?"

"Used to be." He cocked his head to one side a moment as he remembered something. "It's funny. I stopped going to social events. Can't remember why now; but believe it or not my wife had a dinner party at our place at least twice a month, or barbecues in the summer. I can't remember if I stopped going to them or if they stopped inviting me. Probably the latter."

Ami ate her scrambled eggs with fried mushrooms and thought about it. "I read a story once. I can't remember the title. Whole thing took a place at a dinner party. Everyone spilling secrets about each other, and someone got murdered. Almost no one ate anything, but they drank a lot. I remember that."

Remy chuckled. "Well, our dinner parties were a bit dull by comparison. No one died that I recall anyway." He chased down a mushroom and swallowed it. "Must be kind of weird for you learning about life outside the farm and never knowing what was real or not."

Ami nodded. "There were a lot of murders in the stories. I didn't think they were real."

"But now you do, I guess."

"Sister Ryan always said that society outside was evil and corrupt and driven by jealousy. None of us believed her."

"Turns out it's true. Disappointed?" Remy asked.

Ami took a deep breath and then slowly exhaled. "Yes."

"I'll try to prove her wrong," Remy replied. "There are good things happening too. Don't give up on us yet. Back at the motel last night. You can bet that whatever went down didn't start out to go bad. No one sets out to have a bad time, things just go sour sometimes. Someone says the wrong thing or one of the party discover a betrayal or lie they can't live with. Add a gun in the mix and wham, someone dies. There's no coming back from that."

"Sour? You said sour. Is that what happened there?"

Remy finished his coffee and wished he could have another.

"I remember back when I was working at NASA. We were often flying by the seat of our pants. Underfunded, understaffed, facing endless budget cuts. Every launch was a cross your finger's moment. We had yet another countdown delay due to a malfunctioning sensor and we were all exhausted and cranky and people were looking for someone to blame. The stress was immense. We were all on edge. A row could break out just like that (he snapped his fingers), but once we got that bird up into the sky, the tensions just evaporated. At shift change we'd all head to the bar and you could just feel the tensions disappear. It wasn't the beer; it was all that frustration melting away. At least until the next problem and there was always a next problem." He smiled. "I'm pretty sure that's why I ended up with a heart attack. The stupid part is, if I could do it all again, I would sign up in an instant. That was my life for twenty-five years."

"Why?" Ami asked. "If it was so stressful."

Remy smiled. "Because I was part of something big. Important. At least we thought it was at the time. The odd thing was I never wanted to go up into space myself. Aside from my age or fitness, I just liked being there. It's hard to explain but we all took our responsibilities seriously. And sorting out the problems. You can't believe the problems. Computers weren't reliable back then and certainly not as powerful as they are now. It was a lot safer being on the ground than being in space. A lot safer."

Ami suddenly felt a familiar pain and experienced a sinking feeling. Remy saw her expression change. "What's wrong?"

Ami didn't want to say. She'd never had to admit this to a man before.

"You sick? Was it the eggs?" Remy asked.

Ami nearly doubled up with pain. She shook her head.

"I have to go to the..."

Remy dug deep into his memory and abruptly recalled his wife with the same sudden pains. He leaned forward and whispered.

"Is it your period?"

Ami reddened and nodded. "I got to go. Feed Stan."

Remy watched her walk really fast towards the rest room and wondered if she knew what to do. Stupid of him not to have thought about this earlier. Another stop to the pharmacy beckoned. He wrapped Stan's breakfast into his napkin and headed over to pay.

It was another learning experience at the pharmacy. Ami had been surprised at all the sanitary products that were available in that she was totally unaware of. At the farm they just gave out rags and left you to it. She had no idea what she needed and there didn't seem to be anyone to ask, but luckily Remy seemed to know. There were even pills to make the pain go away, but she shunned those. The teachings of Lord Ramesh firmly were fixed in her brain that the pain was to be endured as a reminder of her womanhood. Whatever that meant.

A while later Ami was curled up in the passenger seat sleeping as Remy drove on. Tired and worried about this girl he'd taken on. He had to keep reminding himself that everything was new to her. He needed to anticipate so many things she'd need to know and probably wouldn't want to discuss with him. She stirred and he glanced at her. "Feeling any better?"

Ami nodded. "I'm ok. It's over pretty quick with me. Some girls get the cramps real bad but so far ..."

Remy passed another Civil War battle site marker.

"What do you know about the Civil War? They teach you anything about that back at the farm?" Remy asked after they got back on the highway. Ami noticed they were approaching Petersburg.

She shook her head. "Nothing. Sister Ryan said it was best not to know about the evil mankind can do to each other."

Remy frowned. "Ignorance is bliss, I guess. You ever hear that expression before?"

Ami looked carefully at him. He looked tired. "No."

"Means that some people believe that not knowing how things work out in history will protect you from evil. The trouble with that is that when it happens all over again, such as people wanting the secede from the North, you'll have no idea how it turned out the first time they tried it. Almost seven hundred and fifty thousand soldiers died and thousands more civilians besides. Pretty much everywhere we drive along here is a site of a battle or skirmish. Petersburg had a particularly long and brutal battle."

Ami gazed out of the window as if searching for evidence of the bodies.

Remy sighed. "About ten years ago I made a pilgrimage to many of the battle sites. In truth there's not much to see. But if the same battles break out now, when almost everyone has an automatic weapon and enough ammo to keep slaughter at will, I'd say you could end up with six million dead or more."

Ami frowned. "Six million people?"

"Just a projection based on population numbers. I read it somewhere. The Atlantic, maybe."

"Why were they fighting?"

"Slavery mostly. The South wanted to continue importing slaves from Africa and the North wanted the slaves that were already here to be emancipated, set free."

"What did the slaves want?"

"I'm pretty sure they wanted to be free. No one has the right to enslave someone."

Ami thought about that. "Was I a slave at the farm?"

"Did you get paid for your labor on the farm?"

Ami shook her head.

"Then technically you were slaves. They had to feed you, so you'd continue working, but that isn't payment. You weren't free to leave, so you ran away. If you have been a slave back in 1860 you would have been hunted down and whipped or killed. You had no rights and any children you might have had would become property of the slave owner."

Ami stared at him as she processed this. "Seriously?"

Remy nodded. "The whole economy of the south was based on slavery. The slave owners lived in big fancy mansions and thought themselves superior to everyone else. You can guess how the slaves lived. There's a book on my shelf at home called The Underground Railroad. You should read that. It will educate you about what it was like for black people back then." He glanced at Ami. "That why history matters. There are many politicians now, particularly in Florida and Texas, who don't want kids to learn about this. They said all they're doing is learning about hatred."

"What do you say?" Ami asked.

"What they will learn about is injustice. Never be afraid to learn about the truth. Sometimes it will hurt. Sometimes you'll need to question what you hear or read as there are people out to rewrite history all the time to make suit themselves and their agenda."

Remy rubbed his face. "Ami, I'm going to find a place to park up once we near Petersburg and have nap. You and Stan can go for a walk or have a coffee someplace, but I'll want you to lock me in the cab. I need an hour, I reckon."

"You sure you're alright? You took your pills..."

"I'm a bit short on sleep, remember? I'll try to find someplace interesting for you." He laughed suddenly and pointed to a signpost. "Keystone Antique Truck & Tractor Museum. Just the place for a nap."

Ami looked askance. "Truck and Tractor Museum?"

Remy chuckled. "Just don't let them stick me and this Chevy in the museum whilst I'm asleep. I've been in there before. They've got an impressive selection of vehicles and guess what, you're a farmer. You'll actually know what some of the implements are for."

Ami was extremely doubtful. "What about Stan?"

"Just ask them if it's ok. Point out he lives on a farm. They'll be so happy to get a customer I can't see them saying no. Take what money you need from my wallet and enjoy."

"You sure know how to make a girl happy," Ami said. "Tractor museum. I can't believe it."

Remy took the turn off. "I know kid. But if I'm going to nap, I need to be feel safe. I hope you understand."

Ami put out a hand to his shoulder. "I don't mind. Everything is new to me, remember. Even a truck museum."

"I'll try to find something that you would like next time we stop." Remy promised her as he slowed for a junction.

"I have no idea what that might be" Ami said. "Maybe something with birds or animals? Someplace Stan would like too."

"We'll consult the map later." He turned off the road and smiled as he approached the Truck Museum, happy to see there were very few visitors. "We're here."

Ami shook her head. Well, there was a first for everything. Remy switched off the engine and closed his eyes. He had no idea how he'd even gotten this far he was so tired.

"Enjoy, kid. I promise it's going to be more interesting than it looks."

About an hour later Ami bounced out of the Museum full of smiles. Stan headed to some grass to pee as she walked over to the truck to unlock the cabin door. Remy was still asleep, stretched out on the bench seat at an awkward angle, his head resting on a rolled-up jacket on the passenger side. She went around to the driver's door and unlocked it carefully.

"You were right, Remy. It was amazing. This old guy took me around and explained the entire history of motorized trucks and tractors. Even let me sit on a few. Turns out the tractor at the farm is seventy-five years old. He was astonished I knew how to drive it."

Stan joined her and she heaved him up into the truck and he settled into the passenger footwell.

Ami moved Remy's feet down to the floor and looked at him more closely. He didn't seem to be waking. She felt his pulse. His heart was still beating, but something wasn't right. "Remy? Can you hear me? Are you alright? You want to sleep a bit longer?"

She wondered what she should do. She checked behind the seat for Remy's bag. She knew he had a small pump spray there to stimulate his heart in an emergency. He'd showed it to her a few nights before. She wondered what she was supposed to do with it. Spray it up his nose or open his mouth?

"I'm gonna let you sleep, ok? I'll take us back on the road. No point in hanging around here."

Remy didn't respond. She wondered if he needed a doctor. Be stupid if all he needed was sleep. She wished she knew more about what to do in an emergency. If this was an emergency.

She started the engine and backed up to turn around. The way she looked at it, the sooner he got back home the better. Put a couple of hundred miles on the clock and hope he revives along the way.

"Keep an eye on him Stan." She instructed her dog.

Traffic was busy as she rejoined the Interstate highway. She kept her wits about her and drove at a steady fifty mph. She thought about the old trucks back there, some dating back to the 1920's. The old guy had explained about how important farming was to the rise of American power. How farmers had fed the world during world wars. And how sad he was about how no one really appreciated food or how it got onto their plate. America wouldn't even exist without farmers and their tractors. She hadn't ever contemplated this before, but it was true. She'd spent all her life so far growing food and shared the despair when the weather was either too hot or too wet. No one understood how much could go wrong between planting and harvesting. Fighting the pests, keeping stuff stored properly so that the rats didn't get at it.

She glanced over at Remy. He hadn't moved. Was that a bad sign? Was he in pain? She tried not to think about how difficult her life would be if he died on her. But it was entirely possible he could or would. She admonished herself for being selfish and thinking only about her own needs. And Stan's. What would become of Stan if they didn't have a place to stay? Nothing good. She knew that at least. She had to keep Remy alive and well.

Remy woke with a start at two-thirty in the afternoon. He had a crick in his neck and a desperate urge to go. Took a moment to register where he was and why he was slumped in the passenger seat. He gazed out of the windshield at the view and was surprised to see the Museum has disappeared. He looked for his glasses and found them in his shirt pocket.

There was no sign of Ami, or the dog and they appeared to be parked in woodland. He looked back and there was no highway he could see. It was amazingly quiet. He pushed hard against the door and stumbled out of the truck, heading for the nearest tree to empty his bladder. He was genuinely confused. He had no idea where on earth they were.

Stan came back first and quickly found him, jumping up, happy to see him awake.

"Finally, you're awake." Ami said from behind him. She was carrying some apples in her sweater.

"Found an apple orchard – make a good apple sauce."

"Apples?" Remy asked. "Here? You stole them?"

"I saw the sign. Free apples. Drove down the lane to here. Whole place is abandoned. I think it's old sign."

Remy frowned. "Free apples? It's a bit late in the year for apples isn't it. No one shooting at us? Farmers can be pretty hostile to people helping themselves to ..."

Ami smiled. "The farmhouse is empty, Remy. Some rusted out vehicles. No one has lived here for a while, I think. No one shooting so far. You like apple sauce? We could make a pie when we get home. I love apple pie."

Remy laughed. He briefly wondered if he was dreaming. This was all so unexpected.

"Where are we?"

"Well ..." Ami took the apples to the truck and placed them in one of the containers he had in the back. "I had to turn off the highway. Too many cops. The old guy at the Museum suggested this route might be safer. We might be near a place called Mt Olive. Don't be mad at me. I was just trying to be careful."

"Mt Olive?" Remy was totally confused. He dimly recalled it was in North Carolina.

"You hungry? It's been a long time since breakfast and I'm figuring there has to be a place to eat there."

Remy rubbed his neck. "How long did I sleep?"

"At least three hours or more. I was worried. Didn't quite know what to do. Do I give you that spray somehow? Should I do that if you flake out again?"

"It goes under my tongue. But only one short burst. I don't like using it. It gives me a monumental headache. Show me where we are on the map."

Ami smiled and approached the driver's side. "You want to drive?"

Remy thought about it. "No. I'm still a bit woozy. Lunch sounds good to me. We're in North Carolina. You made good time."

"We'll need to gas up. I think I got lost a bit backaways. We're on Thunder Swamp Road right now."

Remy laughed. "Thunder Swamp Road. Perfect. As long as we're not actually in a swamp. Free apples huh. God bless America."

"There's a whole orchard rotting. No one picked anything. It's a shame, Remy. Let all that fruit go to waste."

Remy nodded. "Farms go bust all the time, I guess. Might be hard to get fruit pickers out here or the bank foreclosed on them." He strolled back to the truck. "Get us to Mt Olive Ami. And watch out for small town cops. Keep to the posted speed limits."

Ami nodded and swung into the driver's seat. Stan leapt up after her and took up his position right next to her.

Remy joined her and slammed the door shut. "Remind me to get that darn door fixed. Been awkward ever since I bought this truck."

"That's a long time for something to be awkward," Ami remarked as she turned around.

Remy chuckled. Ami sounded just like his late wife just then. She'd been embarrassed by the truck. Insisted on using her Ford Edge whenever they went out anywhere together. At least he'd got a good price for it after she'd gone.

"Pickles. Now I remember. Mt. Olive is famous for pickles. We should buy some whilst we're here."

Ami smiled, remembering how they'd tried pickling onions and cucumbers back at the farm. Come to think of it, she wondered what had happened to them. They certainly never got to eat any of them. But that was how it always was. They'd do all the work, and everything would be sent to Charleston.

"Oh yeah, that reminds me. Mr Taylor at the Museum said that if you ever want to sell this truck that you should give him a call first."

Remy smiled. "Maybe I should start my own museum, hey?"

Ami snatched a glance at his face and quickly realized he was joking. "Yeah, but you'd be the oldest thing in it." She replied.

"That's the truth. It hurts. Watch out there's a junction ahead. Make sure you come to a complete stop before you move on. It's the law."

"Yes sir, I guess I need to learn the rules."

"Yeah, you do. Small town cops live to enforce them. You know what? I think I fancy some pizza."

Ami laughed. Remy was coming back to life.

CHAPTER NINETEEN

The Ocean

Ami woke with a start. It took a moment to figure out where she was. Stan was curled up at her feet. Remy had turned the engine off and was staring at her with a smile on his face.

"You slept a long time, kid. Didn't even wake up when I fueled up. How do you feel now?"

She stretched and definitely felt better for sleeping.

Ami realized it was dark and the sky was filled with stars. There was a curious background noise she couldn't place. She rubbed her face and yawned.

"Where are we now?"

Remy opened his door, and a chill wind instantly woke both of them up.

"Look out the windshield. Dead ahead."

Ami stared and saw movement – a flash of white and heard a sucking noise. A half-moon was already on its descent. It had to be late. Another wave crashed against the shore. Ami took in a sharp intake of breath, her heart leapt. "The ocean. We're by the ocean!"

She tried to open her passenger door and struggled to get it to move, then remembered it was locked. She unlocked it and pushed it open wide. Stan was out first, shaking the sleep out of his head. Ami tumbled out of the truck and took her first steps to the ocean, just beyond the dune.

"Go see it," Remy called out. "I'll open up."

"Open up?"

"You'll see. Off you go. Don't go far. And don't go in. It's late. Can you swim?"

Ami shook her head. "Never had a chance to learn."

"We'll have to fix that too. Go on. Enjoy."

Ami ran towards the beach across the dune, loving the sound of waves crashing against the shore. Stan was ahead of her, barking with excitement at new smells and sounds.

Remy stepped out of the truck and stretched, wincing at his sore back. That had been the longest driving session he'd made in years. He glanced over at his trailer home and hoped that it was still intact after the late October storms. He fumbled for his key, trying to recall which one it was on his key chain. Hard to see the red tag in the dark.

The chilly night air had him awake at least. It had been at least four months since he'd last come visited. The trailer would be stale and damp but at least familiar. He found the key and headed towards the front door.

Ami took off her shoes and walked into the waves – shocked at how cold it was. Stan was trying to drink but got swamped and tumbled over, quickly backing away, scared of the waves. Ami broke into a run and ran along the beach, splashing in pools of water and loving the feel of sand under her feet. Stan caught up with her as she stared along the shoreline where, in the distance, she could see apartment blocks and houses lit up by dim streetlights. Ahead of her the ocean stretched away forever and she had an overwhelming feeling of happiness to be here, wherever here was.

She turned the other way and saw some boats had been dragged up onto the sand. Even in the darkness the beach looked exactly like she had imagined it would. She could smell the ocean. She'd never thought about how it would smell. It was exhilarating. A huge wave barreled in from the ocean and she and Stan had to run back to avoid getting drenched. She laughed with sheer joy as she turned to go back to Remy. She kept thinking to herself that this was the first time she really felt free of the Order. Paulo would be sick with envy. He longed to go to the ocean. 'I don't care if I drown, I just want to get to see it and sail away and never look back.' Maybe one day she'd find a way to save him. She'd need to talk to Remy about that.

She tried to remember where she she'd left her shoes as she walked back. "Find my shoes, Stan. Find my shoes."

Stan wasn't exactly sure what she'd requested but showed willing and ran in circles sniffing everything.

Ami arrived at the trailer doorway out of breath but still happy, clutching her shoes.

"Sorry, took time to find my shoes. Stan was useless. Kept barking at the waves. Where are we?" She asked, walking in, closing the door behind her as Stan sniffed everything. The lights were off. Remy was winding something up and looked distracted a moment before he set the object down and turned it on. A dim light pierced the gloom.

"We're home." Remy chuckled. "Well, my other home. When my old house blew away in the hurricane, I was spending more time in Houston anyway and it didn't seem important. But then I got all sentimental about the place and bought this trailer home off one of the Austrian guys on the launch team who was heading back to Europe to work. Cost me more to clear the site, get it towed here and plumbed in for water and power than what I paid for the trailer. I come up here a few times a year when it's too hot in Miami and do some fishing. If we're lucky we might get to see the next Artemis launch to the Moon at Cape Canaveral. It's been delayed three times now."

"Artemis?"

"Rocket launch. My old job, remember? We get a great view from here. Pretty close to Cape Canaveral. Can't tell you how much I've been offered for this lot. It's a double sized, people always wanting to build a mansion on it. I tell them there's no point. Climate change is going to swamp the whole damn coast by 2040 but everyone from the Governor on down is in denial about that."

"Swamp?"

"I guess they didn't tell you about climate change back on the farm."

Ami inspected the kitchen area. "Yep, they did. Lord Ramesh said all of Florida would be under water in my lifetime and whole cities around the world would be gone too with millions dead or fleeing inland. I just thought it was another one of their lies to make us believe only the Order could save us."

Remy shrugged as he turned on the other wind-up lamp. "Sorry to disappoint you kid. It's true. But now isn't a time to discuss it. I can't get the power back on. I know I paid the utility bill but something's not right. I'll look at it in the morning. Your bed is the far end – you just unfold it out. Sheets, blankets everything in the cupboard underneath. Might be a bit damp. There won't be any hot water until I get the power back on, but I'll make us a cup of herbal tea. The kitchen uses propane. If you're hungry there might be a can of tuna or something in the cupboard. But there's a good place for breakfast about two miles away so we can eat tomorrow if that's ok with you. And, oh yeah, run the water for a bit to get any gunge out of it. Can taste funny at first but it's drinkable."

"Are you rich?" Ami asked him.

Remy looked at her in surprise. "Rich? Me. God no. I worked for NASA."

"But you own two houses."

Remy laughed as he looked for matches to light the gas ring. "Other people would look at this old trailer and conclude the opposite. I'm a long way from being rich, kid. But do I care? Not a bit. You'll see when the sun comes up why I keep this place. Sometimes you can be rich without actually having much money. I love it here. Just wish I could afford to build a decent place. My mistake. My insurance had lapsed, and they claimed it was an act of God when the hurricane hit, so a lot of people lost everything except the land and that's under threat now too. I admit, I had it good."

He turned the valve on the propane and lit the gas ring. Ami stared at him as he let the water run a bit before filling a pan with clear water. She remembered Stan suddenly and looked for a bowl for him.

"There's a couple of dog bowls in the other cupboard." Remy told her. "Might be some dog food too but better to use the kibble we've got in the truck." He handed Ami the keys. "Bring in my bag will you and lock up after you."

Ami took the keys and left to get the stuff. Remy looked down at Stan and smiled. "Nice to have a dog back in here again. There's a dog bed in my end. I'll get it for you."

Ami grabbed her knapsack and Remy's bag from the truck. A shooting star streaked across the sky, and she was about to make a wish when she abruptly realized that everything she had ever wished for before had just come true. She was standing free by the ocean. No one was threatening her. No one was going to hurt her or Stan. Remy was looking out for her. It came with an extraordinary feeling of sadness too. What to wish for now? It was the strangest sensation. To be free but feel an immense sense of loss too. She realized she had rarely thought about her mother since finding out she was dead. Was that why she felt so sad? No. What was it? She stood there, still holding both bags and unable to move an inch. She stared at the stars, listened to the steady rhythm of the ocean and was angry with herself. She had no right to be sad.

The trailer door opened, and Stan came out looking for her. Remy was stood there peering into the gloom. "You ok out there? Lucky us. I found some tinned peaches. You like peaches?"

"Coming." She wiped away a tear and headed back to the trailer.

They ate peaches and drank herbal tea as Remy rewound one of the lamps. He smiled as he switched it back on. "Best invention ever. Never need to remember batteries."

"Peaches taste good." She was looking at the ceiling and all the elaborate woodwork. If she didn't know better, she'd believe they were sitting in a log cabin.

Remy watched her taking it all in. "I didn't chose the décor. The guy I bought it from wanted to believe he was living in a log cabin on the mountain slopes of Innsbruck where he was from, so he transformed the interior. Real wood, not the plastic stuff you usually get. Gives good insulation in winter but can get pretty darn hot in summer. My wife, on the one time she came here, bless her soul, condemned it as kitsch, but I secretly like it. I too can pretend I'm living in a log cabin by the ocean. Did you bring the pickles in from the truck?"

"No. They're in the lockbox with the apples. You want to eat them now?"

Remy shook his head. "Never eat pickles after six o' clock. You'll have nightmares."

Ami nodded. "I used to get terrible nightmares. Still do sometimes. Pretty much the same dream. I can't get to Stan and he's either been taken or threatened or once swept away in a flood. I'd wake up choking and sweating. But I've never eaten pickles."

Remy nodded. "Dreams like that haunt you. I used to dream about a screw up at work and the Shuttle exploding. Nothing I could do to stop it. The weird thing is, when the Columbia Shuttle did disintegrate on re-entry in 2003, I was in hospital with a high fever and measles. Maybe it was a guilt thing. I always felt guilty for not being there for the team when it happened. The whole crew lost their lives. Hell, we even knew the foam insulation was an ongoing issue. Flights were suspended for two years after that. Somehow, I survived the first staff culling." He turned to Ami and stood up. "Nightmares are sometimes trying to tell us something, sometimes it's the brain trying to work through a problem. You'll be fine here. If the sheets and blankets are too damp, use the sleeping bag. It will keep you warm. I put the dog bed over there, for Stan, but I'm guessing he'll curl up next to you anyway."

Ami watched him go towards his end of the trailer. "Can I use the bathroom?"

"Go for it. And let me sleep in in the morning. You can go exploring. We'll have a late breakfast at the Breakers. They do killer hashbrowns, nothing frozen, made fresh on the skillet every day. Night Ami."

Ami and Stan got up just after sunrise. They emerged blinking into a warm bright morning. Ami headed to the beach to discover the tide was out and hundreds of little white birds were scurrying along the wet tidal pools searching for something to eat. Everything was new for both of them. The sounds, the smells, the feel of the sand under their feet. Stan ran fast in huge circles, excited by everything he saw or sniffed. Ami stared in astonishment as two pelicans flew by in slow motion. She splashed her face in a tidal pool and tasted the salty ocean water. Stan drank some which he'd probably regret later.

She walked further along the beach and saw a truck arrive at a partially built beachside house. Construction workers jumped out and headed into building. Everything she saw made Ami smile. This was perfection. She found a spot in the dune to watch the ocean as Stan chased birds that rose up as one and settle down a few feet away as if to taunt him.

"Leave the birds alone, Stan. Don't eat the shells. Don't eat anything. I promise I'll feed you once we go back."

Stan ignored her and chewed on everything before spitting it out with regret. He eventually dug a hole and lay down in the cold wet sand panting, pleased with his efforts.

Ami thought about the farm and all the kids who'd still be there. Miserable, probably hating her for escaping. Only Paulo would be willing her to succeed. The rest of them would be expecting her to be brought back beaten black and blue and thrown into the stinking lock-up with the chemical toilet that reeked of rotting shit.

She forced herself to focus on the ocean and what lay on the other side of it. She wished now that she'd paid more attention to the map of the world. She'd never expected to be here, sitting by this vast expanse of ocean, never really believed that it was even possible to be free of the Order. Yet here she was.

Stan was on sudden alert. Two men were approaching. He ran to Ami's side as they walked by. Both of them stared at her but said nothing. They didn't seem interested in her. It was only as they walked further on that Ami noticed they were holding hands. Stan and her exchanged glances but said nothing. Everything was different on the outside, that was for sure.

"Let's go back. You'll be hungry Stan."

Stan was more than happy to return and danced circles around her as she picked up her shoes and began to retrace her steps.

"We're going to have to persuade Remy to stay here a few days," Ami told her dog. "I really, really want to stay."

Remy was lying on the floor when she got back. His tool box was open, and he was pulling up some wires from under the trailer.

"Rats," Remy told her. "Ate through the feeder cable. Must have gotten quite a surprise with his last bite."

Remy rolled over and showed her the bitten cable. He smiled as he began to cut the old wire away. "I'll need to replace this today. You might want to crawl under and remove the dead body before someone I know gets curious. Rats can carry a lot of diseases. Use the plastic gloves in the tool box."

"You sleep ok?" Ami asked him, surprised he was up already.

"Like the dead. Nice to wake up with a warm sunbeam on my face though. It's going to get up to seventy degrees today. You enjoy the beach?"

"I love it here," Ami confessed. "Can I made you some herbal tea?"

"Sure, I'll be done here in ten minutes. We'll go and get us some breakfast at the Breakers. You might want to feed Stan though."

Ami nodded. She was just about to do that. Stan was already standing by his bowl expectantly. "It's beautiful here. I'd want to live here all the time."

Remy smiled. "It is beautiful. Hard to get any work around here I imagine but yeah, I love it. Never could stand Palm Beach with all those billionaires driving up property prices or South Beach with all the tourists all year round. Here is simple, the way Florida is supposed to be lived. I guess one day they'll keep building and it will end up looking like Miami but with luck, not until I'm long gone."

"You should move back here," Ami told him as she filled Stan's bowl and he dived in to gobble the kibble.

"I know. I'm a monument to indecision. Maybe now the Hawk's almost done I can think about it. But hiring architects, finding house builders you can trust and all the hassles with short term loans as I try and sell my other place. A heck of a lot can go wrong and whatever the quote you get, it always doubles. This old trailer will see me out, I think. Hand me that roll of insulation tape, will you?"

Ami looked for a roll of tape and handed it over to him. He began to wrap the exposed wire. He looked up at her. "Rats will eat anything. Plastic, you name it. I'll have to get something to fill the hole they ate through. Last thing we want is for them to start nesting here. Go pick up the dead rat whilst Stan is eating."

Ami was jolted into action. Grabbed some plastic gloves and headed out of the trailer.

Remy reassured Stan she would be back as he continued to wrap the exposed wiring.

Ami returned moments later, hovering at the front door. "What shall I do with them?"

"Them? Jeez. Put them in the garbage. Make sure the lid is on tight. Stan will smell it from a hundred feet away."

Remy was back on his feet when Ami returned and started to wash her hands.

"Two rats. Not a good sign, Ami. Never leave any food waste outside and clear up any dogshit as soon as you can. They breed fast and once they get established, it's hard to irradicate them."

"We had rats in the barn at the farm, always trying to get at the grain store. Had to keep poisoning them. It was hard to listen to them scream."

Remy nodded. "There's no nice way to kill a rat. That's for sure." He headed to the bathroom. "Give me a moment and we'll head on out to eat. Maybe we can buy some fresh fish today and grill them on the stoop. You like grilled fish?"

Ami shrugged. "Only fish I ever had came out of a can."

"The secret is to eat the fish before it gets into the can. Bring in the apples and the pickles – don't want them getting hot in the sun. Oh yeah; and remind me to charge my phone. Maisie will be worried if I don't call her soon. See you outside kid."

Remy locked up and headed to the truck. Ami was already inside with Stan.

"How long have you lived here?" Ami asked him when he climbed into the truck.

Remy thought about it as he started up the engine. "I think I bought the original house here in '88. It needed a lot of work. Hadn't been touched since the forties. It was never really rock solid. Wasn't a bit surprised when the hurricane swept it aside.

"The ocean was filled with furniture and other stuff from all the homes around here for months. Tide kept bringing it back and taking it away. The dunes were bigger before the hurricane. There were palm trees. All gone now. I got back here a day after it hit to find a perfect blue sky, not a drop of wind. I was sifting through the rubble when two cowboys turned up offering cash for the deeds to all the broken properties. Only two neighbors were stupid enough to accept. Those guys must have made a killing.

"My father was born during the hurricane of 1926 in Miami. Most of the original city was blown away or flooded. Nothing new about hurricanes in this state, that's for sure."

He turned the truck around. "Let's go eat."

CHAPTER TWENTY

Remy's Lost Love

Breakers Cabin was busy. Ami was feeding Stan the remains of her toast when Remy rejoined her at the outside table. He didn't look happy.

"What did Maisie say?"

Remy rolled his eyes. "She claims she's been worried sick I didn't answer my phone but she's happy now she knows I'm staying at the trailer."

He buttered his toast and shared his last sausage with Stan who snapped it out of his hands. "Maisie always manages to make me feel guilty. She's one of those people who likes to micro-manage other people's lives."

Ami frowned. "Micro what?"

"An overly zealous nosey parker my wife called her. That was before she descended on me and made my life a misery."

Ami smiled. "Maybe she thought she was helping you."

Remy shrugged. "Yeah, that's what I thought in the beginning. Ah well, at least she's gone."

"But now you've got me and Stan."

Remy grinned. "You I like. Stan too. That's the difference."

Ami felt relieved. "What are we going to do today?"

"Get the trailer fixed up. I need to deal with the scratches and the bullet hole in my truck. Maybe check on Jonny later. I used to go sailing with him and he's good company. You'll like him. Got a lot of tall tales to tell." Remy winked. "Lives on a boat. He used to be one of the NASA rocket engineers. There's quite a few who settled around here once the job ended. Maybe we could sail up to Amelia Island. Amazing bird life there."

"The waitress asked me if I was a snowbird. I mean there's lots of white birds on the beach but why would she ask if I was a bird?"

"Snowbirds are people who come down from the North in winter to live here and elsewhere. They can't face the freezing winters anymore.

Can't say I blame them. But they're usually retirees or people able to work from home as long as they have good wi-fi."

"I've never had a cold winter."

Remy stared at her. "Don't ever volunteer for one. I can't even think if I'm cold. You think you can handle some food shopping today. Get us plenty of vegetables and some sourdough bread or rye, potatoes, and pasta. I'll go to the hardware store and pick you up when I'm finished." He pulled five twenties from his wallet. "I'll need to get some cash too."

He noticed a change in Ami's expression. "What?"

Ami frowned as she stared at the dollar notes on the table.

Remy suddenly twigged what was worrying her. "You've never shopped for groceries before, have you?"

Ami looked embarrassed. "Thousands of things I've never done before. I've no idea how many potatoes or vegetables to buy."

Remy could see how uncomfortable she was with the idea. He placed his hand over hers and squeezed. "We'll do it together. I was just trying to spare you the hardware store. God knows why, you'll probably know more about hardware than me. Shopping for food takes experience. You have to learn how to say no to what looks like a bargain, so you don't buy more than you need. You need to know what will last and what wont. And always make a list. We need eggs, rice, butter, coffee, tea, flour, dog food. And I guess I need to educate you on the dangers of UPF."

"UPF?"

"Ultra-Processed Foods, That's what people eat now. Not only have you got to check everything for the salt and sugar content, but you got to look for emulsifiers and all kinds of 'food additives' as they call that stuff. People actually buy this junk thinking it's healthy. So much to learn about food. Which is why I stick to organic vegetables and read every label."

"You think I'm stupid now." Ami protested.

Remy smiled. "Not in the least kid. You've seen the size of people out there. Most of the food people eat is slowly killing them. You think they read the information on the packets or cook fresh food? People drool about kitchen designs but then order in everything. Makes no sense to me.

"Once you get the hang of shopping, you'll never have to think about it again. It becomes a habit. And it's best to buy for two than one. I'm forever throwing stuff out because I never get around to eating it. Having Stan around will take care of that problem too. Come to think about it, you ever seen a doctor or a dentist?"

Ami thought about it. "Saw one of the nurses from the Order when I was younger. I fell, thought I'd broken my arm. Had a bad fever too. Never seen a dentist. Is that important?"

"No cavities?" Remy asked.

"Holes? Uh-uh."

Remy was impressed. "You don't eat sugar do you."

Ami shook her head. "Sugar is evil. Lord Ramesh was very firm about that."

"He's not wrong. I gave it up twenty years ago. Had to cut out salt too. You may not have liked it much, but those people at the farm were looking out for your gut."

Ami sighed. "We got weighed every month. You go over the average; you got extra work duties. No one ever got fat on the farm, except the staff."

Remy stood up ready to go. "Well, you've got extra duties today, aside from shopping. We have to clean the trailer and get it shipshape for winter."

Ami seemed relieved. "That I can do."

"And I'll get some fresh fish to grill. Busy day ahead for us girl."

Ami wasn't listening. She's spotted a cruise liner on the horizon.

Remy followed her gaze. "Probably returning to Port Canaveral. All the big cruise ships put in there now. None of that was happening when I first moved here. You can catch a ship to the Bahamas or go right down to Rio. Never really wanted to get on a ship with ten thousand people or more. Didn't like the odds."

Ami was still staring. Ten thousand people? It didn't seem possible.

"Try the switch now."

Ami flipped the light switch by the door and a bright light flooded the interior. Remy allowed himself a broad grin. "Next time the rats come they'll regret it. You put the poison where I told you to?"

Ami nodded. "Can I make some soup?"

Remy stood up, wincing with pain as he straightened his back. "Jeez, that hurts. I must find that heat gel I bought a couple of years ago." He turned to look at her. "You can make soup? From scratch?"

"We've got leeks, onions, carrots and some green stuff I didn't recognize."

Remy smiled. "Chop away, kid."

Ami noticed he was still rubbing his back. "You ok?"

"No. Sat in an awkward position that's all. Nothing a well-aimed shotgun won't fix."

Ami frowned. She didn't like that kind of humor. "I used to get leg cramps a lot. Still do I guess, but not lately."

"You have to pull up your toes when that happens, even if that seems impossible. Likely caused by not drinking enough during the day."

Ami was staring at Remy's socks. He noticed what she was staring at.

"Yep, I need new socks too."

"There's a hole in your sweater too. I guess you don't buy much new stuff."

Remy eased down on a chair wincing again. "You got me. But now you've noticed I guess I had better shape up. Must be embarrassing to be stuck with this old hobo."

Ami laughed and shook her head. "Don't buy anything on account of me," she protested.

Remy grinned. "Only time a man buys new clothes is because he wants to impress someone. In my experience anyway."

Ami turned to find a good chopping knife. "You don't have to impress me, Remy. I'm no one."

"Nonsense, you're very special. You are going to have so many men fall in love with you."

Ami made a silly dismissive noise as she began to scrape the carrots. "Are you crazy? I know nothing about love. Nothing at all. Not sure I want to either."

Remy stretched over to a dusty bottle of brandy and wiped a glass with his sleeve. He poured himself a generous helping and sat back in his chair to watch Ami working. He sipped his liquor and seemed to think it was passable.

"I'm going to tell you a story I never told anyone, Ami. It's about love. I'm kinda thinking you probably don't think a man like me ever thinks about love, what with me being an engineer and being a pretty boring old bastard at that."

Ami giggled. "You're going to tell me a love story?"

Remy took another sip of his brandy and sloshed it around his mouth before swallowing, allowing the heat to spread all the way down. "It's my love story. You can say no and I'll shut the heck up, but there just might be something you can learn."

Ami turned to face him, knife in one hand, onion in another, tears already forming.

"Any tears blame the onions, but yes, of course I want to hear your love story. To tell you the truth I never ever heard a love story from anyone. Not a happy one. Is yours a happy one?"

"Hmm, that you'll have to judge for yourself. Love stories always kinda start out happy."

"Is it about how you met your wife?" Ami asked, pushing the onions well away from her as she peeled the skin.

Remy shook his head as Stan settled down beside his shoes.

"Nope. This is a story about a man who lost his head over love. Bet you never thought I'd be saying that."

Ami smiled. "You got any herbs?"

"Top cupboard."

She reached up and found a row of sealed containers all correctly labelled. She let out a little squeal of joy. "Wow, you've got everything."

Remy was staring into his brandy tumbler. "I'd been married ten years when the story starts. I can't say it was much of a marriage. Jean wasn't affectionate at the best of times to tell the truth. But somehow, or another she fell for another man."

Ami turned to stare him in surprise. She hadn't expected that. "She left you?"

Remy laughed. "No, she decided to have a secret affair, but a helpful neighbor told me all about it, even though I didn't really want to know.

"We were living in our old house on this lot back then and I was working at NASA up the road a ways. Jean went to do a paralegal course in Orlando where it just so happens the man she was keen on lived. Her tutor as it happens."

Ami frowned. This wasn't much of a love story so far. "You weren't upset?"

Remy sighed. "Nope. In fact, the total opposite. I was kinda hoping she'd leave me. Jean was ten years younger than me, and I was often away in Houston. She got bored living here on her own. She worked for a lawyer nearby. Anyway, she was gone for a month, and I was suddenly on leave. It was one of those 'use it or lose it' vacations and I learned a long time ago that no one ever says 'thank you' for losing your time off. They just think you're a mug for not taking it. Lesson to learn there once you start work. Always use up your paid vacations. It's your right."

Ami blinked and resumed chopping vegetables. She had no idea about paid vacations.

"Anyway, it was the second day of my vacation, and I couldn't go fishing because of red tide was really bad that year. It's a toxic seaweed that chokes off life in the ocean, stinks too.

"I was walking my dog Dizzy along the beach, a happy go lucky mongrel I found as a pup. Long gone now. There was some shouting and screaming coming from a shack about a mile from here. Dizzy ran over there and began barking. He hated to hear arguing and screaming. I approached; a bit wary because people can be volatile in a domestic dispute. Anyway, this woman came running out of the house yelling. Dizzy backed away but I could see she had been beaten and was bleeding. This half naked guy followed her out ready to beat her some more."

Ami stared at Remy wide-eyed. "What did you do?"

"Normally you wouldn't get involved. The girl could turn on you for trying to help or he could start attacking me. But Dizzy jumped up at the guy to stop him and he was about to start beating the crap out of my dog. So, had to intervene and brought him down. Dizzy had a good hold on his leg, and I may have got a lot of sand in his eyes. The man was blind drunk but that's no excuse for beating anyone. This was nearly twenty-five years ago mind. I wasn't always this old wreck with a sore back. I used to go swimming and work-out at the gym.

"I took the girl back to my place to treat her cuts and let him sober up. She'd been beaten pretty bad, so I bathed her wounds and let her sleep. She didn't utter a single word. Not one. I didn't know her name or if she was married to the guy, nothing. She slept right through the day and didn't wake till the next morning."

"Is this the bit when your wife comes home and ..."

Remy chuckled. "No, sorry, you're letting your imagination run ahead of you. I told you she was away.

"Next morning, I was making breakfast and she suddenly appears in the doorway. No smiles, no thank you for saving her. She just asked where the bathroom was and disappeared.

"About twenty minutes later she reappeared having showered. Still bruised of course. She sat down and ate the breakfast I put in front of her and stroked Dizzy."

Ami washed the leeks before chopping them as she glanced around for a suitable saucepan to make the soup in. "Then the guy who beat her up must have come around," Ami suggested. "He had to be so mad at you for taking her away from him."

"He'd have to find me first. She started speaking after she'd drunk some coffee and spat most of it out. She informed me that American's know nothing about coffee apparently. Which is probably true, if you had grown up in Europe, as she had. I never found out exactly where she was from. She told me she was a nurse. She'd only been in the States for six months. That about all I ever found out about her."

Ami frowned. "And that's the end of your story?"

Remy grinned and took another sip of his brandy. "That my girl was the beginning. The sun came out as it usually did once the ocean haze burned off. There she was at my table, sunlight on her hair. I could see the fine hair on her neck. She was no more than five foot tall, petite with astonishing black-greenish eyes. I can see her now looking at me with a twitch in her nose as she studied me.

"I know that that look," she said finally. "Don't fall in love with me," she said.

"Too late," I told her. I couldn't take my eyes off her.

"I don't want love anymore," she told me. "No one knows how to love here."

I pointed out to her that I was married, of course. I've never cheated on my wife. The girl laughed at me. "All men cheat on their wives," she told me. "Always."

Ami protested. "But your wife was cheating on you."

"I was strongly aware of that. But I also knew that if I cheated as well, there'd be no going back."

"But you wanted your wife to leave you."

"I did. But I also didn't want to give her an excuse to divorce me. I was conflicted. I was clearly totally smitten by this young woman, who probably didn't give a moment's thought to me or the effect she was having on me. I was drowning in my emotions. I never imagined that I, an average boring NASA guy through and through could be experiencing these explosions in my heart. I had an extraordinary love for this young woman and couldn't stop it. It was a runaway train of emotion. I even went to take a cold shower to try and calm myself."

"Was she still there when you got back?"

Remy smiled; his eyes closed as he remembered that moment. "Yes. I told her that she had better stay inside for a day or two until her boyfriend calmed down or sobered up. She agreed but didn't think he'd do either thing. That night she came to my bed. After that I don't think we left the house for five whole days. It was the most intense experience I have ever had in my whole life. She was passionate. I don't know the words. She talked about a lake where she grew up and the poor fishermen and how she longed to escape their simple lives and come to America. I was entranced by her. Never felt like it before or since. She mocked my age and inexperience in lovemaking. She mocked everything about me.

"I was in a state of bliss, finally aware that I only had one day of leave left and I'd have to go back to work. Had she asked me to quit my job and go with her anywhere I would have quit everything for her."

Ami stared at him in wonder. She'd never expected anything like this.

"Then came a knock on the door," Remy said. "It was like the breaking of a dream."

"The boyfriend must have found you." Ami said confidently.

"Worse. It was our neighbor Chester. You'll meet him soon. A man had attacked his young wife. Chester had shot at him, but he'd gotten away. Right away I suspected it was the girl's boyfriend who'd mistaken her for his girl. His wife needed a nurse or doctor fast but wasn't insured and needed help."

"I am a nurse," my guest whispered in my ear. "I will take care of it." She quickly got dressed and went to my neighbor's house. Meanwhile the cops found the injured man who'd beaten the Chester's wife and locked him up. Sure enough, it was the drunken boyfriend.

"She fixed her up and I hoped she'd return but she went back to the shack where I'd found her to find her passport and work documents. I drove over there to ask her to return."

"And did she?"

Remy emptied his brandy glass. "She asked me to make a promise."

"A promise?"

"She asked me to let her go and never to look for her."

Ami was shocked. "But you were in love with her."

"I was, very much so. I really didn't want to make that promise."

Ami located the right kind of pot for her soup. She felt so much sadness for him. "Didn't she love you?"

"For five days she did. She told me that love was too much for me. Too much for her. That she didn't want that kind of love. Nothing so intense can last and it can only lead to pain. She didn't explain, but I understood she wanted something that would last forever."

Ami shook her head. "I don't really understand."

"Intense love can consume you, like a fire. It can't be shared. There's no room to breathe and sooner or later one of you will want to breathe. I'm guessing the man who beat her couldn't stand the thought of losing her, this is what drive him mad. I don't really know. She asked me for bus fare. She needed $27.50 cents. I gave her a fifty and would have given her anything she asked for.

"She said it again. "Promise me you'll never look for me. Never ever."

I promised, pointing out that I didn't even know her name or where she was going.

"But you could have searched for her," Ami protested.

Remy offered her a rueful smile. "No. That's the rule with a promise. You don't break it. Besides, if I had gone looking, that one day I finally found her, I'd be an even older man, pitching up outside her home where her kids and husband are sitting down to supper, or I'd be facing a rifle from a jealous man who wants to run me off his property. No thanks. We had a brilliant five days of love and I'll treasure it forever. Never had it before and will never have it again."

"That's so sad."

Remy shook his head. "No, it isn't sad. It was the best thing that ever happened to me, Ami. The best thing. When the old house blew down in the hurricane it robbed me of the last traces of her. I was sad for a while. I'd lost the place where her bare feet trod the boards or where she drawn a little picture of her lake. But I could still close my eyes and see her smile or remember her whispers in my ear as she laughed at my reaction."

"Then your wife came home."

Remy nodded and sighed. "My wife returned at the end of the month. She told me it was 'over'. At first, I thought she meant our marriage but no, she meant the affair, that I wasn't supposed to know about. We never once talked about it. She went back to her bedroom, and I went back to mine, and we carried on as before."

"So, you never told her."

"Lord no. It was my love story. No one else's. One day I hope you have a love like that and if you do, don't try to prolong it longer than it needs to be. It's like a shooting star. It's not meant to last."

Ami shook her head. "That will never ever happen to me."

Remy rubbed his feet on Stan's warm back. "It will. I promise you. You are going to grow into this beautiful woman and all I can hope is that you'll learn pretty damn quick how to tell good from bad."

"Good from bad," Ami repeated. "And how do I do that?"

"Find someone who respects you, listens to you, cares for you. First signs of jealousy or violence, shouting, pack your bags and leave. Don't look back."

"And go where?"

"As long as I'm alive, you'll always have a home with me. That's a promise."

Ami smiled. She wondered how long that kind of promise was good for with such an old man then cussed herself for being so ungrateful. "I wonder what your nurse is doing now. You think she ever thought about you again?"

Remy shrugged. "I don't know. Maybe she did, but I suspect she forgot about me the moment she got on the bus."

"That's a sad ending."

"But a trueful one. You need any help with the soup?"

"I need noodles. You got any noodles?"

CHAPTER TWENTY-ONE

Moon Shot

The sun was just rising as Ami and Stan were walking on the beach at low tide. Ami walked barefoot and relished this time alone with just the two of them and the ocean. Around her seabirds were getting busy to go feed and there was a light wind blowing her hair.

A jogger was approaching from the opposite way, her dog keeping pace with her as she ran. Ami wasn't sure about this jogging business; it looked kind of sweaty and serious. A beach was to be appreciated slowly in her opinion. The jogger slowed as she drew level and smiled. A tall woman with a ponytail. She removed her AirPods to talk.

"Hi, I've seen you before out here at sunrise. Meant to ask, is that an Australian Sheep Dog?"

Ami stared at her, then at Stan and didn't even try to answer. It was the strangest question she'd ever heard.

"I...er..."

Stan was ignoring them and sniffing the woman's dog.

"Only asked because he's such a beautiful dog with one blue eye and the other grey. Don't see many of these around, for sure."

Ami found her tongue. "He's definitely a sheep dog, but Australian? From where the kangaroos come from?"

The woman laughed. "And other strange creatures. I just love your dog; he has such a noble face and seems so happy."

The woman knelt down and stroked Stan who seemed a bit alarmed at that.

"What's your dog?" Ami asked. "I like his beard."

"Schnauzer. Supposed to be a mini, but she grew up a midi, but it's not as if I'd take her back to the store now, huh. Couldn't live without my Oona."

"Oona?" Ami asked, sounding out the word. It seemed strange to call a dog Oona. "She's pretty."

"She thinks so too. Very demanding."

"I don't know anything about Stan's father. The mother was sickly and had three pups. Two got sold but I hid this one in the barn so they couldn't take it. I think the mother died. She never had time to wean the pups. I hand reared Stan, let him suck milk off my fingers."

The woman smiled. "So cute. I can see he's totally in love with you. I'm so jealous. But I'm pretty sure he's Australian. The short tail is a giveaway. American sheep dogs don't look like this. Guard him well."

Ami nodded and watched the women stand up again and slip the AirPods back into her ears. She glanced at her watch. "Got to keep my pace up. See you around kid. Have a great day."

Ami watched her go, the dog struggling to keep up. She knelt down to hug Stan wondering how on earth an Australian sheepdog ended up being born at the farm. She remembered the battles she'd had to keep him. She slept with Stan in the barn for three whole months and wouldn't have survived without the cook sneaking food to them both and once, she took Stan away with her on her day off to get his shots. Which was ironic as none of the kids were allowed any kind of shots to protect them from any diseases out there. She made a mental note to mention this too Remy one day. Might be important.

She was beaten twice for not giving up on Stan, but he grew quickly and soon learned to growl if anyone approached Ami. He was born to be her protector. The Sister's finally gave in but made sure she got all the shitty jobs on the farm as punishment for her disobedience.

"You think we should try running for a bit?" She asked Stan. He wagged his tail.

Ami set off at a fast pace and Stan was right at her heels, but she was quickly out of breath and crashed into the ocean to cool off. Stan right beside her, doing his best to doggy paddle and stay afloat.

Ami laughed and headed back to the shoreline to lie down – slightly regretting soaking all her clothes.

"Seems we'd both better learn to swim pretty fast if we're going to stay here for a while."

Stan sneezed and rested his head on her legs with a big sigh wondering if it was breakfast time yet.

Remy was late to the breakfast table that morning and noticed Ami seemed unusually quiet when he sat down to drink his coffee and make toast. Stan was watching carefully to guilt him into giving him his crusts.

"You seem a bit introspective today. Still got pains?" Remy asked, tapping the barometer. Pressure was dropping but the sky didn't indicate any rain. He could see she'd put her clothes out to dry on the line.

"You get wet out there this morning?"

"A bit. I got a bit hot running. Next time I'll take my clothes off before I run in."

Remy chuckled. Not quite sure what was going on. "Where are you going today?"

"I want to sketch the old pier and some of the fishing boats. If that's ok with you."

"Of course. Explore to your hearts content. I have chores to do here." He tossed Stan some crusts who snatched them in mid-air.

Ami was finishing up her breakfast. "Woman on the beach asked if Stan was Australian. That was strange. And... I keep feeling guilty that I escaped and left Paulo behind."

Remy stared at her a moment thinking about what he should say. "You said yourself he wouldn't be able to keep up with you. Don't feel bad. You escaped. The longer it is you're not brought back the more it will encourage others to think about escape too."

"But he can't walk far. Not for long anyway."

"From what you've told me, he's resourceful. He'll be rooting for you, Ami. You aren't responsible for him or me for that matter. You have a responsibility to yourself. One day, when you're secure and under my roof, maybe we can make enquiries about him. My lawyer will know how. But not until you're safe. I don't want them to know you're alive. It's better they think bad things have happened to you."

Ami shrugged. She knew this. "It's just that ..."

"You care for him. He was your only friend at the farm. Friendship is important. One of the most important things actually. I only think better of you because your care so much and worry about him. It might be a year or two years before you find out what happened to him, but you can never approach the Order directly. You get that?"

Ami nodded. She understood, but it didn't make her feel any better though. Paulo would have to escape his way. She stood up to grab a poop bag and her sketchpad. Stan was already at the door bouncing up and down anxious to leave again. "Ok, we're going, Stan."

"Take care," Remy told her. "Full moon tonight so there'll be a high tide." He grabbed his phone. "Might be a major rocket launch today. I'll check. Wouldn't want to miss that." He suddenly remembered something she'd just said. "Did you say Stan is Australian? From down under? I wonder how she can tell? He doesn't bark much. Do dogs have accents I wonder?"

Ami saw that twinkle in his eyes, knew he was joshing her and smiled. She grabbed a couple of treats and left without another word.

Remy sighed and had to admit he was jealous of her youth and energy. One day he knew she'd snap under the weight of all that trauma she'd been through. It would manifest itself in many unexpected ways. He hoped he was strong enough to deal with all that and help her through it.

He frowned as he searched for his tools to fix the truck. No way he could smooth out the dent on the hood, but he could rust proof it and give it dab of paint. He found the body filler he needed for the bullet hole and some sandpaper. It felt good to be busy again.

Remy shook Ami awake just after 2am. He was excited.

"The clouds have gone, there's zero wind. It's the perfect time for the launch."

Ami rubbed her eyes; she'd been deep into a strange dream about the farm and having to bring in the pigs. It was hard to shake it off. "What?"

"Just put a light sweater over your pjs, we're going outside." He showed her his phone. It was showing launch minus -5 minutes. "I think they'll launch this time. God knows how many delays they've had in the last three months."

"Launch?" Ami asked, totally confused.

Remy pulled on his sweater. "This was scheduled for September. They're sending astronauts back to the moon, Ami. The Moon!"

Ami blinked. The moon. Huh? Stan slept on. He hated being disturbed once he'd gone to sleep.

"Leave Stan," Remy told her. "Come on, we don't want to miss this. It's the biggest event since the first launch back in 1969."

Still befuddled, Ami grabbed her sweater and followed Remy out of the trailer. He locked Stan in and quickly headed towards the beach. Ami noticed their neighbor Chester was moving that way too with some others all wearing dressing gowns or coats.

"Keep watching the north-east towards Cape Canaveral," Remy told her. "The Orion rocket is huge. This is Artemis, Ami. Four astronauts. One of them a woman. We're finally going back to the moon."

Ami had no idea what she was supposed to feel or look at; but stared anyway. She heard someone shout "Minus Two minutes."

Remy put an arm around her shoulders. "Last time man was on the moon was in December 1972."

"Why?" Ami asked. "Why go to the moon?"

"Because now it's a race. Who controls the moon can control Earth. We can't leave all those rare minerals up there for the Chinese or the Indians or the ice water at the south pole for that matter. We have to stake out our ground, make the rules or there won't be any at all."

Ami frowned; how could anyone control the moon? She didn't understand.

"Space is the new frontier. You never noticed all those satellites up there?" He pointed. "See there's a whole train of Musk's Starlink comms satellites going by right now. Up, right, seventy degrees."

Ami stared at them in wonder. She had seem them go by before, had no idea these objects were actually put there by someone.

"Come the next war, everything we've put there will be a target. If they destroy our satellites, it could make the upper atmosphere impossible to use, all that debris whizzing by at 17,000 mph. It might be impossible to launch anything through it. The whole finance system could collapse with it."

Ami stared into space. She had no comprehension of any financial system, still less one run from space.

"It's a go!" Someone shouted and a people began whooping all around her.

Remy pointed Ami's head north-east again. "This is what I used to do, kid. Launch rockets to send the Shuttle into space."

A glow began to appear on the horizon that quickly grew brighter by the second, the noise of the launch followed seconds later. It steadily grew in intensity. Ami stared with utter astonishment as the rocket slowly lifted off, at first in slow motion then quickly gathering pace. The glow from the burning fuel lit up the whole sky now and people were shouting and waving as the rocket seemed to tilt and head out over the Atlantic ocean.

Ami noticed Remy's fingers were crossed and he seemed to be muttering a prayer.

"How fast is it?" Ami asked as the air began to shake around them with a roar from the rocket engines.

"It will reach 24,000 miles per hour and take eight minutes to reach outer space. It will dump the empty fuel tanks over the ocean, but the main Orion spacecraft will carry on its way to the moon. There's no friction in space, so it won't lose speed on its way to the moon."

Ami and Remy watched intently until they couldn't see the rocket glow any longer. Remy had been counting the minutes in his head. He knew all the stages and the critical moments when things could go wrong.

"What's it like inside the rocket?" Ami asked, suddenly shivering.

Remy exhaled; confident Artemis was well on its way. "Tense, scared, painful, at least until the pressure is off them when they escape Earth's gravity. They aren't in the rocket, they're on the Orion spacecraft module on top of it. That bit will be coming back to Earth. You don't need so much power to get off the moon, it's only got one sixth Earth's gravity there."

Ami processed this information; upset she knew so little about it.

"They got that one up without you, Remy," Chester shouted to him as he turned to go back home.

"They sure did. I couldn't take the stress these days. My hearts racing just watching it take off."

"Yeah, I hear ya. We're heading back to the moon at last man. About damn time."

Ami watched the people all turning to go back to their houses and trailers. "I must get back. I can hear Stan howling."

Remy chuckled. "Well, if that rocket didn't wake him, nothing would. Just think kid, it's been over fifty years since we last got someone up there. So much has happened since then."

Ami shrugged. She had no inkling of what had happened since then or ever really. Was it too late to catch up on history? Where they hell would she start?

"So, it was American's who went to the moon last time?" Ami asked.

"Yep. I remember watching the first moon landing in 1969 on TV. I guess that's when I knew I was going to work for NASA one day. Never deviated from that ambition." He followed Ami back to the trailer. "Of course, we all had a lot of hopes about the future back then."

Ami had hopes too, but none of them involved going to the moon. Stan was certainly howling. That dog just didn't like to be left alone.

CHAPTER TWENTY-TWO

Frozen

Three days later Ami was watching Remy work with the high-pressure washer cleaning the sides of the trailer. He seemed happy as a few years of dirt and salt began to reveal the true color underneath. To Ami's surprise it was returning to a shiny white.

She'd elected to trim the overgrown bushes that covered the yard. By her reckoning it hadn't seen any attention in at least ten years and there was some kind of plan to follow and paths to reveal under all the weeds. She tried to imagine what it looked like with a house on it. Remy had mentioned that he'd planted hardy plants like lavender and such to encourage the bees, but plants needed air and space around them to thrive and much of the lavender had turned woody. She was amazed anything had survived considering nothing ever got watered but figured the moist air off the ocean had helped them live. The houses nearby barely had any plants and the yards seemed so empty of life. She couldn't imagine living without plants around a home and only one neighbor was growing food, tall leeks that needed picking in her opinion before they also turned woody.

The tide was up high. She found the rhythm of the waves crashing against the shore and sweeping back again soothing. She could easily get used to that she realized. She had been reflecting on how she'd got here, living under the protection of this old man who had so easily taken her and Stan in. He was so different to the Sisters and Brothers who ran the farm. There wasn't any of the shouting, no expecting orders to be obeyed or face punishment. None of the daily fear she grown up with. It was like Remy was a different species of human. He asked her opinion on whether she like to do something, as if it was a choice she could decline. There was no pressure on her, and she could go wherever she liked with Stan, not that there was anywhere to go except the beach. She knew he'd worry if she went too far or didn't return in good time. She found she liked that. She could ask anything and get an answer and if he didn't know something he admitted it, unlike Father Tresor who wouldn't ever admit to not knowing something and blatantly lied about everything. She tried to shake thinking about the farm out of her head. She did wonder if they were still looking for her. 'Leave no traces', Remy told her and when they were out anywhere, he always called her Ollie to be safe. She didn't know if she doing 'boy' right or not. The only boy she knew well was Paulo and he was soft and gentle and permanently terrified of what they might do to him next. At least Father Tresor had stopped pestering him since he'd broken his leg.

She looked up, distracted by Stan's barking. He was staring at Remy and barking at him for no reason at all. Remy was still holding the pressure washer but had released the trigger. He was standing incredibly still, his face contorted with pain.

"Remy?"

Remy didn't turn his head. He spoke haltingly. "Get... me inside. If you can. Can't move. I'm stuck."

Ami panicked. She scrabbled up off the ground and ran to his side. She took the power washer out of his hands and lay it down, making sure the water was off. Stan backed away, agitated. She briefly wondered how he'd known Remy was in trouble.

"Stuck?" Ami enquired. She could see he was in agony but had no idea how this could have happened. Had he been stung or something?

"Can't move. Get me inside.... Please."

Ami came around him and pulled one of his arms around her slim shoulders. She'd had to do this when Paulo had first broken his leg.

"Let me take your weight. Lean on me. More. I can take it."

Remy gripped her left arm as he allowed himself to lean on her, afraid his weight would be too much for her, but he was desperate to get inside.

"Can you move one leg?" Ami asked him, bracing herself for his full weight.

Remy concentrated hard. He commanded his right leg to move. He managed maybe three inches.

"Left leg now," Ami instructed him. "Try not to do too much. We can do this."

Beads of sweat appeared on his brow. He wasn't so optimistic. He'd experienced this a few years before. Hadn't done anything physical when quite suddenly his back had seized up. This was exactly the same. He closed his eyes and willed himself forward inch by inch, his lower back protesting with every move, sending shooting pains up his spine and down into his buttocks.

"We're going to turn right a bit," Ami warned him. "We've got to get around to the other side."

Remy knew that only too well. He was on the wrong side of his sixty by fourteen-foot trailer home. He noticed in passing that the anti-hurricane strap anchors looked a tad rusty. He needed to inspect those.

"We're getting there," Ami said tersely, straining under the weight of him. She was glad he was a slim old man. She couldn't have coped with anyone heavier.

Stan stood and stared at them, puzzled at what Ami was doing, letting out little squeaks of worry.

"Are you going to need a doctor?" Ami asked Remy, wondering if there was one in this beach community.

Remy wiped sweat from his eyes and shook his head. "No, a chiropractor maybe. Doctors know nothing about back pain except to give you painkillers. I've been down that route before." Remy gritted his teeth and forced himself onwards. If he fell here Ami wouldn't be able to get him inside. He didn't want to call in help. Most of the houses here were all Airbnb's these days and either empty or filled with strangers who might not be inclined to help. "I'm sorry Ami. This is tough for you."

"I didn't know a back could suddenly stop working."

Remy took a deep breath as a shock of pain pierced his shoulders. "It can and does. I've been lucky so far, only happened once before. Just get me inside and lay me down on my bed."

"That's where we're heading," Ami replied, wondering how she was supposed to lay him down. That was going to hurt.

"I've got some old heat gel in the bathroom. You'll have to rub it into my back, maybe look for some old Advil tablets I've got there. Not like they'll fix anything."

"Don't talk. Concentrate on walking."

Remy nodded. Somehow, they reached the end of the trailer and managed to shuffle their way around it. He noticed how much work she'd done in the yard. It had been a jungle when they'd arrived, now it looked like someone cared about the place. "You did a good job," Remy wheezed.

"Had a lot of practice," Ami answered. "Keep moving. Stan, get out of the way. Go."

Stan backed away as they headed towards the door and the three steps leading up to it. Ami stared at them and realized how difficult this was going to be.

"You think you can do the steps?"

Remy severely doubted it but that was defeatist thinking. He had to do it, no matter what.

"You could turn around maybe. I could haul you up," Ami suggested.

Remy let out a bitter laugh. "I'll be paying the chiropractor two hundred bucks to do that. There's a handle just by the door. I can pull myself up. My right arm is still working."

It took fifteen agonizing minutes and a lot of colorful swearing for Remy to get up one step at a time, allowing for a few minutes of recovery time after each step. He finally made it inside and between the two of them she finally got him to his end of the trailer, where he fell like a ton of logs face down on his bed.

He didn't try to flip over. She tried to make him comfortable then went to search for the gel and pills. She wasn't confident anything would help him.

He was asleep when she returned. She rubbed the gel into his back anyway and left the pills and a glass of water on the floor where he could retrieve them.

She went back to the bathroom to attend to her own needs. Stan joined her, worried and whining. "He'll be ok. Don't worry. We've got work to finish outside. We'll let him sleep. Go on now, you're supposed to be guarding us. Go."

Stan reluctantly left her alone. Ami desperately tried not to think about what might happen to her and Stan if Remy died. Could one die of a bad back?

She shook herself and washed her face and hands and then went outside to finish what Remy had started.

Ami recognized the chiropractor when he came the next day. He was all smiles, introduced himself as Steve and got to work quickly. She was surprised to see it was one of the men she'd seen walking hand in hand with another man on the beach, not that it was any of her business. He didn't treat Remy gently at all. To her it looked like he was trying to torture him, and he protested loudly as the man manipulated his back and then wrapped his arm around his neck and almost snapped it when he got Remy standing again. Remy seemed pleased with the result however and happy to pay him nearly $300 for the hour-long treatment. It cost extra for the house call but there was no way she could have got him out of the trailer again. The man winked at 'Ollie' as he left, but Ami had no idea why.

She made Remy eat her soup and he genuinely appeared happier once the initial shock had worn off.

"That boy knows what he's doing," Remy informed her as he sipped his soup. He was able to sit up in his chair now, sore but a good sore compared to earlier.

"He didn't hurt you? Sounded like he did."

Remy nodded. "I heard something click back into place. I'll be fine later."

Ami was curious. "Why did you call him a boy?"

Remy chuckled. "Any man fifty years younger than me is a boy, Ami. Did you remember to shut the water off? I'm sorry I'm such a burden to you."

"You're no burden. Did you notice anything?"

Remy looked around, then spotted a vase with flowers in it.

"You got me flowers?" He was confused.

"Your neighbor, the old guy called Chester brought them. I told him you were laid up and he said he'd been meaning to pay you a debt for more than twenty years. He said he knows you like African daisies."

Remy stared at the bright yellow and orange flowers; a little bit surprised. "I guess it's never too late to pay a debt. He alright? You said old. He's at least twenty years younger than me."

"Got white hair."

Remy nodded. "Fair play."

"And yes, I put the power washer away. It looks a lot better now."

Remy was surprised and impressed. "You finished the job? Wow. It's aluminum, so it won't rust, and the factory painted it white. My bad for never getting it cleaned before. Nice soup by the way."

"The cook we used to have at the farm taught me how to make soup and stews and roasted vegetables. Nina was the only one ever nice to me. She left suddenly. No idea why."

"Useful skill at least." He looked up at Ami and sighed. "I owe you a great debt, Ami. If you hadn't got me back inside, I think I'd still be stuck out there like a damn statue."

Ami nodded; the same thought had occurred to her. She gave Stan a treat. "Is it ok for me and Stan to go for a walk now? There's some kite flying down the beach. I've never seen kites flying before. Chester said it's spectacular. People come from all over Florida to show their stuff."

Remy nodded. "You go. Have fun. I wish I could see it with you. Anyone been asking you awkward questions."

Ami shook her head. "I'm getting used to being Ollie, I guess. I'm your grandson. So weird telling people that."

"Family is important to people around here. If anyone asks tell them you're living with me 'cause your mother passed away. It's entirely true, so you won't have to tell a lie."

Ami nodded. "Promise me you won't move around? You need help to get to the bathroom before I go?"

"I can do it. You get going. Some of those kites can be huge. It's amazing how they get them into the air. You go. Enjoy. You need money?"

Ami shook her head. "Uh-uh. You haven't got much left by the way. I counted it when I paid the 'boy'."

Remy nodded. "Ok, first thing tomorrow we'll raid the bank or cash machine, if there are any left." He reached for his phone, wincing a little as he leaned forward.

"Go, kid. I need to call my lawyer and some other people before they all think I'm dead."

Ami pulled on her jacket and hauled on out of there with Stan close at heel. She turned to stare at Remy at the door. "I was so scared when your back froze. I've never seen anything like that before."

"And I hope to hell that you don't see it again." Remy replied. "You saved my ass, kid. I won't forget it."

CHAPTER TWENTY-THREE

Kites

A cool wind was blowing but it was perfect weather for kites. Ami and Stan found a rock to sit on to watch them soaring overhead. Remy hadn't been kidding. They were huge! They weren't simple pieces of canvas or whatever tied to a string but giant inflatables. Some were shaped liked monsters, other giant humans, or spaceships. She watched an eagle soar, and someone was trying to get a giant tiger into the air. An octopus swooped down towards her, and she ducked only to see a dragon take its place. There were hundreds of people watching or launching their own kites and someone was selling hot dogs that had all of Stan's attention.

Ami loved watching the kites battling the wind and the happy faces of all the people around her. She was too shy to join in but very happy she came. She had no idea that people did things for fun like this. Her picture of what the outside world looked like was changing all the time.

A boy wearing a hoodie came over towards her and Ami wondered what he wanted. She was uncomfortable with this, but he came closer and seemed to be inhaling a vape. All the staff at the Order were hooked on those so she knew what they were.

He muttered something to her, might have been hi, or just clearing his throat. He had to be about the same age as her.

"Hi." Ami said. "You got a kite?"

The boy shook his head. "Uh." He blew out smoke. It smelled sweet and sickly. Ami looked away to avoid it.

Stan was anxious, wondering who this boy might be.

"You live around here?" Ami asked.

The boy shrugged. Pointed in some vague direction. Ami took it as a yes. She wondered if he'd approached because he thought she was another boy. He didn't seem to be very confident, didn't seem to be very interested in the kites either.

Stan barked as a huge clown shaped inflatable swooped down close to them and Ami laughed as he tried to jump up to bite it. The boy was looking strangely at Stan.

Someone shouted at them from the beach and the boy reluctantly turned and sighed. He glanced back at her as he was leaving and shrugged again. “See ya.”

Ami watched him slouch off towards a tall man carrying something heavy, possibly a damaged inflatable. She stared at Stan a moment. “That was so weird.”

The wind was getting stronger now. More people were arriving and launching their inflatables. There had to be at least fifty or sixty up there in the sky.

“Wish Paulo was here to see this,” Ami told Stan. “He would have loved it.”

After an hour she felt cold and was about to leave when she noticed an old school bus arrive and disgorge about twenty young girls all dressed in bright yellow. She nearly choked. She didn’t recognize any of them specifically, but she instantly knew this was the uniform of The Order. Why were they here? She gripped Stan’s collar; he had already sensed her tension.

She watched as the enthusiastic Order girls pulled out a kite from the back of the bus and rapidly filled it with air. She didn’t have to look hard; she knew it would be an inflatable Lord Ramesh. She’d heard so many stories about the recruiters and what their purpose was and how she was destined to join them when she was sixteen. She’d never seen them in action of course, but here they were, seemingly innocent young women having fun, getting an inflatable launched, talking enthusiastically to the people in the crowds.

She felt giddy and nauseous. What if anyone recognized her? She urgently concentrated on her ‘calmness’ exercises, focusing all her attention on the kites in the sky, many of them anchored to the beach now with heavy weights to hold them in place.

Someone was playing guitar. It was all so innocent, Ami wished she had spoken with people before the bus had arrived.

A young woman from the Order approached her on her rock, thrust a leaflet into her hand with a big broad smile on her face. “Don’t look so sad, you shouldn’t be sitting here alone. Read this and find solutions to your problems. We’re here to save you and guide you to a better life."

Ami stared at her. The woman didn't know she'd been living this better life for eleven years already and hated every second of it. She gripped Stan who was growling under his breath.

"Hope you'll join us at the campfire." She added with an encouraging smile. "They'll be singing, good food and companionship. Don't be shy, no one should be alone."

Ami politely smiled. "My dog's scared of fire and people," she said. "But thanks anyway."

The woman nodded and didn't press it. She moved on towards what she hoped would be a more receptive couple.

Ami was shaking and held onto Stan for dear life. Had she recognized her? Did she know they were looking for a girl with a dog? Did they have a photo of the dog? She didn't think so. She felt sick. Couldn't believe that were here, of all places. But then she knew that this was exactly the place to come. A friendly crowd. Build a campfire, be super friendly. Make people feel good. This had been her mother's life apparently.

She anxiously waited until sunset and was sure no one was watching her before she made her way back up towards Remy's part of the beach and safety. She definitely felt queasy. She was convinced she would throw up any moment. Each step back towards Remy felt like a mile. She turned to the wind and let out a piercing scream.

Stan's ears flattened and he cowered and immediately Ami squatted down to comfort him. "I'm not angry at you, Stan. I can't stand it. They're here. They're everywhere. Where do we have to go to escape them? I hate them, Stan. I hate them."

She couldn't get the feeling of horror out of her head when she'd seen that bus arrive. She had thought she was safe at the beach, but it seemed to her that the Order was everywhere. That's what Lord Ramesh had told them. She hadn't really believed it, but it was true. She counted her blessings for her short hair and dressing like a boy. She knew that young boys were low on the recruitment list. Sister Ryan had been a recruiter before she was assigned to the Farm. She told them that they looked for loners or people with stress issues with good jobs. Especially people who owned their own home or had money but were unhappy. The Order was there for them to gain their trust so they would join up and give up their worldly possessions with the promise that the Order would always care for them, support them, love them. They would find peace and happiness with people that place 'You' in their hearts. As if.

Were the people who flew kites those kind of people? She didn't understand it. Sister Ryan had spent eight years recruiting for the cause. But now she was this vicious monster who punished children for any minor transgressions. How had that happened? Why was it so important to persuade people to give up their money and lives and embrace the Order. She had never understood that or the spiritual nourishment that they were supposed to feel every day, or else.

A huge wave rolled in, and she had to swiftly retreat to the dune. She looked up at the stars and sat there, hugging Stan, unable to move any further. All the damn stupid things that had happened to her at the farm streamed through her mind. She could feel her blood boiling and a heart racing. She tried to control her breathing but even that reminded her of Father Tresor beating her on the head because she wasn't getting it. As if beating you would make you calmer, the bastard.

She stared out across the ocean and a passing crazy thought came to her that she could end all this, just walk out there, and disappear under the waves but that moment passed as Stan licked her face and stared intensely at her as if he was reading her mind.

"It's ok, it's ok. I'm never leaving you Stan. Never. You understand me? You are the best thing that ever happened to me..." She thought about Remy then and sighed. "Aside from Remy. God, where would we be without him, huh." She exhaled, scooped up some sand and threw it to the wind.

A lone pelican flew by in the darkness, it was so calm as it cruised the ocean. It was if it took all her fears away with it.

She somehow made it back to Remy's trailer. He was asleep. She went to the bathroom. She absolutely had to have a shower, as if it would wash away all the fear she was feeling. Her stomach felt like it was going to explode. Stan was scratching at the door to be let in, he hated being excluded.

She stayed in the bathroom for a long time. Cleaner, but still unnerved, sickened, afraid of what might happen next.

"You alright in there?" Remy asked with a light tap on the door.

"Might be someone else might need the bathroom soon. Very soon." She heard Stan bark, his worried yip.

She dressed quickly, flustered she'd spent so long in there. "Sorry, sorry... coming."

Stan made a big fuss of her when she remerged red in the face from the hot bathroom. Remy shuffled past her without a word, shutting the door behind him. She felt awkward about keeping him out of there.

Ami went to the kitchenette and thought about what she'd feed Remy with, she really didn't feel like cooking anything. She felt so down. It was like Lord Ramesh had grabbed her by the throat. Would she ever be free of them? She tried to pull herself together. She was taken back to when she was five years old again, abandoned at the Farm by her mother. She could see her vividly with her flaming red hair and fake reassuring smiles as she told her she would be 'so happy here'. Father Tresor (thinner then) putting his arms around her as she drove away without even a wave or promise that she'd be back. She'd prayed and prayed that it was a terrible mistake and that her mother would return and take her back, but as weeks rolled into months, she finally accepted that she had been abandoned, just like all the other kids. The Farm would be her life now and she should expect no reprieve.

She needed air and went outside into the evening chill and sat on the old wooden chair. Stan pawed her, clearly sensing something was wrong.

Remy returned. He stared at her through the open door and could sense her distress. He put the kettle on. "I don't know what happened out there, but I can see you're a girl in need of some hot tea."

He moved slowly, wincing a little with pain as he did so, and lit the gas to boil the water.

Ami remained silent, looking up at the canopy of stars. Her eyes were filled with silent tears unable at this moment to explain anything or do anything.

Stan went inside and stared at his bowl. Remy could see him worrying the bowl too and filled one bowl with kibble and gave him half a can of dog food in the other, which was gone in two seconds. He made two mugs of tea and gingerly brought one mug out to her before moving back inside to his chair and sitting down with a huge sigh of relief.

He figured she'd talk when she was ready. "You're not hurt, are you?" Remy called out. "I mean, no one ..."

Ami sighed, picked up her mug and headed back inside. It was chilly. "I'm ok, Remy. It's just something I saw... I'm being stupid. I just can't cope right now..."

Remy stared at her a moment and indicated for her to sit down. She closed the door, dropping down on the beanbag.

"Don't know why I think this, but I've been waiting for that dam to break since I met you. You've been through a lot, girl. A heck of a lot. We've been shot at, met all kinds of people who I'd ordinarily avoid at all costs, and you've had to grow up so fast. You haven't had a moment to process the changes in your life or the fact that your mother is dead. You lost that dream of a better life with her. Now you're stuck with an old man with a bad back who you probably think is going to drop down dead at any moment and leave you high and dry. I don't blame you for being upset or for having some kind of meltdown, I'm only surprised you haven't had it sooner."

Ami stared at him but couldn't say anything. She sipped her tea; Stan joined her on the beanbag. Remy ran his hand over his head and ploughed on.

"All the kids my wife used to help had been through a whole lot of stuff, violence, sexual abuse, hunger, beatings, you name it. Outwardly they would look normal but inside they would be churned up, sometimes they blamed themselves for the situation they were in or harm themselves in so many ways.

"She would tell them 'I can help you and get you to see the right people to talk about it, but you have to meet us half way'."

Ami wasn't sure where this was going or if she wanted to hear any of it right now.

"But I didn't really agree with a lot of the stuff she said or did. I know parenting is hard and kids hate discipline, hell I know I did, and you want to rebel. But your situation is kind of different, Ami. You were raised on a farm with all these other kids and most of the staff mistreated you in one way or another. Some might have been kinder but usually it's the bullies who dominate and set the tone. Modern therapy says you have to face the demons, process the negative experiences, and jeez and you had a ton of those. You learned that people can be mean, vindictive, destructive. There are going to be a whole lot of times up ahead when you get triggered by a memory or an incident. Just like today. I don't know what spooked you, but something clearly did. Each time it happens it will feel like you're back there and you'll have a panic attack, feel trapped, you'll experience a whole lot of emotions that will overwhelm you. This making any sense to you?"

Ami slowly nodded and closing her eyes moment, letting his voice wash over her. She found his voice comforting somehow.

"I'm not a tough love kind of guy. I got all that from my father without any of the love. Look at me, I'm seventy-five years old and the scars I got from my father have never left me. Never. I can still hear the sliding sound of his belt coming off so he could beat me, even the sight of him coming home from work used to terrify me. I'm not saying this to make you feel sorry for me – I'm telling you this because none of the things that have happened to you were your fault. None of them.

"You'll never forget the shit that happened but and this is where my wife and I differed, I believe you can put them to one side, lock them away in a box. They'll always be there, every time you get triggered. Stuff from the past or even the recent past. A gunshot goes off, you'll be right back in that hotel room with me and Stan, terrified we might die on the floor there, or driving for our lives on the cornfield, no one will ever believe it, but it happened. You can bet I'll be having nightmares about all that down the road. This is normal. Therapists talk about processing it. Maybe one can make sense of it all, maybe you can't, but every day, you are going towards a future, your future, which no one, absolutely no one can prevent you from choosing. Sure, you'll make mistakes, we all make mistakes, I still make mistakes, but you'll learn from them. You're allowed to remember shit that happened to you, but you cannot let it shape your future. You're in charge of that."

Ami stared at him, Stan's paws on her legs now. She knew she was supposed to say something but what exactly.

Remy leaned forward and reached out a hand to her. She took it. He squeezed it gently.

"I think hugging, holding hands, loving your dog, and living one day at a time will get us through things. I promised you I am here for you, and I will keep that promise."

Ami found her voice at last. "How are you supposed to deal with it. You never know when it might happen. I just saw all those girls getting off the bus from The Order and froze. I thought I was safe here but they're *everywhere*, Remy. I don't know if I can deal with that. It was like – I dunno - like someone pressing a knife into my heart. They didn't do anything to me, nothing but ..." Ami took a deep breath. "They were there... at *our* beach."

Remy nodded, understanding the problem now. "First off, they aren't everywhere. They probably go to places where they think they can attract new members, right?"

Ami nodded.

"I was brought up to be a Christian. My father was a god-fearing, church going, pillar of the community. I went along with it for a while, but I hated it. Everyone we knew belonged to the Church and although the doctrine was supposed to be about a loving and life-giving God, we were taught to dislike, or look down on, all the Catholics or Zionists or Baptists. When the Priest was arrested for abusing the choir boys, I refused to go back. Couldn't believe my folks continued to go. I knew that Christians were everywhere around me and I developed a phobia that they were out to get me. It was stupid but I was about ten years old then and I heard in graphic detail from one of the choir boys what the priest did to the boy, and it shook me. Took me a long time to get over that and absolutely nothing bad happened to me at all."

Ami understood this only too well. "That's what happened to Paulo. He told me what happened to him. Father Tresor didn't really care, boy or girl, he got what he wanted."

Remy sighed. "That boy will never forget it, never forgive it, but if he wants to survive, he has to put it to one side. Never let that dominate his life, 'cause if he does, he won't be able to move forward. You understand?"

Ami nodded. "I worry so much about him."

"I know. But right now, it's all about keeping *you* safe from them. They can never hurt you again, Ami. Y'hear me? I will make sure of it."

Ami looked into Remy's eyes and could see he meant it. "I was really scared on the cornfield, Remy. I really thought we were going to die. You were like kinda enjoying it, I think."

Remy chuckled. "I was determined to survive it. That's all. Refuse to be a victim or a damn statistic."

"Stat what?" Ami asked frowning.

"Every year the incidences of mass shootings increase because everyone is allowed to carry guns. Every victim is a statistic. A number amongst numbers, their names don't matter. That's not how I choose to end my life, or yours."

Ami smiled. "In my nightmares, I want you to come to my rescue."

Remy grinned. "Just call and I will be there." He let go of her hand and settled back in his chair.

Ami rubbed her face. She knew he was trying to help but ...

"We haven't known each other long kid, but you should know that I've spoken to my lawyer and whatever happens to me, you're taken care of. I have to sign some papers when we get home, but know this Ami, I am asking to be appointed your legal guardian. That goes for Stan too. Wouldn't want to leave him out of the picture. You can change your name if you like, take my name. Only if you want to, of course."

Ami was confused. She'd only been half listening. She reached out and began to sip the tea. "Change my name?"

Remy smiled. "You could become a Mitchell, like me. There's something else too."

Ami stared at him barely comprehending what he was saying. "Something else?"

"You like this trailer home, huh?" Remy asked.

Ami nodded. "I love this place. Truly."

Remy smiled. "When I'm gone, it's yours."

"Gone?"

Remy sipped his tea. "You know what I mean ..."

Ami wiped her nose with a soggy tissue. "You're going to die soon?"

Remy laughed, then winced again because that hurt. "No. You don't get that lucky. I've got a bad back, that's all. It will get better. I'm just saying this place, this lot, will henceforth belong to you once I'm pushing up daisies. It's probably going to be more of a burden having to pay property taxes and all the little schemes they keep coming up with to extract money from homeowners, but it will be yours. Not much work around here I know but when you're qualified in something you'll be happy to know you have a safe place to go. A home no one can take away from you."

Ami felt her heart, it was beating fast. She could barely understand what he was saying. "Mine? What about Maisie? Won't she be angry?"

"Maisie's got nearly $200,000 coming to her when my wife's investments mature. She's taken care of and besides, I can leave my property to whomever I like. I'm hoping you won't immediately sell it. Even if you end up working far away from here, it's a great little bolt hole to hide away in, until Florida goes under water, of course."

Ami smiled. He had to mention that. "I love it here. I'd never ever sell it."

Remy was satisfied and sipped his tea. "Good. I'm hoping there's enough left of that soup of yours for our supper. I'm suddenly quite hungry."

Stan was licking his lips, turning circles to get comfortable on a cushion besides her. Ami wiped her eyes and got up from her chair and went over to Remy. She put her arms around him and embraced him, burying her face into his warm shoulder. "I don't really understand what you did or why you think I deserve it; but thank you Remy. Thank you. Please don't die. You're the best person I ever met."

Remy rubbed the back of her head, trying not to let on she was causing him pain. He didn't say anymore, but appreciated she was able to accept what he'd told her.

Ami broke away suddenly, staring at him. "Can I change my first name too? I never really wanted to be an Ami. Nor Ollie. Can I choose my own name?"

Remy smiled. "Of course. Take your time about it, a name is very important and make sure I remember it when you do. Old guys like me take time to remember names."

Ami smiled, satisfied, feeling her spirits lifting. "I'm going to make corn fritters. You like fritters?"

Remy chuckled. "You make what you like. I'll eat it. Fritters. Haven't heard that word in a long time."

Ami headed back towards the kitchenette and explored the cupboards. She'd seen corn flour and a few tins of corn in there earlier.

CHAPTER TWENTY-FOUR

A Music Lesson

On the Friday it was unexpectedly chilly, and Ami was looking for a rug in the old chest when she uncovered a pile of pictures with a slim black disc inside of them. She looked around for Remy and held one up for him to see.

"What are these?"

Remy peered towards her end of the room and broke into a broad smile. "My albums! You found them. Hell, I wondered where I'd put those."

Ami was no wiser. "But what are they?"

Remy considered his answer as he raised himself off the chair. "First, we have to find the record player, then, my girl, you are about to expand your consciousness, be sure you want to do this. Music can be very life altering."

Ami looked at him askance. "Now you sound like Father Tresor. 'Music is evil and will destroy your capacity to reason'.

Remy laughed and shook his head. "Yes, and all that. Music will affect your mind and your soul. That's what good music is supposed to do; and this is good music. Be prepared to be transported to another place."

Ami wasn't sure if he was joking or not.

"What have you got there?" Remy asked.

Ami looked down at the pile and read a title. "Blood Sweat & Tears."

Remy beamed. "Spinning Wheel. Still a classic track. Go on..."

Ami thumbed through the albums. "Sergeant Pepper's Lonely Hearts Club Band. Tapestry by Carol King, Cat Stevens 'Tea for the Tillerman'. Love the drawing. ELO and this one looks weird, San... tana, is that how you say that? Simon & Garfunkel sounds funny and Aladdin Sane. There's at least forty more here. This is all music?"

"Most definitely music. We will find the record player, make some tea, and give you a musical crash course in rock history."

"Rock?"

"Yep, it all comes under Rock Music even though some of would be considered soft rock now. This is what my generation listened to. Your generation has a completely different set of musicians, but you can discover them later. Better to get a foundation course in first so you can appreciate what real talent sounds like."

Remy seemed animated and searched every available closet and box until he found the record player. "Yes!" He cried out triumphantly. "You might hear some crackling; it was hard to keep a record clean and dust free. Must have played each one a hundred times at least. The only way to listen to music in my day was on a record player at home, or the radio. Not AM or course, only FM for music lovers. When the Beatles released a new album, they played nothing else for days. It was an amazing time for music back then. The Sixties was a time of breakthroughs and experiments. It sort of ended when disco came along and well, I'll spare you the pain of that for now." He began to set it up beside the very dusty CD player and connected wires to the speakers. "I see you've got the White Album there. I read somewhere that's worth money these days. So strange to know you've never heard any music till now, other than when we were at the hog roast the other night. You enjoyed that, right?"

Ami pondered that. She remembered dancing but couldn't recall the music at all. Maybe it was too late for her to enjoy music? But she loved seeing Remy so animated and wanting to share 'his music'.

"What if I don't like your music?" Ami asked.

Remy frowned and stood up straight looking very sternly at her. "Then you'd have to leave."

Ami's eyes widened in shock. "Leave?"

Remy let slip a sly grin. "You'll like. I promise you. There has to be something in this pile you'll love. Might even help you make sense of your life. That's what music did for me. We'll start off with Sergeant Pepper by the Beatles. Jesus, I remember lining up for hours to buy that album then racing home to listen to it with two of my school friends. We must have listened to it five times in a row discussing when it all meant and jeez; music was so important to us back then. Someone told me they sold 38 million copies since it was released. That's a lot of vinyl."

"What do I do?" Ami asked as she filled the kettle to make tea.

"Do?" Remy queried, confused.

"When the music plays."

Remy chuckled. "Just listen. Lie back on the bean bag and enjoy. That's what we did. Stan will like it too."

Ami nodded. Sounded odd. Maybe it was like back at the farm when they were supposed to contemplate the universe and tune in to the vibes. She'd always tuned out in those nightly sessions. At least it wouldn't be done in silence with one of the sisters patrolling to make sure they weren't sleeping.

She put a tea bag in each mug and waited for the kettle to boil. Remy was busy cleaning the record and checking for dust on the needle. She tried to imagine him the same age as her waiting to hear this precious record. She couldn't quite picture it.

"The Beatles were four young men from England that caught the imagination of the whole of America. Girls went mad for them, and guys learned to like them if they wanted a girl to like them. It sounds more complicated than it was. My favorite band changed all the time. One time Blood, Sweat and Tears, another day Chicago or The Beach Boys after they released Pet Sounds and got the good vibrations. America was at war and music got entangled with the peace movement. Later I'll introduce you to The Young Rascals and Motown and there's so much to learn."

Ami grinned. Remy was overwhelmed with memories and really excited to hear his old music again. The kettle boiled and she made the tea.

Remy glance up at her and saw her smiling. "Of course, back then we wouldn't be listening to music with hot tea. I drank beer back then, when I could get hold of it. You couldn't buy it until you were eighteen in those days. It's twenty-one now which is ridiculous. I stole my dad's stash."

"Did your father like your music?"

Remy looked surprised. "Him. No. He hated it. Too much noise. He was a Frank Sinatra, Dean Martin kind of guy. Was always yelling at me to turn the music down. That's why I worked so hard to get a college scholarship so I could escape. 'Turn off that crap." He'd yell, even in his sleep I think." Remy grinned. "I never did, at least not for long."

Remy beckoned Ami over. "I'm going to show you how to set the needle. Ok? Volume is preset. All you need is to drop the needle and when it gets to the end of this side, you pull the arm back to this rest point, flip the disc over, give it a quick wipe with the anti-static and put the needle back on."

Ami watched him take his tea back to his chair and settle down in it. "Now?" She asked.

"Now." Remy signaled.

Ami gently dropped the needle, heard the hiss, and watched it engage with the grooves. Loud music blared out of the speakers and Stan ran to the far end of the cabin in fright.

She went over to grab him and together they settled down to listen on Remy's old, battered bean bag as they were introduced Sergeant Pepper's Lonely Hearts Club band.

Lucy in the sky had just finished when there was a banging on the door. Remy angrily got up off his chair, still wincing with pain and stormed to the door. He hated his music being interrupted.

He opened up and his neighbor Chester was standing there holding two cold beers.

"You playing Sergeant Pepper?" he asked. "Couldn't help but hear it."

"Shit man, how did you get so old?" Remy asked, staring at their white-haired interloper.

The neighbor laughed. "Ditto dude. Am I coming in or what?"

Remy stepped aside and the neighbor came in as Remy closed the door behind him. "Find a place on the floor, if you can still get down there."

The man smiled at Ami and dropped to his knees, holding out a beer for Remy.

"Been meaning to say thank you for about twenty years. You're hardly ever here Remy. Where did you go?"

"I'm here now. What happened to your wife? I haven't seen her around."

"Passed away last year. Big C, she got it bad. I'm over it now."

"Sorry to hear that. We're educating Ollie here to good music. So, silence needed if you're staying."

The neighbor held up his hands. "Wouldn't have it any other way."

'Ollie' watched them both with fascination. They obviously knew each other well but had barely said hi to each other since Remy arrived, but the moment the music came on ... it was like there was an invisible connection.

She listened to the music again and closed her eyes as she stroked Stan. It was beginning to make sense to her. She loved the sounds of Mr Kite and could picture all kinds of strange things going on.

The second side had finished, and Ami wanted to hear it all again.

"Never saw them live," Chester complained. "They'd stopped performing before I was five. "You could get about four hundred bucks for that album now."

"Not for sale. It's Ollie's now. He's inheriting the whole collection. Got about fifty more albums back home."

The neighbor was impressed. "You are one lucky kid. Though to be honest I thought you were a girl when you stopped by the other day."

"Inside I'm a girl, outside I'm a boy," Ami told him without explaining why.

Chester rolled his eyes. "I am not even going there. Life is just too complicated these days. In one gender and out the other, hey."

Ami wasn't sure what he meant. Remy didn't comment either.

"What's next?" Remy asked her. "What did you like best?"

Ami got up to put the arm back on the rest. "I liked Lucy and Mr Kite. I want to hear this album next. I like the cover. She showed him Cat Steven's 'Tea for the Tillerman.'

"Now that was my mother's favorite," Chester told them. "God, 'Wild World', must've heard it a thousand times. She left us, y'know. Dad was pretty choked. My sister tracked her down and left to join her. Never saw either of them again."

Remy stared at their guest with astonishment. "I never knew that."

"Never told anyone before. Must be the damn music."

"Should I not play it?" Ami asked, interested to hear his story. She knew twenty odd other kids where something similar had happened to wreck their lives. They couldn't blame the music though.

He held up his hands. "Play it. I'm old now, I'm not going to cry. Fact is, I blamed Cat Stevens for ruining my family and it was nothing to do with him at all. My mother was hippy and hated being confined, I guess. Weirdest thing of all, I married a woman just like her."

He took a slug of the last of his beer. "You're lucky Remy. You're old, but you've got family. I never wanted a family because I didn't want them to be disappointed or whatever. Play it kid. There's some good songs on there. Don't mind me."

Remy handed him the beer he'd given him but not drunk. He signaled Ami to play the next album. "Put the Pepper album back in its sleeve first."

It was midnight before Remy called it a day. Chester had left after Amy had played America's album to them all. She'd loved 'A Horse with No Name' and read the lyrics even though Chester had mocked them a little. "The heat was hot,' he'd laughed, but Ami couldn't disagree, heat is hot, and it was a horse in the desert, it was bound to be dry.

Remy smiled at her when he'd gone. "I loved that song too. Used to listen to it all the time." He yawned. "Know what? That was the nicest evening I've spent in a long time. I watched you trying to make sense of it all."

"I was listening to the words. It's like everyone has something to say. Lots of songs about..." Ami searched for the right words. "Sadness and loneliness. I thought it would all be love songs."

"Artists write songs to make sense of our lives I guess, and most lives are a mess with a moment or two of happiness."

"Really?" Ami asked.

Remy nodded. "Grab any happiness with both hands, kid. Those are the good moments that really matter. I'm going to bed. Don't forget to take Stan out before you go to bed."

They both looked at Stan spread out on the floor. He'd crashed out hours before.

Ami smiled. "If I can wake him up. He likes to sleep."

Remy headed to the bathroom. Ami picked up the empty mugs and the beer cans. She was thinking about happiness. And music and that horse with no name. She was thinking about how wrong it was that she'd never been allowed to hear music and singing at the farm. It wasn't true what Lord Ramesh said, music didn't drive you crazy, it made you think, it made you dream.

She knelt down and rubbed Stan's flanks to wake him up. "Time to pee, Stan. Time to go."

Stan reluctantly stirred, stretched deeply and very, very reluctantly struggled to get up on all fours. Ami kissed the top of his head and whispered in his ears. He flapped his ears and followed her to the door. "Don't you go far," she told him as she opened the door.

Stan sniffed the night air and staggered out. Ami followed him and stared up at the stars, thinking again about Lucy in the sky with diamonds ...

CHAPTER TWENTY-FIVE

Homeward Bound

It was a whole week later before Remy felt he was able to drive again. Ami didn't mind one bit. She'd explored the neighborhood, met various neighbors, most seemed to be from Canada just down for the winter months. She loved it all and the fact that the ocean seemed to change every day depending on which way the wind was blowing. Stan had discovered he liked to swim. She didn't want to leave this place at all, but knew they'd have to. Remy was desperate to finish restoring his car. She'd persuaded Remy to buy her a sketchpad and some pens and had taken herself off to draw the old fishing boats by the ocean and secretly sketches of Remy when he was asleep and Stan, of course. She still regretted having to leave her sketches behind back at the farm, hidden in the barn. Only Paulo would know about those. There had to be at least twenty portraits of him growing up. She found peace drawing. She once drew Father Tresor, but it made her sick to even look at it and she'd burned it he'd looked so evil.

Ami was half asleep as they drove towards Remy's home. She was bewildered by the endless sprawl of homes and heavy traffic. She had no idea where she was. They seemed to have been driving forever. Remy was listening to his music and Stan was lying with his legs up in the air, his belly exposed, completely at ease in the truck.

"Is this where you live?" She asked, yawning.

"Awake?" Remy asked, glancing at her, smiling at Stan's relaxed pose.

"Hmmm. Sorry, I was supposed to be watching you." She felt guilty for having fallen asleep.

"I'm fine. A few days doing nothing seems to have done me good. You hungry?"

Ami thought about it a moment. "Yeah, I am. God, how long have you been driving?"

"We've made good time. Two hours since my last stop. We're close."

"Is this a town or city or what? I get confused by that."

"It's a neighborhood, which is part of a suburban sprawl. We're lucky. It was built laid out nearly a hundred years ago when people liked the idea of local stores and a golf course, not to mention tennis clubs. It's not the beach, I grant you, but my father bought this place off plan in 1970 and was happy here until he died. My wife liked it here. Couldn't get her off the Rivera Golf Course. Never found any interest in it myself; especially with a bad back. My Pa paid almost nothing for this place. He'd die of shock all over again to know how much its worth now."

Ami was fully awake now and shook the sleep out of her eyes.

Remy made a turn onto Shipping Avenue and drove onto the driveway of a small ranch house with an overgrown front law dominated by a large tree. He switched off the engine with a big sigh. He needed a shower, and a stiff drink, then think about food. The house looked ok. He couldn't believe it had been almost a month since he'd left to go to Canada. Never imagined in a month of blue moons he'd be returning with a teenager and her dog.

"I like the tree."

"You'll like it even more when it blooms. Jacaranda tree. It has pretty spectacular purple flowers. It was here before they built the house and luckily, they left it. It gets thirsty but the roots are deep, so it survives. I don't know why people don't plant more trees in their yards. Provides shade and it's good for the planet."

"I love trees."

Remy smiled. "Then you'll love it here. Most of the streets still have trees at least." He struggled with his back getting out of the truck but was glad to be home. "Come on, let's go inside, I'll show you to your room."

Ami was impressed by his home. It seemed huge to her, couldn't believe it was just for one person.

"Put Stan in the backyard. It's dog proof. He can't escape."

Ami was surprised. "You have a yard in the back too?"

"Got a row of cherry trees in the back. If you like cherries this is the place to come in season. If the birds don't get there first."

Ami grabbed her things and picked up Remy's bag as well and followed him to the front door. Stan was there first, curious to see inside.

Remy fumbled with the key. "Any pooping, you pick up. I have some bags by the front door and the back. Special bucket for dog poop in the back."

Ami made a note. She was going to have to get used to picking up poop.

Remy opened up and waited a moment for the trapped heat in the house to escape.

"I try to keep an even flow of air through the house, so we don't use the air-con so much. It's winter now so we're warm but it can get a bit unbearable in summer. That's usually when I head up the coast to the trailer and go fishing. Give me a minute to go to the bathroom and then I'll show you to your room. You'll find some dog bowls in the lower cupboard in the kitchen. He'll be thirsty."

Ami busied herself with watering Stan and getting him into the backyard. She had never expected this. Even the kitchen was bigger than the one at the farm. She had no idea people lived like this.

Remy reappeared. "Want to see your room? I'm hoping Maisie left it tidy."

Ami nodded and followed him down a long corridor. She noticed all kinds of pictures on the wall – a younger Remy with lots of people, all of them smiling.

"Who are these people?" She asked as he opened the end door.

"Astronauts, engineers, people I worked with over the years. Half of them are already gone. I should take them down. Makes this place look like a museum." He pushed open the red door and ushered Ami inside.

"Welcome home, Ami. This is your home now."

Ami stared at her room in total amazement. Remy watched her as she moved around the room examining closets, the bathroom, and the reading nook in the little bay window. She turned to Remy with a puzzled look. "This is just for me?"

"And Stan," Remy answered smiling. "He doesn't get his own room."

Ami sat down on the bed and buried her face into her hands. It was too much.

"You don't like it?" Remy asked, disappointed at her reaction.

Ami looked up at him and wiped a tear away. "This whole room is mine? It could sleep five people at the farm."

Remy exhaled. So that's what it was. "I'm hoping it's going to be just the two of you. I wasn't planning on five."

Ami took a deep breath. "I love it, Remy. I never slept alone before. Not with a door I can shut. And I can paint it?"

Remy glanced around the room and realized it looked a tad shabby. "Sorry, I never got around to doing anything in this room. You can do what you like I guess."

Ami looked around her, her face lighting up. "I want to make everything white and yellow. I always dreamt that one day I'd live in a bright room all of my own."

"White and yellow?" Remy queried. "That sounds cheerful."

Ami nodded enthusiastically. "Can I paint the floor too?"

Remy examined the old floor. It was genuine oak; he really didn't want it painted. "How about a nice white carpet, wall to wall instead."

Ami nodded. "Yes, that would be perfect."

"Better teach Stan to respect it, white can be pretty unforgiving."

Ami looked around for Stan but then remembered she'd put him out in the yard. "I will make sure he understands. No accidents."

Remy smiled. "Ok. I have some frozen dinners in the freezer courtesy of Maisie. I'll get them going."

"And the Studebaker?" Ami asked.

Remy grinned. "I was saving that till last. Remind me to get the steering wheel out of the lockbox."

"And then you'll take me out in it?"

"All being well, very soon, need to get it insured and re-registered. We should make an occasion of it. Drive over to South beach and show it off."

"South Beach?"

"Miami. Hmmm, might be a bit old hat these days. First, I have to make sure the battery's charged, and everything is working as it should. Don't want us to break down on our maiden voyage."

"I can help."

"You can and you will. But first shower, food, the necessities of life." He glanced at her empty closet. "You're going to need some clothes. Your first trip to the mall beckons. I hope you don't die of shock."

"The Mall?"

"It's where money goes to die. You'll see. Best you write down a list of all the things you want."

Ami shrugged. "I already have jeans, shoes, a tee-shirt. I don't need anything."

Remy smiled. "You might change your mind when we get there. Just because I only wear old clothes doesn't mean you have to. Besides we both need to wear something special when we go out in the car."

Ami was bewildered. Too many things to think about.

"I'm going to shower. You can too. There should be soap and shampoo in the bathroom unless Maisie cleaned us out. Pillows, sheets, and blankets are stored in the hall cupboard. Just take what you need."

Remy left her too it. Ami looked back at the big double bed and flung herself across it. She had a room of her own, at last. A whole giant room. And no one was going to take it away from her. She turned over and smiled. Stan was going to love it.

CHAPTER TWENTY-SIX

Paulo

Paulo was sweating in the heat of the kitchen. He was exhausted. He'd been working eight hours straight from lunch to dinner chopping, peeling, frying, stirring, but he was happy. The bounty hunter Jim had asked him what he wanted to do, and Paulo told him he loved cooking. He was hired on the spot by the Italian restaurant they were eating in. He hadn't exactly said that he was desperate for staff, but Paulo quickly realized no one else wanted to work this hard in St Pete for minimum wage.

At first it was just chopping and prepping, then after a week of not messing up, he was allowed to prepare food too. His sauces and soups were a hit immediately with the diners. He had nowhere to sleep at first but had found a balcony on an empty first floor apartment nearby to crash on, washing in the restaurant in the mornings. No one was more surprised than him to actually be paid cash at the end of the week. He stared at the money in wonder. He'd been doing this job for seven years already at the farm and this was the first time he'd seen money.

Franco, the owner recognized a bargain when he saw one and when he realized the boy was sleeping rough found him a room upstairs with access to a bathroom. Promised him, that if he worked hard, he would make him a chef inside of a year. Franco had never met someone so eager to learn and appreciate Italian cooking.

Paulo was surprised that no one mentioned his limp or asked him his age or even asked where he came from. The waitresses were nice to him, and one had even offered to help him with all the hard stuff about getting a social security number and a birth certificate once they were convinced he was 'American born'. He considered himself lucky. Completely shattered most nights but happier than any kid who had escaped the Order had a right to be.

CHAPTER TWENTY-SEVEN

The Golden Hawk

Ami stared at her steaming bowl of mush and frowned. “What are we eating?” She dipped her fork into the microwaved meal, slightly skeptical of the contents.

Remy laughed. “Beats me. Maisie never labelled anything. Some kind of ratatouille I’m guessing with spelt and oats. She was always trying to bring down my high cholesterol. If you don’t like it add ketchup. That’s what I do, or chutney. We have a secret stash I keep in the garage.” He winked at her.

Ami thought about it a moment as she chewed some more. “It’s a lot like the stuff they give us at the farm. Health food.”

“You got it in one. Maisie loved cooking but cooking didn’t love her so much. Everything looks right but somehow... anyway I trusted her to know what is good for me.”

Ami looked thoughtful as she swallowed a forkful. “I’ll cook for you. I want to learn. Do you have any cook books?”

Remy pointed to the shelf above the fridge/freezer. “About forty of them I reckon. My wife would buy them, try one recipe then when it didn’t taste right declare the author an imbecile and that would be that. As you already know I’m not allowed salt or sugar which kind of renders most recipes useless.”

Ami smiled. “I’d never add sugar to anything. Salt’s bad too? Lord Ramesh says a body need salt.”

Remy nodded. “In moderation. Keep to the no sugar path and you’ll most likely never need a dentist.”

Ami ate, Stan patiently at her feet hoping for a tidbit. She looked down at him. “You wouldn’t like it much Stan. Didn’t you eat just ten minutes ago?”

“Dogs never remember they just ate,” Remy commented. “I’m going to set up a meeting with my lawyer for you. She’s not too scary. She’ll guide us with the whole legal guardian process and getting you set up with a social security number and an ID card.”

Ami nodded. "I came up with a new first name too."

Remy was surprised. "You did?"

"Karina."

"Any specific reason why. I like it, but why Karina?"

"Karina was the teacher who taught me to read. I was five and new at the farm. She took me, and another girl called Tabytha to the barn and taught us words and how to write them. We both adored her, and we were heartbroken when she suddenly left. Something bad must have happened to her, I think. She was very anxious that we didn't tell anyone we could read. She said reading was like a secret escape passage and she was right."

"What happened to Tabytha?"

Ami frowned trying to remember. "Someone took her to hospital. She had scarlet fever, I think, and they were scared she might infect all of us. I heard later she got better, but she never came back to the farm. I was very lonely after that, but I had Karina's secret pile of books to read. She kept them behind a wooden panel in the barn. Bet you didn't read Charles Dickens when you were seven. I don't think I understood some of it but for a while I lived in old England, and it was a story full of orphans and thieves and somehow, I felt better about being an orphan. Even though my mother wasn't actually dead then."

Remy smiled. "I've read at least two Dicken's novels. Tale of Two Cities and Bleak House. Seven is pretty early to make sense of it all but he was a master story teller. Some of the words and expressions must have seemed so strange to you."

"I remember Mr Pickwick, and someone called Fezziwig and Mr Scrooge. I hated him. I loved the names. I can still see them in my mind and then poor Oliver Twist wanting more. That I understood very well. I was always hungry."

"Well in our Dicken's scenario, we have to get you into the system. You can't work without a social security number. The lawyer, Joanna might ask you awkward questions."

"Questions?" Ami looked worried.

Remy nodded. "I can't be there for legal reasons. She has to make sure you're doing this of your own free will. This is to protect me as well. She'll ask you about the farm, what you want to do with your life. She'll be suspicious you're after my money. That's her job to be suspicious."

"I'd never ..." Ami began to protest. Remy held up his hand to stop her.

"I know. You know. But her job is to make sure. It might seem harsh but it's all for your own good. If she agrees to process it, all your problems go away."

"I will work," Ami stated. "I'm not afraid of hard work."

"I don't doubt you for a second."

"And school?" Ami asked nervously. "Will I have to go to school?"

"At first, I thought you should but then I remembered you can get accreditation on-line these days. In fact, you can probably finish out school entirely on-line. You might be surprised how far ahead you are compared to many kids. One step at a time, Ami. We'll both be going through a learning curve. And don't worry about money. We'll work out something between you working, learning on-line and needing personal stuff. I invited you here and so that's on me. One way to pay me back is cook something better than Maisie."

Ami laughed. "That I can do. It's not so bad after the first mouthful."

Nevertheless, she still had butterflies in her stomach about seeing a lawyer and talk of school and just about everything really. What if the lawyer didn't like or believe her? She was scared to appear ignorant and be laughed at. That was what worried her most of all.

Remy gave her a reassuring smile. "You'll see, everything will work out. Never be afraid to ask me for something you want. Never be afraid to say no or be unable to tell me something that's bothering you. I will never judge you, never belittle you. I want you to have the best life you can and when I'm gone - which I have zero intention of doing anytime soon, you'll be safe, secure, and happy you made the best of everything."

Ami hated the word 'gone' but her emotions were crashing around inside her. This was her big opportunity to have a good life. The one she'd promised herself she'd have. But did she deserve it? She wasn't sure. Something really bad could happen and she could be dragged back to the farm, or worse become one of those girls with fake smiles recruiting new people to the Order.

"Tomorrow, I'll show you the neighborhood. Lots of people come here to eat and experience the local charms. There's even a bookshop, which you'll love. Lot of history here in the Grove. A long time ago you could catch a Pan Am seaplane to South America right down by

Dinner Key. Wish I could have seen that."

"Seaplane?"

"A passenger airliner that takes off and lands on water. Only small ones take off on water now but must have been an amazing sight back in the thirties." He noticed she'd only eaten half her portion. "We finished?" Remy asked. "We have a lonely vehicle awaiting our attention."

Ami grabbed another mouthful and abandoned the rest. "I'll finish it later." She was excited to see Remy's car.

Remy flicked the garage lights on and there it was. A gleaming, almost perfect Studebaker Golden Hawk in showroom condition (bar the missing steering wheel).

Ami stared at the car in wonder. It was so much better than the one she'd seen in Richmond. "It looks brand new," she whispered in awe.

Remy grinned, pleased at her reaction. "It does. New leather, new carpets, seven coats of paint. Hard to believe it was once in pieces on the garage floor here."

"How many years did it take?" Ami asked, gingerly opening a passenger door to peer inside. "Smells like ... I don't know what it smells like, but I like it."

"Money," Remy chuckled. "That's what it smells like. We'll get the steering wheel attached in a couple of days and get it ready for the road."

Ami glanced back at Remy sighed. "It's truly beautiful."

Remy beamed. "It is. My late wife considered this restoration a monumental waste of time, but now it's almost ready, I don't resent a moment. Not even the time spent cussing the rusted screws that wouldn't come out or were stripped or the time I nearly crippled myself messing around with the cylinder head. It's frustrating trying to find spare parts and caused endless delays, but I never gave up. I just couldn't. I had to finish it."

Ami came over and gave him a hug. "I can't wait to go out in it. You're right I can't go in these clothes. I need something special, has to be white to match the car. Nothing else will do."

Remy grinned. "I guess I'll have to dig out my father's old sports coat. It's cream, but he was very proud of it. We'll be like two movie stars driving down the highway."

Ami wasn't entirely sure what a movie star was, but she understood anyway. Stan wandered in licking his lips.

"Can Stan come too?"

Remy thought about it. "Only if he wears socks. No scratching the leather allowed."

Ami laughed and bent down to hug Stan. "Hear that, Stan. You're going to be wearing socks. You're going to be a star too!"

CHAPTER TWENTY-EIGHT

The Lawyer

They walked along Virginia Street from Remy's house to his lawyers building in the Grove. Stan wanted to sniff everything, and Ami was curious that every lot was different and some houses, most really, had clearly been torn down to build condos. She loved the tree lined streets. She pointed to a bright purple creeper that covered the walls of one house.

"Bougainvillea." Remy informed her. "It's great to look at but a bitch to prune. Sharp thorns. It's growing on my back wall at home, only mine's more orange."

"I love it. So sad they've torn down all the homes like yours."

"Last ten years has been brutal for tear downs. One day when I'm gone, they'll tear down my place and cram an apartment block on the site. But I'm hanging on as long as I can. I like this neighborhood precisely because it isn't built up."

"That would be tragic," Ami told him and meant it.

They approached the lawyers building and Remy pointed out the crowds around all the restaurants. "People come from all over to eat here. Most of the locals go to Berries on 27th. It's a well-kept secret from the visitors."

He noted with disappointment that the flower store he used to go to was now a Starbucks. He turned to Ami with an encouraging smile. "I'll walk you up, then come back down and take Stan for a walk."

Ami shook her head. "Don't go. I'm terrified."

Remy squeezed her shoulder. "She won't bite. She might ask some awkward questions though, like if you've transitioned, since you're dressed as a boy."

Ami stared at him confused. "Trans what?"

Remy sighed. "A lot of kids, girls in particular want to be boys now."

"Why?"

Remy shrugged. "That's not something my generation can quite fathom, but it's a fact. Tell her exactly why your dressed as a boy and she'll understand your situation better. Don't hold back. It might help you oddly enough, she'll understand the pressure you're under not to be recognized by the Order. I've sent her a photo of your mother's death notice in the local paper. It's useful as it lists you as surviving her."

Ami bit down on her lip. She had wondered about that. Somehow it only made her feel worse. She looked at Remy and Stan, dizzy with doubts. "You really want to be my legal guardian? I mean, I might turn out a mess. I might be just like my mother and ..."

Remy squeezed her shoulder again. "You would never abandon a child. You ran away and took your dog. You're strong and determined. I have every faith in you that you will turn out just right. Now let's get going. She won't appreciate us being late. By the way, she's a sucker for spaniels, so be nice to her dog."

Ami nodded, for some reason this made her feel a lot better. She trailed after Remy into the four-story building and into a freezing cold lobby. They took the elevator to the top floor.

"When you're done, wait for me outside Starbucks." He gave her ten bucks. "Buy yourself a coffee."

Johanna, the lawyer closely observed Ami as she nervously sat across the desk from her stroking her over enthusiastic spaniel.

"He can smell Stan on me, he's an Australian sheep dog." Ami said. "So someone told me."

"That dog of yours is a long way from home." Johanna remarked drily.

Ami tried not to stare at the woman's red hair piled up on her head, wondering if it was natural. She looked impatient, like someone forced to do something they didn't want to do.

"You like dogs then." She observed.

Ami nodded. "I love Stan. He saved me. I was so unhappy but from the moment he was born at the farm he was devoted to me."

Johanna remained impassive and scribbled some notes. "How would you describe your relationship with Remy?"

"Relationship?" Ami asked confused.

"What is he to you?"

Ami thought about it a moment. "Kind, thoughtful, he loves Stan too. I never met anyone like him before. He won't admit it, but I think he's been lonely for a long time."

"So, you think you'd be his carer?"

Ami frowned, was this a trap? "He doesn't need a carer. He can look after himself. He wants me to stay. I didn't ask, if that's what you mean. I never asked for anything except a toothbrush and a sketchpad."

Johanna looked at her more carefully. "You have good teeth. Did they have a dentist as this farm?"

Ami nearly laughed; it was a stupid question. "No doctors, no dentists, no sugar. Tough luck if you got sick. The power of prayer will cure you."

Johanna allowed herself a flicker of a smile. "And if it doesn't?"

"They die or someone takes them away," Ami answered. "We'd never see them again. I got sick once. Really bad and I couldn't breathe and was vomiting..." She took a deep breath remembering. "Sister Ryan told me to prepare to die and think myself into a happy place."

"A happy place?" Johanna asked gently.

"That's what were trained to do. Project yourself into a happy place. I guess I projected feeling better. I sweated so much the other girls had to change the sheet five times that night but in the morning the fever was gone."

"So, no one called a doctor or..."

"The Order doesn't permit outsiders. Even the teachers who came in belonged to a different chapter of the Order. I got lucky I guess."

Johanna scribbled more notes. Ami wondered what she was writing.

"Tell me, Ami, whose idea was this legal guardianship."

Ami shook her head. "Not me. Stan might have something to do with it. He doesn't want to lose Stan."

"Your dog."

Ami nodded.

"And do you want Remy to be your guardian?"

Ami smiled. "I do. I know it sounds selfish, but I sleep alone with Stan for the first time in my life, not counting when I was in lockup."

"Lockup?"

Ami shrugged. "The jail on the farm. I disobeyed an order. I just couldn't kill the chicken. I'd raised her from a chick. They make all the kids raise a chicken or a lamb and then after a while cut their throats. I refused."

Johanna blinked, furiously scribbled some more notes. "Describe this lockup."

Ami pictured it. "It's an old pigsty with a metal gate. No bedding, no water, a hole to piss in and you only get a meal every other day. There's no electricity and it stinks. Freezing cold in winter as there's no glass in the window either."

"How long where you in there?"

"Two weeks the first time, then another two weeks because I still wouldn't kill the chicken. They killed it anyway and made me eat it. I went sick for a week."

"How old were you when this happened?"

Ami had to think about it. "Ten, maybe nine. It's hard to remember how old you are because the Order doesn't celebrate birthdays. Don't celebrate anything except the Solstice in June and the harvest in September. Once Stan was born, I knew if I ever was thrown into lockup again, they'd kill him. Father Tresor hated Stan. Stan would growl at him if he ever came near me."

"And you were at this farm from the age of five?"

Ami nodded. "My mother left me there. I never saw her again."

"And when exactly did you decide to suddenly go looking for her?"

Ami took a moment to draw breath. "I knew Father Tresor was building up to having his way with me. He kept on touching me and rubbing up against me when no one was looking. I'm not blind, I know what he wanted, and he'd already gotten other girls pregnant. I've seen them after he's finished with them, they're like broken. They disappear pretty quick when they start showing when the Sisters find out. I don't know where they go.

"I was on cleaning duty for his office and dreading his return from town when I found my file. Didn't even know I had a file, but I guess every kid there had. I found letters in there she had written me. I didn't have time to read all of them but there was an address on one of them. She said she regretted never coming to see me. The moment I had that I decided to leave. Couldn't tell anyone, except Stan, of course. Left early in the morning when I was sure everyone was asleep. It's a long walk to the road."

Johanna made more notes. "Father Tresor, you said. He was a priest?"

Ami shrugged. "The man in charge is called Father, the other men are called Brother, and all the women are Sisters. That's the Order."

Johanna frowned, then wrote it down. "So, all in all you spent ten years there."

Ami nodded. "I think I'm sixteen soon. I arrived the day after my fifth birthday, but I can't remember the exact date. Just remember crying a lot. Weeks probably."

"And you never tried to run away before?"

"Thought about it a million times, but the ones who ran were always brought back by the cops and stuck in the lockup for a month or more."

"However, this time you ran."

Ami closed her eyes; it didn't seem to her that this interview was going well. "I had to go. I was next. I knew it. The moment I found my mother's address I knew it was a sign. I had to go. Stan followed; he wasn't going to let me go without him."

Johanna frowned and looked back at her notes.

"And Remy Mitchell just happened to be there."

Ami nodded. "It was raining hard. I was soaked and Remy was taking a piss at the side of the road, he has to pee a lot. Stan ran on ahead and jumped into his cab. Stan loves riding on the tractor and well when Remy saw me, he said get in. I wasn't sure, but Stan has good instincts about people."

Johanna looked at another document on her desk. "Has Remy promised you anything?"

Ami sighed. "He said I can have his trailer home when he's gone, but that was just his bad back talking. He's better now and I'm sure he forgot that already."

"So, you don't think he'd go through with it."

"Remy doesn't owe me anything. I'd never ever take anything that wasn't mine. He's a good person. I don't want him to die. No one as nice as him should die. I promise I'll take care of him and make him proud. I'm a good worker. Not afraid of hard work."

"And boys?" Johanna asked, looking at her directly.

"Boys?" Ami asked, puzzled.

"What if you meet a boy or a girl, I suppose I must ask. What then? Wouldn't Remy be a bit inconvenient for you?"

Ami twigged what she was asking. "I ... I don't really trust anyone."

"But you trust Remy."

"Of course. We've survived being shot at, him passing out at the wheel, to tell the truth I never want to leave him. He saved me and I saved him, and I will take care of him. No one ever paid any attention to me, ever and he's like the first person who thinks I could be someone, could be worth something."

Johanna noted the passion in her voice and glanced at her computer screen a moment. "I checked on your birth mother, Ami. She registered your birth in Orlando. You were born there on February 5th. It doesn't state the name of any father. I have requested her death certificate, which would officially confirm you are an orphan and therefore Remy would be able to be your legal guardian. You could also be formally adopted, if you wanted to be. Would you be alright in taking his name?"

Ami blinked. "His name? Yes. I want to. I want to change my first name too, so the farm can never ever find me."

Johanna nodded. "That's possible. Please write the name you wish to be known as. Initial it. You might be interested to know that Federal investigators are looking at the Order and have already visited the farm following Remy's tip off. Sadly, the children were removed just days after you ran away. The farm staff are being interviewed and will no doubt confirm your story. Once they have a court order, they will visit this Lord Ramesh's estate in Charleston where they believe the children were taken. Apparently, they found graves at the farm. Do you have any idea of who might be in those graves?"

Ami frowned. She'd heard rumors of course. But never seen any graves and she was sure she knew every inch of the farm.

"I never saw any graves but there were stories about babies and ..." She tailed off. She didn't want to think about it. "If anyone died, they were cremated at the back of the barn. It's against the Order rules to dig a grave."

"You witnessed a cremation?" Johanna asked.

Ami nodded. "Like I said, you didn't want to get sick at the farm. Was it wrong to cremate them? Lord Ramesh said it was a purification ceremony. We all said prayers for a successful transformation."

Johanna tried to hide her reaction to that. "I'll pretend I didn't hear any of that and leave it up to the FBI. Ami you are aware that Remy is a lonely old man, right? You're here today so I can ascertain that you will not abuse the privilege that he is affording you. He's very honorable and old fashioned. I would like to think that you are honorable too."

Ami dug her fingers into her hands. Was this going better now? "I swear I am. I wouldn't let anyone harm him. I promise. I want him to be happy and proud of me."

"Put your preferred name, pronoun, and signature on this form. I will submit if for authorization in due course. Congratulations you have been appointed a legal guardian."

Ami was amazed. "That's it?"

"That's it. There are formalities but you will get confirmation in the mail."

Ami stared at her open mouthed. "I feel sick," she whispered. "I feel..."

"No one has any claims on you now. By sheer chance and a possible intervention by God, you happened on the one man who gives a damn. Don't abuse it. I will be checking on your progress. I am Remy's lawyer, and I will protect him. If you have further questions, I'm here and I answer emails ... eventually."

Ami took a deep breath. "Remy was going to teach me about emails."

Johanna laughed. "Don't rush. There quite enough of those out in the universe. I'm sure you'll be teaching him about stuff in no time at all. Off you go. Take things slow, you have a big hill to climb. Was there anything you wanted to ask?"

Ami rose up in a daze and made her way to the door wondering about this 'big hill'. She turned briefly and said, "There is one thing. I had a friend, Paulo. I left him behind. If he's in Charleston, I'd like to know. Remy says I can't make contact, but I'd just like to know he's safe. Paulo Mancini."

Johanna wrote the name down. "I can make no promises. From what I hear that Order of yours is well protected by the politicians they contribute to. You can ask Remy what that means, but I will try. You take care of that man, y'hear?"

"I will. And thank you, thank you."

Johanna offered her a brief surprised smile. "Duly noted."

CHAPTER TWENTY-NINE

Want chocolate with that?

Ami came down from the lawyer's office with her head spinning. What had been agreed? What did legal guardian actually mean? Did she have responsibilities now?

There was no sign of Remy or Stan. She didn't really want a coffee, but the sign said the outside seats were for customers only, so she felt obliged to go inside and buy one. What she really needed was some alone time to think about what had happened to her and about all those questions from the lawyer.

It was empty inside. The Barista stared at her expectantly as Ami stared at the list of choices. It was bewildering.

"So, what would you like?"

Ami grimaced. She wasn't sure at all. She desperately looked for a sign that just said 'coffee', she had no idea what Flat White or Latte or Chai or even an Americano meant never mind short, tall, grande, and venti. She was paralyzed by the choices.

The Barista looked at her more carefully. "Your first time in here?"

Ami nodded, not sure she was allowed in. "I'm not even sure I like coffee."

The Barista smiled. She couldn't even remember the last time they had a newbie in the building. "We've also got tea, chai, juices, hot chocolate."

Ami seized on hot chocolate. She'd tasted chocolate once at the farm when they were sat around a fire, one of the Sisters had a rare moment of sharing. "Hot chocolate," Ami barked to stop all the choices coming at her. "I'll try that."

"Wow, you never had hot chocolate before? Want whipped cream with that and syrup?"

Ami shook her head and mumbled "No." Only the Sisters got the cream on the milk at the farm. Paulo said that was why they were all so fat. "Just hot chocolate please."

"We've got marshmallows if you ..."

Ami backed away. "No, no..."

Marshmallows brought back horrible memories of the same camp fire. Toasting them and each kid being made to eat them straight from the fire and burning their mouths. The Sisters laughing at them as they spat them out, some crying in pain. She remembered it tasted like a hot sweet slug and shuddered.

"You ok?" The Barista turned her head to check on her as she prepared the drink. "We don't get many first timers in here. I remember my first time, too much choice right."

Ami nodded, wishing she could disappear.

"Your name?"

Ami looked puzzled.

"So I can write it on the cup."

Ami was about to answer Ami but stuttered out a "K.K. Karina."

The barista wrote it on the cup.

Another customer entered with a small child in tow. Ami felt relieved the focus was off her. She took out the ten dollar note and showed it to the Barista. She took it and handed back some change. She pointed to the end of the counter. "Wait for it down at the end."

Ami complied and patiently waited, thinking that every time she would be going into any store it would be like this. She didn't think she'd ever get used to it. She must look so simple to the girl behind the counter, then berated herself as she remembered Lord Ramesh's word that simple people should be respected and helped. She closed her eyes. How would she ever empty her head of all the teachings of Lord Ramesh. Or forget all the mean things they ever did to her.

She took her steaming cup of hot chocolate outside, relieved to be alone again. She resolved to keep a diary of everything she'd done, everything she did must be written down, so she'd know how to behave in the outside world. Even that thought needed correcting because she needed to remember she was free now – she belonged to the outside world.

The hot chocolate tasted too good. It had to be bad for her. The Sisters were always saying anything that tasted good was bad for you.. Probably something to do with sugar.

She saw an ambulance go by, sirens blaring, driving fast. It was quickly followed by another. She instinctively knew something bad had happened nearby. A cop car flashed by, and Ami wondered if there had been another shooting. Then she had a sudden thought that Remy might be involved. He was out walking Stan.

Now she began to worry. Where were they? She didn't want to disobey his order to wait for him at Starbucks but what if something bad had happened? So bad it needed two ambulances. She was just trying to decide whether to go when Stan came running towards her, trailing his lead. He leapt up on her desperate to say hello, trembling like he did if he had been frightened.

"Where's Remy? Where's Remy, Stan?"

Stan was hot, panting, his eyes full of panic. Ami abandoned the remains of her chocolate, grabbed the lead, and headed back the way he'd come from.

"Find Remy, Stan. Find Remy."

They ran four blocks before they caught up with the ambulances stopped outside a huge liquor store. Two ambulance crew members were wheeling a woman out of the building on a gurney. Ami couldn't see if she was alive or dead. The other ambulance crew was leaving already, no doubt called to another job.

Stan pulled her towards the curb and Ami reluctantly followed, still not sure whether Remy was involved in any of this. It made no sense as to why he would be.

That's when she saw two legs sticking out under an old car in the parking area. Remy's easy grip shoes attached to the feet. She could hear his voice. 'No, try it the other way. Needs a new clamp either way. I have to go, the dog's escaped."

Ami approached the car and knelt down. "Remy?"

"Pull me out, Ami. I can't move. Pull me out."

Ami made Stan sit and on pain of death move from that spot. She grabbed Remy's ankles and pulled. Remy slowly appeared, his face covered in grease, but otherwise in good shape. There was another man under the car trying to fix something and cussing loudly.

Remy sat up, surprised to see Stan. He looked a bit shamefaced. "Jeez, I'm sorry, Ami, but Stan just bolted when ambulances arrived, sirens blaring. I thought he was tied to the bike rack there." He pointed to the rack but then saw how it was bent and Stan must have pulled hard enough to get free of it in his panic to leave.

She wanted to scream at him. He'd let Stan escape! Ami helped him up, stomping on Stan's lead in case he got any other ideas. She was extremely angry with Remy but tried to keep it in check. Didn't he know by now how important Stan was to her.

She took a deep breath, biting on her bottom lip to contain her fury. "It's ok. He found me; he ran the right way."

Remy looked very guilty. What if Stan had run the other way? There were many very busy roads. "I'm so sorry kid. I went under the car to help but then I couldn't move. If it wasn't for the sirens ..."

The owner of the old car finally stood up wiping grease off his hands. "I guess someone had a heart attack."

"Happened so fast." Remy said. "Damn, I know you're angry with me, Ami. I don't blame you. I was careless. Just wanted to help a guy out and ...."

Ami blinked away a tear. Stan was ok. He'd run like this before when the farm tractor had backfired. She'd had to search every inch of the farm for him. He'd run miles, not a thought in his head except to get away. Same at the hotel in Richmond after the gunshots. He was mortally afraid of loud noises.

Remy glanced towards the car owner. "Meet Jet. He owns this old Thunderbird here. 1956. It's a beauty. What do you think? European style in those days, clean lines."

Ami wasn't in any mood to appreciate yet another old car but held her tongue. Stan was safe. He'd run back towards the lawyers building. Sheer chance she was there to greet him.

The man, Jet, who owned the Ford nodded towards her. "Sorry your dog got loose, kid. Must have been terrifying for him. Sirens make my heart race too."

Ami offered a weak smile. It would be long while before she'd trust Remy with Stan again, if ever.

Remy took Ami's arm. "We should go. I can't apologize enough about Stan. I'm so sorry, Ami. I know I messed up."

Ami relented a little. "He does get scared easily."

Remy remembered where she'd been. "How did it go?"

Ami was jolted back to the moment. "I think ok. It was over so fast."

Remy frowned. "So, am I your Guardian now?"

"Guardian?" Ami asked then frowned. "I think maybe I should be *your* guardian."

Remy took that on the chin. "Yes, I deserve that. I know you're angry with me. I can't apologize enough. Remind me again what you want to be called. I'll have to practice it ten times a day, more probably."

Ami smiled. "Karina." Just saying it out loud sounded strange even to her. "Karina. No more Ollie. I might keep my hair short though. I'm getting used to it."

Remy just smiled. He waved at Jet who was getting back into his Thunderbird. "Good luck man. Maybe see you at the showground."

Jet grinned. "Looking forward to seeing your Studebaker."

"Showground?" Ami asked as they walked back to Remy's home, Stan's lead firmly gripped in her hand.

"Pinetree Concours d'Elegance auto show. There will be medals up for grabs. Remind me to see if we can get a late entry. It's not like the one in Palm Beach. There's a show in Boca Raton next year we could drive to. The holy grail of collector's shows is at Pebble Beach, but that's in California and way too many miles for me to drive or the Hawk. One day maybe we could drive all the way up to the South Bend Indiana and enter the Concours there at Copshalom Mansion. Check out the Studebaker National Museum too." He glanced at her. "Maybe when you get your driver's license. It's a long drive for me."

Ami was surprised. "Can't wait for that. Make sure you enter the show. You'll win easily."

"You think? They'll be other cars there, and they'll all be pretty damn keen to win a medal too."

"When is it?"

"Two weeks, I think. We'd better get polishing and get you that white dress."

Ami nodded, calmer now. She wasn't sure who to blame the most, Stan or Remy but she didn't need shocks like that. Living without Stan was not an option.

"I'll need to call Hagerty and get her insured, bet that will cost me plenty. Owning a classic car ain't cheap." He sighed and glanced at her again.

"I'll take you to Bal Harbor to get that dress. My wife was a big Nordstrom fan."

Ami didn't care where they went, as long as she could get a white dress.

"Stan will have to stay home or in the truck. You're about to discover that Florida isn't as dog friendly as you'd like. Did you like Johanna, by the way?"

Karina wrinkled her nose. "She's scary. Even her hair is scary."

"Yep, but she's honest. A good woman. Looks out for me. She wouldn't have said yes if she didn't like you."

Ami was surprised he thought she liked her.

"You hungry? We need to celebrate. I'm thinking fish. We have to celebrate you becoming a Mitchell."

Ami smiled. "In that case I'm hungry."

Remy nodded. "Good, remind me to talk about an allowance. As soon as we get you an ID and you turn 16, we will set you up with a bank account. Don't want you to have to ask for money to buy essentials. My father made me work for pocket money. I had a list of duties this long," he held his arms out wide. "He was a pretty mean man most of the time, but always paid the pocket money. Must have been a shock for him when I moved out and he had to pay the going rate for people to do all that stuff."

"I can work."

"You will. Gaining a respect for money is an essential skill. Did she find out your birth date?"

Ami nodded. "February 5th."

Remy smiled. "You're an Aquarian. That figures."

"A what?"

"Your star sign. To be discussed. Maisie was obsessed with star signs but Virgo, so we were never destined to get along. My wife was the same. She only liked three star signs and mine wasn't among them."

Ami had no idea what he was saying but smiled anyway.

"I discovered I like hot chocolate today." Ami remembered to tell him.

Remy laughed. "Good on you. Discovering what you like is important, then you'll need to learn what is good for you and what isn't. Those two things are often incompatible."

Ami nodded. "I was afraid of that."

As they waited to cross the road Remy abruptly turned and drew her towards him for a hug. "Forgive me being stupid and old and letting Stan escape. I'll never let it happen again."

Ami hugged him back. "Stan's got a lot to learn too."

Remy nodded. "He does, but the main thing is we're a family now. Sounds strange when I say it but that's what we are. The three of us will make it work, ok?"

Ami closed her eyes a moment content to be held, then drew back as he smelled of oil and grease. “We need to get you clean before we go eat.”

“That bad huh? His Thunderbird looks good up top, but underneath is a mess. Too bad. You have to pay attention to all the details if you want a medal.” He broke away. “Karina, we’re going to Monty’s, the best fish restaurant in in the Grove. Clams, lobsters, Mahi-Mahi, and swordfish fresh from the ocean. They’ve got it all. You’ll love it.”

“Ok.” Ami was surprised to discover they were back at Remy’s house already. She looked across the road at the cramped condos built onto the lot and frowned.

“Never let them tear your house down, Remy. It’s so pretty. Promise me you’ll never let them do that.”

Remy chuckled. “I’ll do my damnedest.”

Amu smiled and finally let Stan go to explore the front yard. This was the start of a whole new life.

CHAPTER THIRTY

Concours d'Elegance

The garage door rose stiffly. It had been a long time since it was last opened. The newly minted Karina sat serene in the front seat in her oh so perfect white dress, white scarf, and white gloves (Remy had insisted). Behind her an excited Stan stood wearing his white socks, that he'd already tried to chew off and only a very firm final warning from his mistress made him desist.

Remy was wearing an off-white sports jacket, straw hat, tan trousers, and his comfortable suede shoes. She'd never seen him look so smart and it made him seem so much younger.

He opened his door and slid into place, closing it firmly after him, satisfied at the sound it made. He glanced at her. "I'm nervous," he confessed. "Can't believe this is finally happening."

Karina was excited. "Are we going to move?"

Remy took a deep breath and started the engine. It caught first time. It was louder than he remembered.

He eased the car out of the garage until they were well clear of the doors. He pressed the button and the doors closed without a hitch. "We are at launch Minus 1. You ready?"

"I've been ready for hours," Karina answered. "How far do we have to go?"

"About thirty miles or so. Optimal cruising speed will be around fifty-five, be prepared for anything."

"Let's go!" Karina shouted. "I want you to win a medal."

"If there's a medal for best polishers then you will have it my girl. This car has never ever looked so good."

He drove to the end of the drive, checked for traffic, and moved out onto the road.

"See if you can find us some music. You're the DJ." Remy told her.

Karina switched on the radio and hunted for a station she liked. She'd had good practice whilst polishing the car. "This ok?"

Remy listened for a moment and was surprised. "What d'ya know, they still play Tom Petty."

They drove through the neighborhood, windows open, Karina's white scarf flying around her. They saw people pointing and staring and Remy was happy to see his car was getting a good reaction. The engine seemed to have settled down too, just low burble at 30 mph. Remy was listening carefully. "Eight cylinders, a lot of smooth power under that hood. Built like a battleship."

"What's it like to drive?" Karina asked.

"A lot easier than the truck. You'll get your chance when you turn sixteen."

"Not many months now."

"What will you want for your birthday?"

Karina shook her head. "I've got everything I need. I'll make a cake. Never made a cake before."

"We shall make the best cake. I'm thinking we'll invite Maisie and her boyfriend over."

Karina made a face. "She hates me."

Remy smiled, there was probably some truth in that, even if Maisie had never met her. "Yeah, but she'll want to see the girl who's got me twisted around her little finger."

"Twisted?" Karina queried.

"She's suspicious it all happened so fast, but she doesn't know what you and I have been through, or your history at the farm." Remy indicated he was joining the highway and began to accelerate. "Here we go. Say a prayer for the Golden Hawk."

Karina looked back at Stan who'd curled up on the backseat rug, one sock missing already. She looked around the interior with pride. "This is a beautiful car."

"Wait till we get to the showground. You'll see a hundred collectors' vehicles. This is like a day of time travel for you."

Karina frowned looking at him. "Every day is time travel with you."

Remy grinned, watching his speed to match the other traffic. "We're living in my future. When I was a kid, I imagined a completely different future to what we've got, but if you think about it, everyone thinks they're living in the present, but this was always someone's future."

Karina stared at him and shook her head. "You're crazy. You know that right?"

Remy smiled. "Just think what your future will be like in 2080 or 90. Then try explaining what 2025 was like to your grandkids. They'll shake their heads and pity you, probably. You did what? You ate that? No way."

Karina smiled to herself, yes explaining her life to anyone when she seventy or more was going to be impossible. She got it now. 2025 was Remy's future and they were going there in a car that was nearly seventy years old, a car that looked like the future back then. Her brain hurt just thinking about it.

A SUV drove alongside them, and people inside started taking photos, waving, and smiling. "Nearly seventy and she still turns heads," Remy said with a grin, as they watched the SUV speed away. "This is why we drive her."

Start me Up by The Rolling Stones came on the radio and Remy turned the volume up. He was happy.

"Oh wow - you weren't kidding," Karina exclaimed as they drove into the old showground. Remy flashed his entrance ticket on his phone. They gave him a number and a sticker for his windshield, and they were pointed towards which row to go down. There were at least one hundred old cars lined up with people strolling by and examining them.

"We're in the Studebaker section," Remy informed her as they negotiated the rows, heads turning as they drove past other vehicles. He turned to Karina a moment. "Your job is find me a washroom PDQ. Got it?"

Karina nodded. "On it. Can I look at the other cars after."

"That's why we're here. I'll stay here a while. Go check out the Chevy Roadster next row. Oh, I see there's some old Jaguars. Nice. Go steal an E-Type for me." He chuckled then winced. "And find that washroom fast."

Karina smiled. She was beginning to understand what was cool and what wasn't in old cars. Remy backed into his slot. "Don't let Stan pee on any hubcaps, they'll get a bit antsy about that kind of thing."

Stan was anxious to get out, sniffing the new smells. Karina noticed he'd gotten all his socks off now.

"You are a very naughty boy," She told him. He wagged his tail and licked her face.

They were parked up beside an Avanti, the owner giving it a quick rub down.

Remy gave it a cursory glance. "Stiff competition today."

Karina laughed and opened her door, Stan leapt over her to get outside first.

"I'll go find the washroom. Back as soon as I can."

Remy switched off the engine and patted the dashboard saying a silent thank you to the Studebaker for getting them there in one piece. He thought about his father momentarily. How he'd loved this car, more than his wife, certainly more than his son.

"It's back in one piece Dad. I hope you can see it."

Ami (he hadn't really gotten used to saying Karina yet) was knocking on the roof.

"Four rows over, directly behind us. Better get going. I'll watch the car."

Remy took a deep breath and climbed out of the car, praying he could make it in time and there was no line up. He couldn't even say thank you. He just walked off as fast as he could. Karina and Stan watched him, both a little concerned as they saw the tension in his face. "Hope he makes it Stan."

People stopped by to look at the car and Karina smiled as they peered inside. She reached for Stan's rug; it wasn't quite in keeping. Then found his socks. She showed them to him. He hung his head for a microsecond then wagged his tail.

"Don't think I won't be putting them back on later, dog."

She cast her eyes around the showground, amazed at how many people were here. She prayed no one would ask her any questions. Too late a man wearing a white straw hat stopped by.

"Is this yours?" He asked.

"My..." she had to think a second how to call Remy..."my grandfather's."

"Nice restoration job. That real leather?"

Karina nodded. "Yes. Hand stitched. Took ten years to restore it."

"Good polish. What's the milage on this?"

Karina knew that answer. "Nearly 10,000 from new."

The man seemed impressed and moved on, she noticed he was writing something down as he walked. She worried she said the wrong thing.

Remy finally returned. He looked very relieved. "Never let me leave the house without a spare pair of trousers again. That was touch and go. How are we doing?"

"People are looking."

"Good. Look out for men in straw hats, they'll be the judges. You and Stan go explore. See if you can find that guy with his Thunderbird, we met the other day. Enjoy yourselves. There's a Stanley steamer towards the back row. Bet you didn't know some vehicles ran on steam a hundred years ago."

Karina didn't know if that was unusual or not but tried to look impressed. She attached a lead to Stan and set off. Determined to judge for herself what was best.

Remy watched her go before greeting three people who were keen to know about his car. "Is this a genuine Golden Hawk?"

"Right down to every nut and bolt." He replied with some pride.

So many old cars, so many people. Karina wandered down the rows, Stan at her heels bewildered by the range of vehicles. Some old motorcycles too and even ancient pick-up trucks that she remembered from the museum she went to. She paused besides a bright yellow Packard Station Wagon, the sign read 1947. She was about to move on when she heard a familiar voice. She turned and gasped; Father Tresor was walking towards her with two young girls in front of him. Her heart nearly stopped. She swiftly hid behind the Packard grabbing Stan's collar. Her legs and hands were shaking, and she wanted to be sick. Had he seen her? She heard the girls giggling, didn't they know what a monster this man was?

They all stood admiring the Packard. She wanted to crawl under it. Stan was confused at her change in demeanor, but he wasn't reacting to Father Tresor which confused her. Normally his hair would rise and he'd cower. She looked around her to where she could run to. A Model T Ford was stranded mid row, a man trying to get it started. She sneaked a look back, Father Tresor was now inside the Packard, the owner had approached. Karina panicked; she should run but didn't want him to see her.

"This is quite a restoration. Nice finish." Father Tresor was telling the owner. "My Grandpa had one of these, wouldn't part with it."

One of the girls came around the back and saw Karina squatting there. She smiled and put a hand out to stroke Stan, who dutifully licked it.

"Cute dog," the girl said.

Karina wasn't sure how to respond.

"Dana?" Father Tresor called out. "Where are you?"

The girl smiled at Karina as she left. "Coming daddy."

'Daddy?' Karina was confused. Father Tresor had a family? Since when? Something seemed to click in her head. The child wasn't afraid. Stan wasn't afraid. Her legs still shook and she still felt sick. She took another peek inside the vehicle and could only see the back of his head as he listened to the Packard owner. This was a different Father Tresor. How was it possible? She took a deep breath and ran as fast as she could towards the stranded Model T and took refuge behind it, looking back as Father Tresor got out of the Packard and was surrounded by smiling people who all wanted to shake his hand.

"Didn't know the Mayor was a classic auto fan," the man who owned the Model T remarked. He was watching Father Tresor greeting more people who all seemed so happy to see him.

"Mayor?" Karina asked, her voice barely recognizable.

The man looked at her uncertainly. "Been Mayor for a year now. Some people like him, but like all politicians he's big on promises and I've not seen any changes."

"A year?"

"Mayor Hernandez won by a landslide. You feel like giving me a push?"

"Push?" Karina queried, then understood what he was saying. "Sorry, sorry, I was spooked. I ..."

The man looked at her more carefully. "You ok? You look very pale."

"I'm fine. I'm ok," she answered, taking in a deep breath to regain her composure. "Where do you want me to push?"

Remy was growing anxious. Ami, he meant Karina, had been gone more than an hour. He'd been busy showing off his car and time had slipped away. He heard someone click on the PA loudspeakers, getting ready to make an announcement.

"Afternoon everyone, welcome to the 10th Anniversary of the Pinetree Concours d'Elegance. The judges had made their first rounds, and a shortlist has been selected. Will the following vehicles please raise their hoods for inspection. Numbers: 4, 17, 52, ... oh I missed 28, 97 and 105. Final judgement will be declared at 5pm and Mayor Hernandez will award medals to the three finalists. Ladies and Gentlemen, this has been a fantastic turnout this year and thank you for supporting us and our charity 'Children's Cancer Life Fund' it's a wonderful cause and we've raised damn near $100,000 this year, so thank you all. Make sure you stay for the cook out and the amazing All-Star Swing Band. There will be dancing. Thank you."

Remy sighed. Couldn't remember his number but was pretty sure it wasn't on that list.

Suddenly Karina and Stan were upon him. She wrapped her arms around him and hugged him tight. "105, Remy. You're number 105."

He stared at her. He could see she had been crying but didn't understand why. She was being all happy and sad at the same time. Stan was pawing his leg to be included too.

"Got to get the hood up. Are you ok, girl? What happened? You've been gone so long and ..."

Karina broke away. "Get the hood up. Come on. Sorry I was gone I..."

Remy walked back to his vehicle and bent down to release the hood catch. He realized he needed to go again. "Hold the fort. I have to go. Tell me what happened when I get back and don't disappear."

Karina watched him go and went around the front of the car to raise the hood. She was still shaky. Still trying to process how sick she'd felt, how weak, just because someone look a bit like and 'sounded' like Father Tresor. She'd thought herself strong and had left the farm behind her, but one voice had reduced her to rubble. She couldn't believe it was that easy to wreck her life. Being with Remy made her feel so safe and here she was, still shaking. She should have known when Stan didn't react that she was being foolish but...

She suddenly realized she was being surrounded by men and one woman in white hats. The judges were here. She stepped aside as let them bury their heads into the engine bay.

To her great relief Remy returned to answer any questions and she and Stan retreated. Stan seized an abandoned hamburger and scoffed it before she could say no. She looked down at him and smiled.

"I'm hungry too. What do you say we go get Remy a coffee and maybe a sandwich?"

She had a twenty-note tucked into her bra. Remy's idea since dresses didn't exactly have pockets. Stan was alert for any other food dropped on the ground now, he was definitely up for it.

They returned to find Remy fast asleep in his car, his hat skew on his head. The hood was down and although some people were still drifting by looking at the vehicles it was definitely less busy this end as the swing band was playing on the far side of the showground. She gave Remy a gentle shake.

"I brought you a coffee. Got us a chicken sandwich to share."

Remy opened his eyes and blinked a few times. Couldn't believe he'd fallen asleep.

He grabbed the coffee took a moment to recover his equilibrium.

"You alright?"

Karina pressed the coffee in his hands, then broke the sandwich in two. "Didn't have enough money for two sandwiches. They wanted nine dollars for a chicken sandwich. Coffee was five."

"Jeez, I remember when I could get a coffee and sandwich for a buck. Just proves I'm old, that's all." He sipped his coffee and gratefully swallowed it. His throat was dry. He looked up at the sky and the huge cloud formations. "Going to rain in an hour or so, if it doesn't pass over." He glanced at Karina eating her food and remembered.

"Something happen to you today? Want to talk about it?"

Karina shook her head. "Just ghosts. I got spooked, that's all. I'm ok now."

Remy didn't press it. "Those judges sure asked a lot of questions. I'm not sure I gave the right answers. One of them knew his Studebakers inside out."

"You got shortlisted, Remy. That has to be a good sign, right?"

Remy drank his coffee and nodded. "Yeah, that was a good feeling. One of the shortlisted is a Mercedes 300 – it's rare. They've done a good job restoring it."

Karina didn't know what it was or why it was impressive. "I still like yours best, although I did like a cute little Mini. Must have been so scary to drive one of those. So small."

"Must be a special import. They were never sold here, I don't think." He looked at his phone. "Not long now. Want to walk down to the bandstand?"

Karina smiled and helped him out of the car. "Don't forget to lock up. Do you need to pee before we go?"

Remy laughed. "You know me too well now. Of course, I do. I just had coffee."

Remy got busy with locking the car and then headed off to the washrooms. Karina and Stan followed. A welcome breeze was getting up and the band seemed to have gotten louder all of a sudden.

They linked arms as they walked towards the bandstand, pausing only to admire a shiny blue Alfa Romeo Spider. "Like it?" Remy asked.

"It's very cute. I think I'm beginning to see a difference in cars now."

"That's what's been lost lately. Almost every new EV they shove at us looks like every other. You mentioned a ghost? I wasn't listening properly earlier."

Karina sighed. "What's the expression? Being scared of your own shadow? I'm not as tough as I need to be. That's all."

Remy nodded. "It might take a long time to put everything that happened to you in the past. Hell, I still wake up sometimes in the middle of the night remembering something or someone being mean to me or some slight at work or worse an argument with my wife. Might have happened thirty years ago, but it's still locked in my damn head, nothing you can do about it. Just make sure your life is going forwards. The Order will always be in your past, but you are making your own future now. Don't you forget it. You are in control."

Karina said nothing but squeezed his arm a little tighter as they approached the bandstand.

"Two minutes," Remy told her.

They watched a woman approach the microphone and signal to the band to wind it up.

Karina tensed as she watched the Mayor climbed the steps to the stage. Now she looked properly he was a lot shorter than Father Tresor. She felt foolish she'd been so afraid.

"Welcome everyone to the Concours d'Elegance prize giving. The judges tell me it was a tough call today and I want to say to everyone that we love hosting you all and it was a brilliant showing of some of the finest automobiles in the world. Well done all those people who have spent months and years restoring and keeping those cars on the road. Long may it last."

There was a strong applause for that sentiment.

"So, on to the medals. Mayor Hernandez will be awarding them today and he promises to bring his Grandpappy's old Packard to the showground next year for the 11th Concours d'Elegance. Be looking forward to seeing that here, Mr Mayor."

The Mayor waved and smiled as only Mayor's do.

"In reverse order. We have in third place with a Highly Commended 1955 Lincoln Coupe owned by Mr Jake Closter. Come on up sir."

Karina watched the man make his way through the crowd to the stage. The Mayor shook his hand and handed him a medal he showed to the crowd who cheered.

"One down," Remy whispered.

"Next up, second place goes to Jack and Geraldine Fenwick, long-time supporters of this event and winners in 2023 with their beautiful and very rare Facel Vega 500. Highly Commended."

There were many whoops in the crowd as a husband and wife climbed up the steps and Geraldine even scored a kiss from the Mayor as he handed over the medal.

"And now for the Best of Show..."

Karina squeezed Remy's hand. "It's got to be you, Remy. It has to be you."

Remy wasn't sure, the Mercedes 300 looked pretty damn impressive when he'd ambled over to take a look.

"Come on up Mr Remy Mitchell with his beautifully restored Studebaker Golden Hawk. There's sad story that goes with this car, his pappy, Jordan Mitchell died at the wheel some years ago now, but here it is, brought back to life after ten whole years of restoration and what a wonderful job Remy did. Well done."

Remy was stunned. Not so many people cheered but one woman seemed very excited and shouted, 'Go Remy'.

Karina steered Remy to the steps and made sure he got up there safely into the embrace of the Mayor. The medal was awarded, Remy showed it to the crowd and got a better response this time before Mayor quickly launched into a speech about the importance of preserving the past to protect the future.

Karina hugged him at the bottom of the steps and many people congratulated him, clapped him on the back and then suddenly there was an older woman embracing him with some enthusiasm. He seemed both shocked and happy to see her. He turned and introduced her to Karina.

"Beth this is Karina. Karina this is Beth. She was my wife's best friend."

Beth was grinning and studying Karina carefully. Remy could see he needed to explain.

"I'm her legal guardian now. She's living with me."

Beth embraced her. "Finally, he's got his own way. You are a lucky girl, Karina. Poor Remy wanted to adopt so many times but she who must be obeyed said no. I hope you are taking good care of this man."

Karina was bewildered but smiled and answered, "I am."

Beth beamed. "I can't believe you finally got the Studebaker finished. This poor man, Karina, hid in his garage for years trying to complete the car. Of course, we all knew it was to avoid Jean. I really want to know your story Karina and just how on earth you two found each other. Come on, the bar is open. We need to celebrate this."

Remy felt dizzy. Beth was like a whirlwind, a true force to be reckoned with. Not heard a word from her since his wife passed. He had a recollection she was fan of old cars too and owned a '71 Datsun 240Z she somehow kept on the road.

"Beth teaches art at the Community College," Remy told Karina. "Tell her about your batiks."

Karina looked blank for a moment, then realized Remy was giving her a cue to help her talk to this woman. The very last thing she wanted to do was talk about herself but the batiks and her sketches, she could do that maybe.

For his part, he hoped Karina could survive Beth. She had the knack of extracting every bit of information from a person and you wouldn't even know why you told her everything.

Stan stayed close to Karina, unsure about this new person but still keeping an eye out for a stray hot dog on the ground. He was ever the optimist.

It was almost ten o'clock before they left the showground. Remy was exhausted. Karina hugged Stan on her lap to stop him from removing his socks. Remy glanced at her.

"Sorry about that. She's quite a force huh?"

Karina laughed. "Exhausting. I feel as though she squeezed me dry. She can drink too, huh."

"Yeah, I forgot that about her. I'm glad her niece is coming over to drive her home. Beth and my wife did everything together. I might as well have not existed. Last I saw of her was weeping at my wife's funeral. I was always surprised I never saw her again after that, but I shouldn't have been. She was never much interested in me."

Karina yawned. "She invited me to come to her class on Tuesday."

Remy was surprised; but pleased. "You must go. Beth can open a lot of doors for you. Doors I couldn't possibly open. She's well connected."

"But I'm not trained or anything. It will be embarrassing."

Remy shook his head. "She wouldn't have asked you if she didn't think you had something. She's a good teacher. I should have called her earlier about you. She'll help. If she rates you, she'll move heaven and earth to get you into the system."

"System?"

"As she explained, she doesn't give a damn about your lack of schooling or grades. If you have talent, there are exceptions to the rules."

Karina winced. "So, all I need is talent. What if I'm no good."

"I've seen your sketches. I know you think they're secret, I peeked. I'm no artist but I'd say you have a good eye, girl."

Karina was annoyed he's peeked but didn't quibble. She'd left her sketchpad in the kitchen, of course he'd peeked.

"If you ask me, and I know you aren't, I think you have talent coming out of every pore. Never feel you aren't good enough. Let Beth guide you. If you're good, she'll make sure people know about it. If you need guidance, she'll provide it. I can give you a home and put food on your plate, but she can give you confidence. Believe me, she wouldn't have invited you if she didn't like you."

"I don't think she liked Stan."

Remy chuckled. "Stan stole half her hamburger. Entirely our fault we didn't bring food for him."

Karina thought about this. Beth had given her a whole new set of anxieties. Not school, but 'Art Class'. Hadn't she explained enough about how terrified she was of being with kids who might mock her ignorance about life, everything. She couldn't believe she'd agreed to go.

"You'll be ok. I believe in you, girl. What are we going to do with the medal?"

"Put it in a frame over the fireplace," Karina suggested. "I'll do it."

Remy smiled and patted the steering wheel. "She deserves it. Best of Show. My old Dad would be ecstatic."

"Watch the road, Remy."

"I'm watching. Big day to remember. I'm glad you were there."

Karina put a hand on his arm a moment. "It was a good day. Best of Show, Remy. Best of Show."

CHAPTER THIRTY-ONE

Hubris

Remy was watching CNN waiting for news about the astronauts orbiting the moon when a familiar face came up on screen. Longhorn, the billionaire, and host of the hog roast. He was being led handcuffed from his mansion by the FBI. TV cameras were covering the event. He was ranting about being a victim of a deep state witch hunt. He looked slightly manic with his white hair all over the place. The TV reporters were saying he was being charged for hoarding weapons, rocket launchers and supporting domestic terrorism. All of which Remy knew was true but he worried about the consequences. His supporters were going to be mad. After all he was supposed to be financing this 'National Divorce' thing – and clearly supplying the weapons.

Karina called him from the kitchen where she was making supper. He got up from his chair and joined her.

"Remember the hog roast?"

Karina was tending the mushroom omelets she was making and putting some spinach in the microwave. Remy marveled at how quickly she had mastered his kitchen.

"Ready in a minute. Don't criticize. First omelets I've ever made."

"Wouldn't dream of it. Make sure it's cooked on the outside before you scoop it up."

Karina glanced back at him. "Hog roast? Where I learned to dance?"

"And Stan puked up the pork."

Karina winced at the memory. "Ewww. Anyway, what about it?"

"The FBI just arrested Longhorn, the guy who hosted it, on terrorism charges."

Karina didn't seem surprised. "Wasn't he the guy who wanted to start a war or something?"

Remy nodded as he sat down at the table and took two forks out of the cutlery jar. "Civil war. Remember the shooting on the highway?"

"When we raced across the cornfield? Yeah, I was so scared. Stan just fell asleep. Couldn't believe it."

"FBI say it was his people blocking the highway and doing the shooting."

Karina served up the omelets and added the spinach to their plates. "Always someone shooting someone it seems."

Remy nodded. "The thing is, he was the main guy, the moneyman behind this Civil War idea. His supporters won't be happy to see him arrested. There could be trouble. Might be like the whole MAGA January 6th thing all over again."

Karina placed his food in front of him. She didn't know about any January thing.

Remy looked at his plate impressed. "Looks great."

"Made too much, I think."

Remy shook his head. "It's perfect and I'm starving. All I did was go shopping and trim some trees. Somehow worked up an appetite."

Karina plonked herself down and looked Stan who was waiting for tidbits.

"I just fed you. Remember?"

Remy was frowning as he ate. "I'm thinking we'll spend New Year up at the trailer. What do you think?"

Karina broke out a big smile. "Stan and me are ready. Just say when."

Remy nodded. "Remember they were talking about things kicking off in the New Year? It will be the anniversary of January 6th insurrection. Might not happen now they've arrested Longhorn. You can be sure the FBI will be arresting more pretty soon. But..." he ate another mouthful. "Call it intuition, I'm pretty sure they are going to see this arrest as a call to arms. A challenge. If there's going to be bad stuff happening, I'd rather be up by the trailer than here."

"Bad stuff? You mean more shooting?"

Remy nodded. "A lot more shooting. A lot of people are going to have to choose a side pretty fast or be labelled 'the enemy'. They'll be looting, all kinds of crazy stuff."

"What about the Hawk? You going to leave it here?"

"It should be safe in the garage, I think. They're trying to defend the old ways, not destroy them."

Karina frowned as she ate. "You're serious about this."

Remy nodded. "Yeah. I was at Ace hardware yesterday – had at least two people tell me 'Something in the Air' with a wink, like they take one look at my truck and think I'm part of it. Thunderclap Newman is getting a lot of plays on some local stations I notice. It's a song for revolution, 'Something in the Air'. Not very subtle, but there were a heck of lot of people buying survival stuff and so-called hurricane protection for their windows. Hurricane season is over. I think people in the know are getting ready for trouble."

Karina sighed. "All my life I've been waiting for this revolution to start. Lord Ramesh kept on saying the change is coming. Be ready. That's why they made sure we knew how to fix things, grow things. Father Tresor would tell us that first they'd cut off the power and then the food supply. Learned how to dry food to preserve it and salt food. Stick it in jars. Beans. It was always green beans. Never got to eat any. It was sent to Charleston."

"All essential stuff, kid. My mother used to bottle summer fruit, so we'd have it to eat at Christmas. Frozen food killed that off, but some people still do it." He finished his omelet and thought more about it. "I'll stock up on essentials and survival stuff too. Just in case."

This all sounded pretty normal to Karina. "Don't forget Stan's survival food." She was just glad they'd be at the ocean. That made her happy."

"You finish painting your room?" Remy asked her.

"And yours. You'll have to sleep in the guest room tonight. Pretty strong smell."

Remy smiled. "Wow, you've been busy. You work hard girl."

Karina shrugged. "Your room looks a lot brighter. Bigger somehow. Don't worry I covered everything, like you said."

"Thank you. I'm sure it looks great. You ready for Beth's class tomorrow?"

Karina sighed. "I don't know. I'm scared to go."

"Don't be. You wanted the chance to see what it's like being in a classroom. Beth will take good care of you. She started up this whole Art Therapy thing a few years ago for kids and adults with mental issues or y'know, problems adjusting to changes in life. She's got good instincts about people."

"I didn't think you liked her."

He shrugged. "She was my wife's friend, and I didn't really come into the equation. Either way, I'm taking you there and I want you to try it."

Karina kept her silence about that and got up to clear the dishes.

CHAPTER THIRTY-TWO

Art Class

Tuesday came and the weatherman said it could go to 87F. Another perfect day in paradise. Karina felt nauseous. Could not believe she'd agreed to go to 'Art Class' and wanted to cancel, fall ill, anything rather than go.

Remy made her eat breakfast that tasted like sawdust in her mouth and then drove her to Art School. Stan couldn't believe he was being left with Remy and Remy had to swear three times and cross his heart that he wouldn't let go of the dog lead.

Finally, she was abandoned at the curb, and she nervously made her way into the building which seemed fairly relaxed with not many students hanging around in the lobby. Only now did she realize that she didn't know Beth's surname. Had no idea where to go and stood there like a lost soul clutching her sketchpad and pens. She wanted to flee and then realized she had no idea on how to get home. She'd never ridden a bus.

"Can I help you?" A student asked her.

Karina stared at her, taking in the creased t-shirt, blue streak hair and men's shorts that covered most of the girl's skinny legs.

"Um, Beth's art class," she mumbled shyly.

The girl stared back, taking in her sketchpad and pens clutched tightly in her hands. "She's tough. I hope you can take criticism."

"You know her?"

"I ought to, I'm her niece. You must be Karina."

Karina blinked, shocked someone, a total stranger knew her name. "I, y, y, yes."

"I knew it. Beth said you were a natural. I like your hair. I can never cut it that short, my ears stick out."

Karina followed her down a long corridor, noticing art work on notice boards and a few students who didn't seem to be doing anything, everyone dressed in so many different colors and wearing weird shoes.

The girl turned back towards her a moment. "Is it true you've never been to school?"

"We had classes at the farm," Karina replied defensively.

"But you didn't like have to go to an actual school."

"No."

"I hated every single moment of school. So lucky to get accepted here. You're not the youngest student here by the way, there's a child genius. He's ten, I think. Already has his first degree in Math. So weird."

They continued walking for a moment then stopped outside a red door covered in graffiti and stickers.

"This is it. My advice, sit at the back and listen before you do anything, she likes that."

"Listen?"

The girl nodded. "You can go in; class starts in about five minutes."

Karina was about to thank her when she abruptly ran off to join a group of students. Swallowing hard, Karina entered the classroom, all eyes turned towards her. She desperately wanted to be invisible, but she narrowed her eyes and walked towards the back, as suggested. She found herself a chair to sit on and placed her sketchpad and pens beside her on a ledge. There didn't seem to be any desks.

No one spoke to her. She looked around and saw there was an older woman sitting on a stool with a shawl wrapped around her front and center. No sign of Beth. She wondered if this was all a terrible mistake, she shouldn't have come.

Beth entered in a rush, quickly followed by two students who went straight to their chairs. Beth was dressed in blue fisherman overalls with a strange cap on her head. She spread some papers out on her desk and looked around the room with a sigh. She took out another paper and handed it forward. "Good morning. Sorry to see not everyone is here. Forward the attendance sheet, initial your name, you know the routine. If you don't sign, you're not here and if attendance doesn't improve this class could be cancelled next term. Please let people know. If you don't know the arts are under attack from the bean counters, you do now. Is Karina here?"

Karina winced. She didn't want to be noticed. "Here." Her voice seemed to squeak she was so anxious.

Beth nodded. "Good. It's life drawing today. Susan here," she glanced over at the older woman. "Susan is not just a life model, but a well-respected local artist. I'm looking for light and shade. I want to see a real living person on the page. You have seventy minutes, starting now. Then we shall discuss. Got it? Light and shade."

Karina relaxed. Life-drawing she could do. She bitterly regretted leaving all her sketches behind in the barn, but it was raining, and it was a last-minute decision to run. They would have all turned to mush anyway. The only old person she had sketched before was Remy, asleep on his lazy boy with Stan on his lap. She wondered about light and shade, what that meant exactly. She reflected on most of the kids she'd sketched at the farm, and they were like blank pages. No lines on the faces, some scars maybe and bruises. But the old woman was full of lines, and she realized with some shock had removed her shawl and was naked under there. Her wrinkled breasts and a scarred torso testament to a life lived. This was way beyond her skills. She looked around the room and everyone had started sketching already, she hadn't even reached for her pens.

Beth didn't come near her. She seemed to be busy with paperwork.

Karina opened up her sketchpad and closed her eyes. There was something in Susan's expression, something in the shape of her eyes, and those hands with shiny brown skin and how on earth did you do any art with such long nails?

Karina opened her eyes momentarily. Seized her pens and glanced at the light and shadows behind the woman and began to draw an outline. Fixing an image in her mind.

Suddenly Beth straightened her back, checked the time, and stood up.

"Times up. Lay down your pens."

Karina was shocked. Times up? But she'd said seventy minutes, she was nowhere near finished. She looked down at her portrait and immediately wanted to redo the hands - why oh why were hands so hard to do? She glanced at the clock on the classroom wall, she couldn't believe seventy minutes had passed. How the hell?

Beth was walking among them, examining each sketch making non-committal noises. She held one sketch up done by a boy with scarlet hair and nose rings.

"Note Nico has successfully used the light, but it is a little harsh don't you think, a little bit cruel."

Karina noticed Susan was dressing. She didn't seem curious about the finished results. Suddenly Beth was upon her and held out her hand for her sketch pad, taking it back to her end of the room to examine it in the light.

"Our visitor Karina here has had no formal art education, in fact very little education at all. But I want you all to see what a real artist can do."

She revealed the sketch to everyone in the room and there were loud murmurs of appreciation and a couple of 'wows'.

"I watched Karina very carefully," Beth was saying. "She didn't copy Susan, she hasn't drawn what we can all see, an older woman sitting on a stool. She has drawn a person, found her very essence, it's almost beautiful. Needs work on the hands but look more closely. This is a real person on the page."

She looked down the row at Karina and smiled. "Karina, I hope you will keep coming here. I know you're not formally enrolled, but I am sure the whole class will welcome you and as you learn techniques here, we shall learn from you."

Karina was astonished as people clapped her. She wanted to die of embarrassment. They liked what she had done. No one had ever liked anything she'd done before, no one.

Everyone gathered around her sketchpad and examined her drawing, then someone opened it up and stared at her other sketches of Stan, the fishing boats at the ocean and Remy asleep, the Studebaker.

Beth called her down and she approached cautiously as someone handed back her sketchpad with a muttered 'amazing.'

"Everyone, I want to talk about today. About how we inhabit a person to reveal their personality on the page. I'm guessing Karina you don't really know how you achieved this?"

Karina's heart was racing. They were all looking at her. She had to say something but what? "I..." She closed her eyes. "I become them."

Beth allowed herself a small moment of triumph. She looked around at all the other students. "She becomes them. Wow. What you don't know Karina, and I was watching closely, you barely looked at the page as you sketched, in fact I think your eyes were closed."

Karina heard a sharp intake of breath from some of the students. She didn't want to open her eyes; it was safer to keep them shut.

"It's not unknown. She literally glanced at Susan, closed her eyes and felt her way to being Susan, being old."

"Like a shaman," some student suggested.

Beth liked that. "Yes, that might hold water. She imagined what it would look like in her head and simply worked away at it."

Karina opened her eyes. They were all still staring at her. "I do have a problem with hands. Probably feet too."

"This we can help with. Nyla will work with you on that. That alright with you Nyla? Nyla is good with fine details. You can both learn from each other." Nyla offered Karina an encouraging smile.

"Ears," someone said. "I have a problem with ears."

Suddenly everyone was talking about their own issues and Karina found she could breathe again. Would she come back? Is this what school was? She didn't feel scared anymore.

Beth placed a hand on her arm. "You did well, Karina. I knew you would. Remy asked me to come over for lunch on Saturday. We will talk more then. I want you here every Tuesday till the end of term. That all ok with you?"

Remy was waiting for her with Stan who went crazy to see her again.

"Didn't manage to lose him this time I see."

Remy grinned and hugged her. "Did it go ok? How was it?"

She shrugged. "Ok, I guess."

"Will you go back?"

She nodded. "I think so."

"I told you she wouldn't bite."

Karina smiled and buried her head into his shoulder. "Thank you, Remy. Thank you for everything. Can we get some potatoes and leeks? I really, really want to make some soup."

They walked back to the Chevy truck and Karina looked up into the sky and suddenly sensed she had some kind of future. She looked down at Stan trotting beside her. Had she really had her eyes closed to sketch that old woman? How strange was that? Paulo has always told her she completely disappeared when she was sketching but she'd never understood what he meant. She didn't know what it signified but people smiled at her, made her promise she'd come back, and she had a tiny inkling that right now she might actually belong somewhere.

"And onions. We'll need onions," she added as they reached the truck.

CHAPTER THIRTY-THREE

CODA

Brother Grace patiently sat on a very worn, slightly sticky leather armchair in a grim bedsit. He didn't like the smell of the place at all, the whole room stank of stale food from the Fried Chicken store underneath. From the look of the room, it seemed to him that Father Tresor had run out of money and luck.

He checked the time. He figured Tresor would have got off his shift at Walmart twenty minutes ago. He was confident he wouldn't stop off at the bar, the man was a wine drinker, and it was way too expensive to drink in a bar. Five sad empty bottles of Oak Leaf Cabernet stood in the kitchenette. Didn't he know cheap wine was bad for the liver?

He closed his eyes a moment. Punishment comes to those who transgress the rules. From the condition of the room, punishment had already started. But if Father Tresor thought he'd find redemption back at the Order it wasn't going to happen. Lord Ramesh had heard the testimony from the children from the farm in person and been shocked. Sister Ryan would serve five years of humiliation and servitude for her transgressions. But it had been decided there was no way back for Father Tresor. Stealing another members identity had been the last straw. There was nowhere for him to belong. You cannot redeem the devil.

Brother Grace heard heavy footsteps on the stairs. A key turned in the door which swung open. Father Tresor didn't bother with the light switch. He wearily entered, set his bag of groceries down on the floor and turned to close the door. He paused a moment. Instinctively he turned back, a particular odor had caught his attention, aftershave, he didn't use aftershave. He flipped the light on.

Brother Grace smiled from the armchair.

Father Tresor's eyes were drawn to the Baretta M9A3 in Brother Grace's steady hand. He also noticed the attached silencer.

"Welcome home, Father Tresor."

Sam Hawksmoor

The Sam Hawksmoor Novels – https://www.samhawksmoor.com
(All available on Amazon and Kindle)

We Feel Your Pain - so you don't have to – Hammer & Tong 2020
ISBN-13: 979-8-69908-7693
The first Delaney and Asha investigation: Their role is to keep the city safe from unscrupulous people. When something looks too good to be true – it's a scam, right? But what if the scam works? What kind of scam is that? Want to live a life free of pain? How much would you pay for that?
**Number One in the Delaney & Asha series*

The Book of Ashes – Hammer & Tong 2022
Some secrets are meant to be kept forever
ISBN 979-8-837434-952
It was supposed to be a simple 'find a missing writer' case. Wolfie Sigurdsson had been paid upfront by Brin Martinet to write a biography of his father, the former Olympian shooter Arnold Martinet, photographer – now living in a secure dementia facility. Easy money for Wolfie, but he hasn't delivered. When Delaney finally tracks Wolfie down in a remote surfing town in a freezing New England he claims he's been watched, told not to write a single word. But by whom? What secrets has Wolfie uncovered? He won't tell.
**Number Two in the Delaney & Asha series*

Mission Longshot - Hammer & Tong 2021
How far would you go to save one life?
ISBN-13: 979-8- 73565-1390
Jarred awake after 23 years in a life-pod on colony-ship Nova, Celeste discovers she's the only survivor - a trillion miles from home. Celeste knows she is now alone forever. Stella is testing a light-speed ship in 2057. The only chance they have to save Celeste. On her return, the Moonbase has vanished. On Earth Florida is no longer flooded. Impossible since climate change. Gerry, Kali, and Jolene, out hunting aliens. It's Millennial New Year's Eve 1999. Stella accidentally went back in time 57 years. Saving Celeste just became the biggest longshot of all.

Girl with Cat (Blue) – Hammer & Tong
ISBN-13: 978-1-5451-56629
War, secret tunnels, pre-historic monsters, and airships. Two London's

separated by tunnels filled with monsters. Two identical teenage girls who should never meet… an amazing fantasy story. *Shortlisted for the International Rubery Book Award & Honorable Mention in the Writer's Digest 26th Book Awards*

Another Place to Die: Endtime Chronicles - Hammer & Tong
ISBN-13: 978-1-5028-35437
Think you can survive the next lethal pandemic? Kira and her dog Red try to escape the virus and the Firestarter's who follow. Be ready for the next pandemic! (A Sam Hawksmoor & Sam North novel)

J&K 4Ever - Hammer & Tong
ISBN-13: 978-1-5306-24225
60 years after the apocalypse. Jeyna and Kruge are two young orphan lovers determined to stay with each other despite it being forbidden. They must escape into the unknown. Behind them will come cruel Enforcers ready to hunt them down.

The Repercussions of Tomas D – Hammer & Tong
ISBN-13: 978-1- 4910-32015
Tomas accidentally goes back in time to London in the Blitz. The day after he disappears, his girlfriend Gabriella wakes up to realize she's the only one who remembers that Germany was supposed to have lost the war...

Marikka – Hammer & Tong
ISBN-13: 978-1- 5119-94224
The Girl who ran from the fire - The Boy who crashed the car & Anya, the girl who can read objects – An intense story about a father's search for his missing daughter.

The Repossession of Genie Magee - (Book One)
ASIN : B093LM4LG1
2nd Edition - Hammer & Tong 2021 Genie Magee is imprisoned in her own home and Rian, her boyfriend, has to bust her out on the eve of a great storm. They run straight into a trap where scientists are running lethal experiments on runaways who may not be as dead as they think. *Winner of The Wirral 'Paperback of the Year'*

The Hunting of Genie Magee - (Book Two)
ASIN : B093LJLB2X
2nd Edition now back in print - Hammer & Tong 2021
$10,000-dollar reward for the capture of Genie and each of her friends. Who now owns their DNA? What is the secret buried in Radspan?

The Heaviness of Genie Magee - (Book Three)
Hammer & Tong (Published as Rüya in Turkey)
ISBN: 978-1-49750-8033
Rian is snatched along with many other genius kids to work on Cary's anti-gravity theories. Genie has just 48 hours to save them from ruthless kidnappers.

This is the 12th Sam Hawksmoor novel. A former Program leader for Creative Writing Master's at Falmouth and Portsmouth Universities.
Sam writes his first drafts by hand. This novel began in France and was completed in Miami thanks to the generosity of good friends. Em in Florida and Lionel and Catherine in Biarritz.

https://www.samhawksmoor.com

Acknowledgements

To 'Kitty' for feedback and her long-suffering support; and many thanks to first readers Walli Leff and Marlene Steiner in New York for their sensible and useful feedback. Also, to podcaster Sara Troy in Canada for her feedback and live interviews.

And lastly thanks to Em Robson in Miami for enabling me to do my final research there. Some people have Paris, we have a rather terrifying stuck elevator moment at the Westin in Cape Coral when everyone in that potential coffin (17 of us) realized we were seconds away from death.

Printed in Great Britain
by Amazon

47562449R00139